Here's what some of the characters had to say about their involvement in Bayou of Pigs:

"We wanted to help stop the spread of communism and make money for ourselves."

>—Mike Perdue, the Texas mercenary who organized the invasion of Dominica

"Kill commies for money. That's what it was all about."

>—Bob Prichard, a Vietnam vet recruited for the mission

"It was almost like a Rambo movie."

>—Brian Alleyne, a former Dominican cabinet minister

"Harebrained, crackpot ... unsophisticated, undermanned, underfinanced, ill-led, misdirected and adolescent."

>—Lawyer Frank Fay

"High finance, deals and the burning ambition of certain North American nationals to turn Dominica into a crooks' paradise."

>— *The New Chronicle*, Dominica

"I don't think you could make up a story as interesting as this."

>—Mike Howell, captain of the ship hired to transport the mercenaries to Dominica

"Imagine what you could do if you owned your own country."

>—Wolfgang Droege, Perdue's lieutenant

BAYOU OF PIGS

Also by the author:

Cold Terror
The Martyr's Oath

BAYOU OF PIGS

THE TRUE STORY OF AN AUDACIOUS PLOT TO
TURN A TROPICAL ISLAND INTO A CRIMINAL PARADISE

STEWART BELL

WILEY

John Wiley & Sons Canada, Ltd.

Library and Archives Canada Cataloguing in Publication Data

Bell, Stewart, 1965–
    Bayou of Pigs : the true story of an audacious plot to turn a tropical island into a criminal paradise / Stewart Bell.

Includes bibliographical references and index.
ISBN 978-0-470-15382-6

    1. Political crimes and offenses—Dominica.   2. Sovereignty, Violation of—Dominica. I. Title.

HV6295.D649B45 2008   364.1'3209729841   C2008-902156-8

Production Credits
Cover design: Jason Vandenberg
Interior text design and typesetting: Tegan Wallace
Cover images: Stockbyte, Rubberball, Photodisc, Stewart Bell
Printer: Friesens

John Wiley & Sons Canada, Ltd.
6045 Freemont Blvd.
Mississauga, Ontario
L5R 4J3

This book is printed with biodegradable vegetable-based inks on 55-lb. recycled cream paper, 100% post-consumer waste.

Printed in Canada

1 2 3 4 5 FP 12 11 10 09 08

Knocking off a bank or an armored truck is merely crude.
Knocking off an entire republic has, I feel, a certain style.

—*Frederick Forsyth,* The Dogs of War

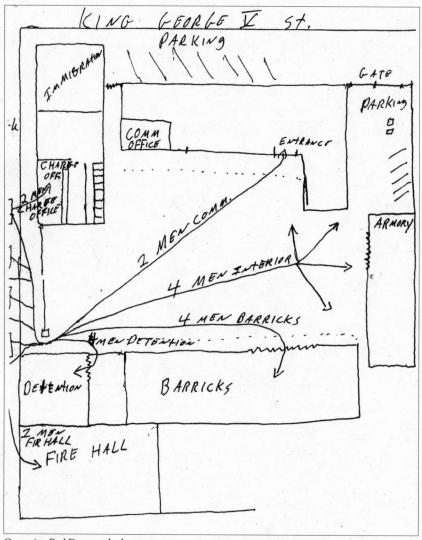

Operation Red Dog attack plan

Contents

PART III—Soldiers of Misfortune

Prologue

Toronto, Canada
April 13, 2005

WALTER WOLFGANG DROEGE answered a knock at his apartment door at two-thirty in the afternoon. It was Keith Deroux. He was standing in the hallway carrying a blue Pan Am Airlines bag with a loaded revolver inside.

Keith was a relentless junkie. He'd been buying cocaine from Wolfgang for six months. The $305 he owed was carefully recorded beside his initials in the 8 1/2 x 11-inch notebook that Wolfgang used to track his clients' debts.

Even though it was midafternoon, Wolfgang wore nothing but a T-shirt and underwear. He had no use for clothes. All he did these days was sell drugs out of his apartment, and the job had no dress code. His clients were desperate. They didn't care if he wore pants.

The neighbors suspected he was up to no good. Visitors would come and go at all hours. His apartment on the second floor of 2 North Drive was a regular drive-thru, but the Toronto police drug squad apparently knew nothing about it. Although Wolfgang was one of those cryptically referred to as "known to police," and his FBI file warned he "should be considered armed and dangerous when not in custody," it had been years since his last run-in with the law.

Except for the large quantity of cocaine in his closet and the marijuana in his freezer, Apartment 207 was otherwise ordinary-looking—750 square feet, with a single bedroom, a TV, and an armchair by the window. The only hint of Wolfgang's troublesome past was his signed photograph of the German far-right leader Ernst Zundel. And then there were the files on the bookshelf beside the sofa that contained the membership lists of the Heritage Front, an organization Wolfgang had once headed. More Heritage Front files were stored on his computer.

Wolfgang had started dealing drugs after leaving the Sandstone correctional institution in Minnesota, where he'd served two years for his crimes as a mercenary. Keith was a regular customer. He'd called on his cell phone early that afternoon and said he wanted to come over to buy cocaine, but it was a lie. By the time he got to Wolfgang's apartment, his head was spinning. He'd been drinking hard liquor, gulping Tylenol 3s and snorting coke. On top of that, he was in methadone withdrawal. He was shaking like an old man.

Wolfgang let Keith into the apartment and went to get the cocaine, but when he turned his back, Deroux reached into his flight bag and pulled out the Rohm .22.

"Are you alone?" Keith asked.

"Ya," Wolfgang responded, with the German accent he had never quite shaken.

"I don't believe you," Keith said.

He ordered Wolfgang into the bedroom and told him to open the closet door, to make sure nobody was hiding inside. Keith was inspecting the closet, satisfying himself that it was really empty, when Wolfgang bolted. Keith fired, but he was a lousy shot and, even at fifty-five, Wolfgang was too quick for the quivering hand of an addict.

The first bullet hit the wall by the front door.

The second was also a miss. It sailed through the open doorway and into the hall.

Wolfgang ran for the stairwell.

He turned to look back just as Keith pulled the trigger one more time. The bullet struck Wolfgang in the chest, but he kept running. He was almost at the stairs when Keith got off one last shot. It hit Wolfgang square in the back of the skull. He fell face down on the carpet.

It all happened quickly. Wolfgang probably did not have time to think about who might have sent Keith to kill him, and there was no shortage of candidates, seeing as he had spent his entire adult life militantly taunting, provoking, offending and plotting.

The FBI Terrorism Section's file on Wolfgang notes his travels to Libya, involvement in the Aryan Nations and the National Socialist Party of Canada, illegal weapons, drug trafficking and his use of false identities, but the most remarkable entries concern his mercenary activities.

Wolfgang and a Texas soldier of fortune-type named Mike Perdue had once organized a military coup on the island of Dominica, a country probably best known today as the setting for Johnny Depp's *Pirates of the Caribbean* films. On November 3, 1978, Dominica became the Western hemisphere's 30th nation. At the Independence Day ceremony in Roseau, the capital city, Prime Minister Patrick John, the opposition leader Eugenia Charles and Princess Margaret watched as the Union Jack was lowered and the flag of Dominica was raised, a circle of stars surrounding a Sisserou parrot. Centuries of French and British colonial rule were over, but Dominica's troubles were only just beginning.

Within months, Wolfgang and Perdue were working on a plan to invade the island. They called it a strike against communism, but their motives were mainly financial. They wanted to steal the country and turn it into a crooks' paradise. The North American far-right wing was involved, along with the Mob and financiers in Las Vegas and Mississippi. So was the island's ex-prime minister, his army chiefs and a gang of Rastafarian guerrillas. Some believe the CIA was in on it, too.

It was one of the most audacious heists ever attempted, and until now the true story behind it has never been fully told.

This is the story of that coup. It is the story of how a Texan kicked out of the U.S. Marines and a militant Canadian Nazi teamed up to topple a Third World government for profit, adventure and power. It is a story about the Cold War, greed, revolutionary politics and the ethics of foreign military intervention. It is also the story of two federal undercover agents from New Orleans and their confidential informant, who stumbled onto the biggest case of their lives.

And it begins and ends on the island of Grenada.

Part I

Everyone Wants an Island

Basic requirements for the mercenary are few and simple: strong personal motivation and an equally strong, agile, and controlled mind and body.

—*Paul Balor,* Manual of the Mercenary Soldier:
A Guide to Mercenary War, Money and Adventure

1

Members of the People's Revolutionary Army in Grenada

St. George's, Grenada
March 13, 1979

"THIS IS MAURICE BISHOP SPEAKING."

The voice coming through the transistor radio interrupted the calypso and reggae songs that played all night on Radio Grenada.

"At four-fifteen this morning, the People's Revolutionary Army seized control of the army barracks at True Blue. The barracks were burned to the ground.

"After half-an-hour struggle, the forces of Gairy's army were completely defeated and surrendered. Every single soldier surrendered, and not a single member of the revolutionary forces was injured."

Maurice Bishop had waited a long time for this moment. A tall, handsome lawyer with a stylish, black beard and a head full of revolutionary ideas, Bishop had quietly built a guerrilla army that trained in Cuba and Guyana. Then he waited to pounce. All he needed was the right opportunity, and then his rival handed it to him.

On March 12, 1979, Prime Minister Eric Gairy flew to New York for meetings at the United Nations. Comrades across the island were told to prepare for the revolution. Early the next morning, Bishop contacted his military commanders and said the code word that signaled the start of the coup d'état: Apple.

Commander Hudson Austin led the assault against the True Blue Defense Force barracks, where 100 sleeping soldiers were arrested. The rebels seized the Radio Grenada studio, renamed it Radio Free Grenada and began broadcasting public service announcements and revolutionary propaganda.

The rebels were armed with shotguns, pistols, rifles, Molotov cocktails and whatever else they could find. They met little resistance. They attacked the police headquarters in St. George's, and the airport. At the rural outposts, the police either ran away or hoisted their white vests and shirts in surrender. Cabinet ministers were roused from their beds with guns pointed in their faces, and the Mongoose Gang secret police unit was rounded up and jailed.

"At this moment, several police stations have already put up the white flag of surrender. Revolutionary forces have been dispatched to mop up any possible source of resistance or disloyalty to the new government," Bishop's voice boomed over the radio as the coup d'état was in its sixth hour. "I am now calling on the working people, the youths, workers, farmers, fishermen, middle-class people, and women to join our armed revolutionary forces at central positions and to give them any assistance which they call for.

"Virtually all stations have surrendered."

PRIME MINISTER Eric Matthew Gairy suspected his rival was up to something. Three crates of ammunition had been smuggled to the island from the United States the previous September, labeled as petroleum jelly. Two members of Maurice Bishop's New Jewel Movement had later been arrested in Washington for trying to ship more. Gairy thought a coup was probably afoot but he had left the island anyway, thinking that, after so many years in office, he had been divinely chosen to rule.

Slim and dapper with a thin mustache, Gairy was a mystic. His office was filled with magazines about UFOs and spirituality, as well as a mummified donkey's eye, strange powders and saltpeter. He believed that aliens had been visiting Earth to help mankind. He also believed he could make his political opponents suffer sleeplessness and anxiety by transmitting Love Waves with his mind.

A sharecropper's son, Gairy had left Grenada as a young man to work in Trinidad before moving on to the oil refineries of Aruba, where he unionized the workforce, angering the island's Dutch administrators. He returned in 1950 and formed the Grenada Mental and Manual Workers Union, which organized the island's farm workers and fought for higher wages. His Grenada United Labour Party soon dominated the British colony and Gairy became Chief Minister in 1954. His political career suffered a brief setback in 1962 when the British Foreign Office discovered that $1 million in state funds had somehow vanished, as if by one of Gairy's acts of dark magic. Gairy was suspended for corruption but returned to power in 1967 as prime minister and was soon lobbying the United Nations to take action on what he called "a matter of great concern to Grenada"—UFOs.

MAURICE BISHOP ARRIVED back in Grenada in 1970 after completing his schooling in Britain. Bishop was six feet, three-inches tall with a big smile and big ideas, part of the generation of students deeply moved by Fidel Castro's Cuban revolution. He studied law in London, where he was exposed to Marx, Mao and the Black Power movement. Upon his return, he began agitating for political change and was arrested at a health workers' demonstration, which only raised his profile. After Eric Gairy was re-elected in 1972, the opposition formed the New Jewel Movement. (Jewel was an acronym for Joint Endeavor for Welfare, Education and Liberation.)

By the time Grenada became an independent nation in 1974, Gairy was a corrupt strongman intolerant of dissent. His armed forces and police broke up demonstrations with force. Among those killed by the police was Bishop's father, Rupert. Gairy's conviction that he was divinely prophesied to rule, and his preoccupation with space aliens, led *Time* magazine to invent a unique label for his administration: a warlockracy. From his mansion atop Mount Royal, Gairy studied the supernatural and made life difficult for his rival, using both the powers of the state and the powers of mysticism, but he never let his concern show. "Lots of people have tried to get rid of me and they are lying in the cemetery," Gairy told the *New York Times*. Gairy had more celestial issues than political dissent to deal with. During his 1978 address to the U.N. General Assembly, he raised the topic of ufology, calling on the world body to "play an active and leading role in coordinating research on the UFO phenomenon."

While Gairy was searching the skies for flying saucers, Bishop was meticulously plotting revolution. New Jewel Movement members infiltrated the police and military and were just waiting for their chance when Gairy flew to the United Nations to once again lobby for international action on UFOs. It was now or never.

Bishop was convinced that Gairy was preparing a slaughter. He thought the prime minister had left the island because he did not want to be present when his security forces wiped out the New Jewel leadership. He wanted an alibi.

"Before these orders could be followed, the People's Revolutionary Army was able to seize power," Bishop explained in his radio speech. "This people's government will now be seeking Gairy's extradition so that he may be put on trial to face charges, including the gross charges, the serious charges, of murder, fraud and the trampling of the democratic rights of the people."

The first coup d'état in the English-speaking Caribbean was largely bloodless, with only three dead.

By 10:30 a.m., when Bishop made his inaugural radio address, Gairy's rule was all but over and the Isle of Spice was on a path towards Marxism. Once the dust settled, Bishop intended to set up a Revolutionary Council and establish ties with Cuba and the Soviet Union. He promised to form a People's Revolutionary Government, and referred to himself as the People's Leader.

Bishop was certain that Gairy would not surrender the prime minister's office without a fight. Gairy would try to mount a counter-coup; Bishop was convinced of that. He was also sure that Gairy would hire foreign mercenaries to do the job.

"We know Gairy will try to organize international assistance, but we advise that it will be an international criminal offence to assist the dictator Gairy," Bishop said in his broadcast. "This will amount to an intolerable interference in the internal affairs of our country and will be resisted by all patriotic Grenadians with every ounce of our strength.

I am appealing to all the people, gather at all central places all over the country, and prepare to welcome and assist the People's Armed Forces when they come into your area. The revolution is expected to consolidate the position of power within the next few hours.

"Long live the people of Grenada."

2

Mike Perdue

Houston, Texas
May 1979

MIKE PERDUE LIKED to tell war stories.

Some soldiers come home from combat and keep it all to themselves, but Perdue seemed to enjoy talking about roaming the battlefields of Vietnam, southern Africa and Latin America. He wasn't afraid to tell people he was a mercenary. Everyone needs a paycheck. Besides, it was hardly a new profession. It was as old as war itself.

The Greeks hired themselves out to the pharaohs of Egypt. The Vikings fought for the Byzantine Emperors. Ireland's Wild Geese soldiered for the French. And during Africa's post-colonial upheaval, mercenaries flocked to Angola, Benin, Botswana, the Comoros, Congo, Lesotho, Mozambique, Namibia and Rhodesia. By the 1970s, mercenaries were identified with independence of spirit, the "last free men," with their own magazines such as *Soldier of Fortune*, the "journal of professional adventurers."

With his thick, brown mustache, solid forearms and dark aviator sunglasses, Michael Eugene Perdue would not have looked out of place on the cover. At five feet, eleven inches and 200 pounds, he had the solid physique of a bodybuilder, the fruit of hours spent at the gym near his house in the Bayou City, Houston.

Perdue's adventures were set in places like Rhodesia, where Ian Smith had recruited white mercenaries by placing ads that promised "fun" in the Bush War against black liberation groups. Some of Perdue's wars were closer to home. He told stories about running guns into Nicaragua, where the pro-American president Anastasio Somoza Debayle was in a losing civil war against the leftist Sandinista National Liberation Front.

And Perdue talked about fighting in Uruguay, where left-wing Tupamaro guerrillas, also known as the National Liberation Movement, were waging a campaign of kidnappings and assassinations, and had even killed an FBI agent. To battle the insurgency, Uruguay had joined forces with Argentina, Bolivia, Brazil, Chile and Paraguay in Operation Condor to kill leftist revolutionaries. There were rumors of American involvement, so no one questioned Perdue's story.

Thirty years old and between jobs, Perdue was intrigued when he heard about Grenada. He had spent enough time in the West Indies to know that overthrowing the island's ill-equipped revolutionary militia would not be difficult. Grenada was the smallest country in the Western hemisphere. It was only twenty-one miles long and twelve wide. There were icebergs in Antarctica bigger than that. He could do it. But after that he swore he was going to quit. One more coup and he'd be set for life.

On the maps, the West Indies looked like fragments of green glass shattered on a blue tile floor. South of the familiar pistol shape of Florida lay Cuba, Jamaica, Hispaniola (Haiti and the Dominican Republic) and Puerto Rico.

After that, the islands looked infinitely smaller. Even their group name, the Lesser Antilles, suggested a relative unimportance, but with a few exceptions each was, or would soon become, a fully independent country with all the powers and burdens and opportunities that accompany nationhood.

The southeastern islands of the Caribbean are called the Windwards. Perdue studied the archipelago. He kept the maps in his black briefcase, along with his Government Model Colt .45. The islands were a new outpost of communist expansion, and Perdue was about to make them a battleground for foreign mercenaries.

"This is my last job," he said.

MIKE PERDUE LIVED in a tastefully decorated house in Houston's Montrose neighborhood, two miles south of the Buffalo Bayou. Howard Hughes had once lived nearby. So had Lyndon B. Johnson, the 36th president of the United States, who had flooded Vietnam with American combat troops, saying that, "If we allow Vietnam to fall, tomorrow we'll be fighting in Hawaii and next week in San Francisco." Perdue used similar logic when he talked about his military career and mercenary jobs.

Anyone who visited Perdue's house on Marshall Street could tell the mercenary business paid well. The house was full of antiques. He shared it with his close friend Ron Cox. They had known each other for a decade and had moved south together from Indianapolis. Cox wasn't a mercenary. He owned a business less than a mile away on the Westheimer Road strip, called the Final Curtain. Cox sold wholesale design drapery.

At Christmas, Perdue would drive up to Kentucky to visit his mother, Flora, at the Wheel Estates trailer park in Louisville. Flora was originally from northern Tennessee. In 1935, she'd married a bootlegger named "Popcorn" Henry Asberry Perdue. They were living in Crawfordsville, the Athens of Indiana, when Mike was born. He was still a baby when his sister decided to marry. She was thirteen. Flora approved but Henry said no. They began to quarrel often and Henry soon abandoned the family.

"We were kind of a piss-poor hillbilly family," says Bill Perdue, the eldest of the five Perdue children. With the kids in tow, Flora moved to Lafayette, Indiana and Jackson, Michigan before returning to her hometown, Portland, Tennessee, where she got a dollar-a-day job at a shirt factory. "We always had clothes on our backs and food in our bellies. She did a good job," Bill says. "My mother raised four boys and a girl. Mike's problem was he was a baby at the time. My mother could never say no to him. He was her favorite. My mother never told him 'no.' He could have anything, he could do anything and nothing was ever wrong."

At Halloween, Mike would dress up like a soldier. He kept cats and would carry them around by the neck. "He killed quite a few cats," Bill says. "He didn't have a conscience at all really." Mike went to high school in Gallatin, Tennessee, a town best known as the home of Dot Records, which produced some of the most popular American recording artists of the time—Lawrence Welk, Pat Boone, Liberace, the Andrews Sisters and Freddy Fender. It was also just 100 miles north of Pulaski, Tennessee, birthplace of the Ku Klux Klan.

Even at a young age, Mike Perdue drifted towards militancy. In his teens, he formed a youth gang inspired by the Klan that would beat up blacks and break into vacation homes along the Tennessee River. "That was Tennessee at the time," Bill Perdue shrugged. "It was a way of having power, I guess."

The police soon caught up with the gang. Mike was arrested for breaking into a house and his mother couldn't afford a lawyer like the other boys' parents. He was sent to state prison, where he passed the time lifting weights. He told his brother he killed a black inmate by holding his head in a toilet bowl. "I guess this black guy had approached him and said he was going to kick his ass," Bill says. Mike was never charged in connection with any such incident and Bill does not know to this day whether the story is true. Mike was released after a year. "That's when he really took to a life of crime. They didn't straighten him out. They just showed him better ways of doing it."

Flora met her second husband, Jim Carter, in Gallatin, but when Mike found out he was beating her, he lost it. He phoned his brother, who got in his car and drove straight to their mother's apartment. When Bill Perdue got there he found his stepfather cowering in a corner and Mike standing over him.

Bill picked Jim up by the collar.

"Don't do that to my mom," Bill told his stepfather.

"Bill," Jim said, "do whatever you want. Just don't let Mike at me again."

On February 19, 1968, when Mike was still in high school, Henry Perdue gassed himself to death in the camper trailer he called home. Less than two months later, on April 1, Mike enlisted. All three of his brothers had served in the armed forces. Bill was in the U.S. Air Force. Bob and Jim were in the Army. Mike rounded out the family service record by joining the Marine Corps.

AFTER HE LEFT THE MARINES, Mike Perdue never really held a steady job. His brothers all worked with their hands. Bob was a diesel mechanic and Bill worked at the auto plant. But not Mike. "Just badass lazy," Bill says. He drove a truck for a while and worked at a mental hospital. He tried his hand in the drug trade, trucking marijuana up from Texas, but he got swindled out of his money. Then he met a woman in Houston who told him how easy it was to defraud banks.

It was a simple, devious scam. Perdue would drive around until he found a letterbox with the flag raised, its contents awaiting pickup by the U.S. Postal Service. He'd steal the letters and find one with a check in it, maybe a utility bill payment or a birthday gift for a grandson. He'd copy down all the information on the check and then he'd go to the bank. He'd give the teller the name and corresponding account number and withdraw their cash.

Sometimes he didn't even have to get out of his car. He'd just pull up to the drive-in teller. "He'd drive through and they would hand money out the window," Bill Perdue says. "He was kind of like a flim-flam man. He didn't work but he always had a pocket full of money." In Houston, the toughest part of his day was his workout at the gym. He didn't even have to take care of the house. His roommate did that. "This Ron Cox was an excellent housekeeper," Bill Perdue says. "Hell of a nice guy. He really took care of Mike, about like his mother did."

The neighbors on Marshall Road liked Mike and Ron. They were always willing to lend a hand. Whenever they mowed their small front lawn, they would cut the grass next door as well. "They were very nice men and were good neighbors," one woman says. Mike told them he had served in the military and liked guns. He said he had a collection of handguns in the house and told people to come over if they ever got scared. He'd protect them.

He didn't tell them about the guns buried in his garden.

THOSE WHO HAD LISTENED to Mike Perdue talk about his fighting days knew that every minute of his soldiering life had been spent battling communists, but he was not one of those you could ever call a true believer. He didn't seem to believe in much of anything. All that mattered was making as much money as possible in the easiest possible way. He would lie, cheat and steal, if that's what it took. He would even put on a uniform and kill. Asked how his brother got involved in the mercenary profession, Bill replied: "Easier than working for a living."

Perdue liked to read *Soldier of Fortune* and *Special Weapons and Tactics* but, in May 1979, he picked up a weekly news magazine and leafed through its glossy pages. There was an Islamic Revolution in Iran and a human rights crackdown in China. Congress was talking about bringing back the draft. The only good news was in the Middle East, where Israel and Egypt had made amends. Book reviewers were raving about John Updike's new novel, *The Coup*.

But what caught Perdue's attention was an item about the revolution in Grenada. He knew almost nothing about Grenada. He had vacationed in the Caribbean but back then Grenada wasn't exactly a popular tourist draw, with resorts where you could lie on the beach and gulp rum. The article described Maurice Bishop as a leftist revolutionary. Washington was worried about him. It was bad enough that Castro held Cuba, the northernmost island in the Antilles chain. Now the southernmost of the Antilles had fallen to the communists as well. The Soviets had the Caribbean in a vise grip. U.S. shipping and air lanes were said to be at risk.

From such a solid footing, Moscow and Libya could meddle in Central America, fomenting revolution and propagating anti-American unrest. Grenada was not a big country but it had strategic value to the Soviets: it not only gave them another friend in the Americas, it was also 1,600 miles closer to Angola than Cuba, and could therefore serve as a base for spreading communism in West Africa.

There was a long tradition of U.S. intervention in the Caribbean. In the United States, some called the region America's Lake. President Theodore Roosevelt had come up with a doctrine, called the Roosevelt Corollary, which asserted the right of the United States to exercise "international police power" in the Caribbean and Central America. "All that this country desires is to see the neighboring countries stable, orderly and prosperous," he wrote in 1904. Interventions followed in Cuba, Nicaragua, Haiti and the Dominican Republic.

13

So when Mike Perdue read that the deposed president of Grenada was seeking arms and foreign mercenaries to take the island back from the Marxists, he thought he might be just the man for the job. Eric Gairy wanted to stage a counter-revolution and Perdue was confident he could do it. "It was just an idea that I came up with," he said. How hard could it be to topple Grenada's idealistic new regime? As the legendary mercenary Colonel Mad Mike Hoare said, "Literally, thirty or forty well-armed, ruthless men can overthrow a stable government."

Soldiers of fortune like Hoare had stirred outrage in the developing world. Dictators and despots were hiring their own private armies to consolidate their power at the dawn of African independence. The United Nations tackled the issue in 1977; an addition to the Geneva Conventions explicitly denied mercenaries the right to be treated as combatants or prisoners of war. The U.N. was also working on an international treaty against the recruitment, use, financing and training of mercenaries. The agreement's aim: the "eradication of these nefarious activities."

Nefarious activities were what Mike Perdue did best. All he had to do was talk Grenada's exiled prime minister into letting him organize the coup. And Mike was a good talker. "He had the gift of the gab," Bill says. "He was a very personable and funny guy, too." He could talk people into almost anything. Some people are just like that. The stories he told about Vietnam helped. Who wouldn't listen to a man who had been wounded in combat twice, and lived to fight another day in the jungles of South America?

PERDUE FOUND ERIC GAIRY in San Diego. Gairy was staying at a friend's house and passing his days in exile discussing his theories on UFOs, which he believed he had seen several times, and dreaming of the demise of the "young, weed-smoking drop-outs" who had ousted him. He was determined to return to power. "This cannot last," he told a *Los Angeles Times* reporter a month after the coup. Unless Maurice Bishop was stopped, he added, the Caribbean "will become a nest for communist activities."

Perdue called him up, using a phone number he got by canvassing newspaper reporters who had interviewed the ex-prime minister. Gairy was willing to meet, so Perdue got some money from a friend in Texas and flew 1,300 miles to southern California.

They met at a hotel. Perdue explained his credentials and said he would be willing to assemble a mercenary force to retake the island. The counter-coup would be swift and decisive. All he needed was a contract that would make it worth his while.

Gairy did not enter into a formal agreement with Perdue or give him money. He was noncommittal, and neither accepted nor declined the proposition, but Perdue sensed that Gairy was interested, and that was good enough. He decided to begin planning the invasion of Grenada. He would overthrow Maurice Bishop and return Eric Gairy to power. The mystical Gairy would get his country back and Perdue would make enough money to retire—and he'd have another war story to tell.

3

Aarne Polli and Wolfgang Droege (right)

Toronto, Canada
August 1979

MIKE PERDUE KNEW that if he was going to stage a coup d'état, he was going to need money, mercenaries, guns—and a contract. He felt he had at least made a start on the last item on the list but he had work to do. Getting money and guns was not going to be that difficult, but he needed help finding manpower, so he turned to a charismatic Louisiana native he had met a few years earlier, the former Imperial Wizard of the Ku Klux Klan.

Perdue went to hear David Duke speak in Texas and approached him afterwards. "He came to one of my public meetings, that's how I met him," Duke says. "I didn't know anything about him; he wasn't a friend." Perdue told Duke he was putting together a force to invade Grenada. "He gave me the impression he had experience in these types of things."

Duke had left the Klan in 1978 and he wasn't interested in toppling foreign governments by force, but he gave Perdue a few names and numbers to get him started. One of them was in Canada. It was the phone number for a house with steep steps and a small front porch on Kingsmount Park Road in Toronto, and it belonged to a man named Donald Clarke Andrews.

Don Andrews had mutton-chop sideburns and walked with a limp. He lived in an old brick house on Toronto's east side and, between shifts as a hospital kitchen supervisor, published a newsletter called the *High Sierra Club*, a mimeographed recruiting bulletin that connected mercenaries with those in need of their unique skills. He was also a leader of Canada's militant far-right movement.

Andrews was just out of prison when Mike Perdue called the house to enlist his support for the invasion of Grenada. "He said the guy there wanted to get back into power, Sir Eric Gairy," Andrews recalled. Perdue told him he was assembling a team of mercenaries for the job, "which I thought was a fair thing," Andrews says.

Andrews was already familiar with the events in Grenada. Every strident anti-communist knew about it. He didn't hesitate. He immediately assigned two men to work with Mike Perdue.

"BASICALLY, I'M AN UNDERDOG FIGHTER," is how Andrews once described himself in an interview. "Anyone that's got any goodness in them, I'm on your side."

A Canadian government report describes him as a "cult-like" figure. Some just call him a racist.

Andrews owned a couple of rooming houses in Toronto as well as the Mansion, which is what everyone called his home. Every week, right-wing radicals like Wolfgang Droege would gather in his living room to hear him lecture on racial politics and the evils of communism. His followers were known as the Androids. "Jealous people called them Androids because they did what I asked them," he explained.

Born in Sarajevo, Andrews was the leader of the Nationalist Party of Canada, the latest of the right-wing groups he had formed since moving to Canada in 1952 and changing his name from Vilim Zlomislic. At the age of twenty-five, Andrews co-founded the Edmund Burke Society, named after an archconservative British Member of Parliament. The Burkers were supposed to be a thorn in the side of the Reds on the far left. Whenever the Reds held a protest, the Burkers would be there staging a counter-protest. But the Burke Society rapidly drifted into anti-Semitism and white nationalism, and changed its name to the Western Guard in 1972. Its mission was to "preserve and promote the basic social and spiritual values of the White People." Its symbol was the Celtic cross and Andrews was its leader.

Western Guard members crashed leftist meetings wearing fake Hitler mustaches and shouting white power slogans. Its members greeted each other with arms raised, Nazi-style. Andrews called it the Roman salute, arguing it predated fascism. When the Guard celebrated Mussolini's birthday, the Toronto Marxist committee demonstrated outside Andrews' headquarters, carrying picket signs that read "Ban the Western Guard." Andrews and his members stood on his balcony, giving the Nazi salute and pelting the protesters with eggs and bricks. At Toronto's CityTV studio, a Guardsman interrupted a performance by the Jamaican band Crack of Dawn, shouting that blacks should be sent to Africa. The band's nine-year-old singer was slapped in the face and Andrews was arrested, accused of kicking a band member's wife in the stomach. Andrews was acquitted, but before dismissing the court, Judge Farquhar McRae told a story about a piano. If you only play on the white keys, he said, the result is discord. The same happens if you play just the black keys. To get harmony, you must play them both. "Now that's the story," he said. "Goodbye."

Spray paint was one of the Western Guard's favorite tools. "Hitler was right," "Keep Canada White," and the Nazi slogan *"Juden Raus"* (Jews Out) began appearing on fences around Toronto. Andrews blamed a splinter group. A Western Guard member named Armand Siksna became the first person charged under Canada's 1970 Hate Propaganda Act when a Toronto police officer caught him with a can of spray paint in his hand, standing in front of a slogan that read, "Down with Jews." He was acquitted.

Andrews was a troublemaker but he was also an ideologue. He was well read and could comfortably cite historical references to back his political theories. His fundamental belief was that power belonged to white people and that non-white immigration was eroding that divine right. "White people," espoused one of his flyers, "Canada belongs to us." The party's Toronto Manifesto called for an immediate halt to "colored immigration" and a program to "repatriate" non-whites "to countries or areas where their own race is the majority." "You don't want Toronto to become another Detroit, Buffalo or Calcutta," one pamphlet read. "Don't be forced to flee to the suburbs for safety or fear to walk your street at night. Don't be an alien in your own country!"

The Guard thought it was destined for mainstream politics. Andrews even ran for mayor of Toronto in 1974. He finished a distant second—although he beat out a clown named Rosie Sunrise and a superhero called Rik the Universe, whose platform consisted of recipes for frogs' legs. But he caused the political equivalent of cardiac arrest when it was pointed out that, under city regulations, as runner up, Andrews would have taken control of Canada's largest city had Mayor David Crombie died in the two weeks prior to election day. The headline in *The Toronto Star* read: "Toronto Was a Heartbeat Away from Fascist Mayor". The rules were quickly changed.

Don Andrews was impressed when he came across the writings of David Duke. Andrews sent him a letter, and in 1975, drove south with Wolfgang Droege to meet the Louisianan. Andrews and Duke were similar men in some respects, both intelligent and yet smitten with beliefs that made them intellectual outcasts. Both also hoped to hold political office in the most multicultural cities in North America— Toronto and New Orleans.

Although they had their differences of opinion, Andrews and Duke were engaged in the same fight to transform their beliefs into a mainstream political movement, and so they helped each other out. The Canadians showed up at Duke's rallies south of the border, and when police in Ontario went after Don Andrews and the Western Guard, Duke sent a letter to the attorney general, Roy McMurtry, protesting his "anti-white policies": "[You have] betrayed your race and nation by subservience to international Zionism and the state of Israel. Take heed that your nefarious anti-white activities are being monitored and recorded by our international Klan movement. If you persist in your treacherous activities against the white race I can assure you that there will only be grave consequences."

McMurtry showed the letter to police. "They wanted to arrest him, but I said no," the minister says. "They could do what they wanted; I wasn't instructing them one way or the other except to say, 'I don't want to give the son of a bitch that sort of notoriety.'"

For the most part, however, Duke kept out of trouble, but Andrews seemed to seek it and the Western Guard eventually collapsed under the weight of his zeal. He plotted to attack an Israeli soccer team visiting Toronto for a tournament (the scheme was never carried out), but that wasn't what landed him in jail. "We did do it," he admitted in an interview, "but I wasn't convicted of it." Rather, his 1978 conviction was for possession of explosive substances and mischief, for painting swastikas and racial slogans on synagogues. The judge sent him to prison for two years and banned him from the Western Guard, so when he was released, he formed a new organization with a similar platform, the Nationalist Party of Canada.

Don Andrews had a reputation in the far right and he knew some mercenaries through his newsletter, so it was only logical that when Mike Perdue approached David Duke about an anti-communist coup, it was Andrews' name that came to mind.

Andrews gave the Grenada plan some thought. He got some books from the library and read up on the Caribbean. He quickly came to two conclusions. First, they had to move fast, before the Cubans settled in and made the island impenetrable. Second, the operation could not be mounted from the United States or Canada.

"Too many spies around here," he said.

For the coup to have any chance of success, it would have to launch from an offshore base. And he knew just the spot.

IT WAS AARNE POLLI who introduced Andrews to Dominica. Polli was one of the many young men who hung out at the Mansion. A Canadian of Estonian heritage, he grew up in Toronto and spoke cryptically about having once worked for the U.S. intelligence establishment. He had been drawn to Andrews' stance against communism, but then his friends drifted into fascism. "Everybody wants to be the fuehrer," he sighed. He thought the parade of organizations formed by the extreme right was comical. "Every time you get two of these guys together and a six pack, you get another organization."

Polli had his fingers in a few business ventures. He had a contract giving him a 30-percent commission on a deal to buy a dozen

Caribou airplanes from Tanzania. Another contract promised him a 10-percent finder's fee for the sale of Alaska gold, and he was in on another scheme called the "Ghana loan gold barter transaction." His friend Dennis, a businessman in Ottawa, had also been looking into investing in a small island called Dominica. It was possibly the least developed of all the Caribbean islands, with no industry to speak of except bananas. Dominica was a breathtakingly beautiful place, with volcanic peaks and rain forests, but tourists hardly ever stopped there. Anyone with any business sense could see it had huge potential—real estate, tourism, forestry.

Dennis was particularly interested in the timber. Dominica has some of the best oceanic rainforests in the West Indies. It was a valuable untapped resource, but aside from local harvesting for cooking fires, the island had no logging industry. There had been several attempts to make a go of it, dating back to 1909, but the island's geography and inaccessibility made it so costly to log the forests and get the lumber to buyers that nobody had ever been able to make it work. Together with Polli and a Las Vegas physician named Ted Thorp, Dennis had been trying to get permission to harvest hardwood and export it. A feasibility study found that about one-third of the island's timber was commercial grade, meaning the wood was perfect for railroad ties. If they could get a contract with a railroad company, all they had to do was get the wood to Key West. The numbers weren't great, but they figured they could break even. If they got a contract, they could at least get bank financing.

When Andrews heard about Dominica from Polli, he took an immediate interest. He had his rooming houses in Toronto, but he had been thinking about investing in the Caribbean. He wanted a base of operations somewhere offshore. He had already invested $6,000 in a coffee business with a Frenchman from Guadeloupe. They were going to grow coffee in the mountains of Dominica, but the plan fell through and Andrews lost his money. Now that a coup against Grenada was in the works, he thought that Dominica might prove useful in another sense.

He checked a map. Only a short stretch of sea separated the two islands.

Dominica was small, remote and within striking distance of Grenada. Anyone who planned to invade Grenada was going to need a place to assemble, train and launch. Dominica seemed like the natural staging area. If he were to set up a company in Dominica, Andrews thought, he could bring down mercenaries and guns without arousing suspicion. They could prepare for the attack without fear of scrutiny. "I thought I'd use that opportunity to build up a business and bring the mercenaries in," he says. A foreign-owned business would provide the front they needed for their covert activities.

Andrews needed to know what was going on in Dominica. He needed to do reconnaissance, so he contacted a Belgian who had replied to one of his *High Sierra Club* classifieds. His name was Roger Dermée and he was the real deal. He had fought in Algeria and Katanga. "He was a genuine Congo mercenary," Andrews says. Dermée flew to Dominica and quickly settled in. He began teaching French at a school run by nuns and, in the evenings, worked as a hotel chef.

Andrews also asked Aarne Polli to go south to work with Mike Perdue. Polli paid $479.20 for an American Airlines ticket with an open return date. At seven the next morning, Polli took off from Toronto airport for LaGuardia. From there he flew to Miami and Barbados before arriving in Dominica at 6:30 a.m.

He landed on an island in chaos.

4

Roseau, Dominica, 1981

Roseau, Dominica
August 29, 1979

HURRICANE DAVID WAS BORN off the West Coast of Africa. The tropical heat cooked the ocean waters, and the rising air began to swirl, propelled by the Earth's rotation. The trade winds blew the spiral west, and then it veered north, towards the island of Dominica.

It struck land at 9 a.m. The palms began to dance and the coconuts shot off the trees like cannonballs. Gusts that peaked at 175 miles per hour ripped apart the shanties. Roofing and shutters filled the sky like spinning kites and entire farms of banana trees toppled in unison. In the Botanical Garden, a fat baobab flattened a yellow bus.

The island had not seen a storm so destructive in a century and a half, and it could hardly have come at a worse time. Not a year had passed since Dominica had gained its independence from Britain and nationhood had turned out to be a struggle. The government had been forced out by popular unrest, and the economy, dependent almost entirely on the export of bananas, was faltering. Already one of the poorest of the Caribbean islands, Dominica was in crisis. And then along came David, as if extreme weather had been sent to finish the place off once and for all.

Radio broadcasts warned the hurricane was coming, but the forecasters predicted it would hit Barbados. When David suddenly changed course for Dominica, the locals couldn't believe their misfortune.

"God must be a *Bajan*," they said.

Even as they awaited the storm, some thought the high mountains would protect them. The mountains had always been the island's guardians. Morne Watt, Morne Trois Pitons and Morne Diablotins, the Mountain of Demons—they formed a natural fortress that for centuries had sheltered the Caribs, escaped slaves and pirates. The forested slopes made the island a nightmare for invaders, military conquerors and colonists, which may be why locals joke that were Christopher Columbus to return today, Dominica would be the only place in the New World he would still recognize.

The Lesser Antilles are the chain of small islands on the eastern rim of the Caribbean Sea. On the map they look like a tail appended to the four big islands of the West Indies. First inhabited by Arawaks, the islands were conquered by warring Caribs from South America around 1200. Almost 300 years later, while searching for a passage to Asia, Columbus reached the northern Caribbean and left a company of soldiers at Hispaniola. Columbus returned to Spain but quickly sailed for the Caribbean again, this time taking a more southerly route. On Sunday November 3, 1493, he sighted land, an island that jutted from the warm seawaters like a rough green gemstone. He named it after the day of the week on which he had found it: Dominica.

Columbus sailed his seventeen-ship flotilla north to Guadeloupe, Montserrat, Antigua and St. Kitts, and on a third voyage in 1498 he reached Grenada, Tobago and Trinidad, which became the first Spanish settlement in the Eastern Caribbean. The European land grab had begun. The British settled St. Kitts and Barbados. The Dutch staked a claim to St. Martin. The French landed at Martinique and Guadeloupe. Dominica lay between the two French islands, but it resisted colonization. The Caribs drove off the first Europeans and it was not until the early 1700s that French settlers were able to build their coffee estates. The French lost Roseau to the British in 1761, and the two powers fought on and off over the island, until France formally ceded it to Britain.

On the plantations carved out of the jungle, coffee gave way to sugarcane, a more labor-intensive crop. To meet the demand for farm workers, land owners began importing slaves from West Africa. The British and French transported a staggering 3 million slaves to the West Indies. But Dominica is a ragged island full of hiding places and slaves fled the plantations for the mountains and valleys. The British fought several wars against the escaped slaves, known as Maroons, until the British Parliament abolished slavery in 1833.

As the islands around it prospered, Dominica remained stuck in poverty. The slow pace of development so concerned the British that they sent a commissioner, Sir Robert Hamilton, to study why it was "more backward and less developed than almost any other of the islands ... and why its people were less prosperous and contented than Her Majesty's other West Indian subjects." Farming was Dominica's mainstay: sugar, coca, limes, bananas. In addition to the large plantations, islanders cultivated small plots and sold their crops at the Saturday market in Roseau. Tension between the big landowners and farm workers came to define Dominican politics, and following the Second World War, the Dominica Labour Party formed to push for better working conditions. Edward Oliver LeBlanc led the party to election victories in 1961, 1965 and 1970, but in the early '70s everyone was talking about an ambitious young union organizer named Patrick Roland John.

PATRICK JOHN WAS A POPULIST. He could rouse a crowd with his speeches, waving and gesticulating to make a point. He was best known as a sportsman. He played cricket and represented Dominica in soccer. He was an athletic powerhouse, although he is extremely short in stature. On his passport application form, he wrote that he was five feet three-and-a-half inches, but the passport itself puts him at five feet one inch, shorter than Napoleon (whose troops once attacked the island). The BBC described him as "small in stature but large in ambition," but in Creole, they say, *Piti hach ka bat gwo bwa*. Little axe cuts big trees.

From modest roots, John became Roseau's mayor in 1965 and served as Minister of Home Affairs. When LeBlanc stepped down as colonial premier, "PJ" was the popular choice to replace him. His campaign used a masterful slogan that played on both his size and his humble origins to position him as a man of the people. The slogan was: The Little Man.

Not everyone liked Patrick John. He had a political rival by the name of Mary Eugenia Charles. They clashed at just about every level. Aside from the obvious male-female divide, John saw himself as an advocate of the common man, whereas Eugenia Charles was the daughter of J.B. Charles, a wealthy businessman who had been mayor of Roseau and a member of the Legislative Assembly. While PJ was schooled in Roseau, Eugenia Charles had been educated abroad. After graduating from the Convent of the Sisters of the Faithful Virgin, she studied law at the University of Toronto and went on to the London School of Economics. She returned to Dominica in 1949 to open a law practice.

Never a supporter of the Labour Party, she wrote anonymous newspaper columns denouncing its policies. Her writing so unsettled the government that it introduced legislation aimed at silencing the press. Charles led opposition to the law, which she called the "shut your mouth bill." It passed anyway, but her supporters, who called themselves the Freedom Fighters, went on to form their own party, the Dominica Freedom Party, and Charles entered the legislature as their representative. Charles had a talent for political theater. When the premier tried to introduce a parliamentary dress code, she showed up in the legislature wearing only a bathing suit, a gift from a visiting Canadian friend, purchased at the Eaton's department store in Toronto.

The Labour Party demonized her. They called her the Wicked Wallhouse Witch, after her family residence south of the capital. They made fun of her because she was unmarried and childless. For her part, Charles bristled at the government for its lack of punctuality. Meetings scheduled for ten in the morning would invariably fail to convene until well after eleven. Eugenia Charles was a "powerful lady, the Iron Lady of the Caribbean," says Parry Bellot, a Dominican journalist, educated in Vancouver, Canada, who served as her press secretary. "Strong leader. She'd bulldoze her way through a lot of things. She could be rough with her language, use some cuss words," he says. But she had integrity and a practical nature that drove her to get things done.

DESPITE THEIR MUTUAL DISDAIN, Patrick John and Eugenia Charles agreed on one issue: the Dreads.

The Dreads were militant Rastafarians. Like Jamaica's Rastamen, they wore their hair in long matted ropes, talked about exploitation and liberation and worshipped Emperor Haile Selassie of Ethiopia, whom they considered the Messiah.

Everything the Dreads associated with colonization or the white man, including Western medicine, imported or processed food and clothes, they renounced and rejected. They would walk naked along the side of the road—not *on* the road because asphalt was a tool of colonial oppression.

And they smoked a lot of marijuana. They grew it on remote farms in the hills east of Roseau which they guarded using guns they bartered for ganja. "According to Dread philosophy it is more or less a God-given gift to grow whatever plant you can grow on the face of the Earth," says Fordie Algernon Maffei, a former Dread everyone calls Algie. "Anyone trying to interfere with God's gift is the devil." The Dreads combined the spiritual elements of Rastafarianism with the political jargon of the Black Power movement and the zeal of 1970s leftist revolutionaries. It was a potent mix. They were radical and violent. When the mood hit them, they would descend from their hilltop camps with rifles and cutlasses to raid the plantations for food and attack farmers, whites, tourists and police. "They are a bunch of uneducated, misguided youth," says Gene Pastaina, a former police inspector who later became the island's Director of Public Prosecutions. "They had no philosophy in mind. They're ignoramuses."

Algie Maffei was one of them. Algie grew up in Fond Colé and at one time played soccer with Patrick John at Windsor Park. He served briefly in the militia, the Dominica Defence Force, but he quit and went to sea to work on the banana boats that deliver the island's most valuable export. "I like guns," he says. "I liked guns since I was small." His troubles with the police began when he was a teenager. By the time he was twenty-one, his rap sheet included convictions for shooting with intent, assaulting police, indecent language, resisting arrest and "throwing missiles." "I admit I am a violent man within my rights," he explains. "To defend myself is my right."

In 1970, Algie was arrested for marijuana possession. Released on bail, he went straight to the docks and stowed away on a cargo ship that sailed north to Canada's St. Lawrence River. He jumped ship in Trois Rivières, Quebec and hitchhiked to Montreal. The driver dropped him off on rue Ste. Catherine amid St. Jean-Baptiste Day celebrations. He didn't know anyone, so he started asking around for the only Dominican he knew in Canada, Rosie Douglas. Like Maurice Bishop, "Brother" Rosie was a young West Indian who had left home to study. The son of a wealthy coconut plantation owner, Douglas was in Canada to study agriculture but he was more interested in political science. At Sir George Williams University in Montreal, where he was president of the Association of British West Indian Students, he led an anti-racism sit-in that lasted two weeks and ended with a riot and a fire that caused $2 million in damage. Douglas was arrested.

He was out on bail, awaiting a ruling from the courts, when Algie came to town and met a woman who just happened to know Douglas. Algie dialed the number she gave him and before long he was living at Douglas' girlfriend's apartment. Algie had paid little attention to politics in Dominica but he liked what Rosie had to say about socialism and black power. "I learned a lot from Rosie," Algie says. "Rosie gave me a lot of books." The books that Douglas recommended to his followers ranged from Lenin to Stokley Carmichael. "It was a matter of the black man taking control of his destiny," is how Algie sums up the message. The first book Algie read was *Black Skin, White Masks* by Martinique-born black consciousness thinker Frantz Fanon. Published in 1952, it is described on the jacket as "the unsurpassed study of the black psyche in a white world." As a Dominican in Montreal, Algie identified with his argument. That summer, Algie and Rosie drove to Toronto. Twice, Algie tried to cross the border into the United States near Niagara Falls, and both times he was turned back. "So I just gave up and went back to Montreal," he says.

The Quebec courts gave Rosie a two-year prison sentence for his role in the student riot and he spent the time writing *Chains or Change: Focus on Dominica*, a manifesto for the island's Black Power movement. The book ranted against the "lackey hypocritical" and "imperialist" Canadian government that had jailed him and was preparing to deport him back to the island. Douglas blamed Dominica's problems on "white boy" and an education system that taught "the works of crackers like Shakespeare—the racist." Blacks who did not support Black Power, he called parasites. "Black Power means Black people doing everything within their power to break the back of white power to uplift the Black race," he wrote. At the core of the book was a call for an immediate Marxist revolution in Dominica modeled after Cuba. "Brothers and sisters, we have suffered long enough—we are demanding change, not at the next election in 1980, or in the life hereafter, but NOW!"

Algie visited Douglas in prison as much as he could, but it was difficult. Algie had a wife now and a newborn son. Algie was watching a hockey game on television between the Montreal Canadiens and the New York Rangers when the police came to his door with a warrant. "They came in and they started ransacking the place," he says. "They said they were looking for arms, ammunition and explosives." He believes they were acting on information provided by the Dominican police and Rosie Douglas' driver, Warren Hart, whom, it turned out, was an undercover agent planted by the Royal Canadian Mounted Police, which considered Douglas a national security risk. Canadian immigration told Algie he was going to be deported back to Dominica. He got a lawyer to appeal the deportation order, but he was frustrated with the way things were going in Canada. He went to visit Douglas in prison. "I think I'm returning to Dominica because Dominica is where I am needed," he said.

He returned home in 1974, just as the Jamaican Rastafarian movement was making its way to Dominica. Men who had sported Afros were wearing their hair in dreadlocks, listening to the music of Bob Marley and Peter Tosh and smoking marijuana religiously. In Dominica, however, there was a hardcore faction of Rastas called Dreads. "The Dreadman is also a Rastaman but the reason they call it Dread is he will not accept this [idea that] when you get slapped on one cheek, you turn the other," Algie explains. Algie grew his hair out in dreadlocks, started eating off the land and smoked what he called "spliffs," sometimes two or three times a day. "Marijuana is a sacred thing," he explains. "You are supposed to smoke marijuana and give praise to the Almighty." He grew his own marijuana, and farmed bananas, yams, tannia and dasheen on his land near La Plaine.

"I wanted to be seen as a revolutionary," Algie says. "The fact that capital was held by a few and the poor were getting poorer had a part to play in the idea of revolution."

He did not like Patrick John.

"To a certain extent he represented powers that protected those with capital," he says.

PATRICK JOHN AND EUGENIA CHARLES went head to head in national elections on March 24, 1975. John and his Labour Party easily defeated Charles' upstart Freedom Party. In addition to serving as premier, John made himself Minister of Security, and Colonel of the Dominica Defence Force. The DDF was created in the late 1800s to help British troops defend the island and maintain internal order. It was a volunteer force of no more than thirty personnel, but Patrick John transformed it into a full-time, professional army legislated to "maintain the integrity of the boundaries of Dominica" and "assist the police force in the maintenance of law and order during civil disturbance." Charles was against turning the DDF into a paid militia, but as Leader of the Opposition, she was powerless to stop it.

Dread violence was getting intolerable. The Dreads kidnapped young girls, terrorized farmers and attacked whites, including an American who was shot dead and a retired Canadian couple found murdered in their house. The Dreads would spit on tourists, stone them or steal their cameras. Tourism plummeted. The government responded by passing a security law. It was called the Prohibited and Unlawful Societies and Associations Act but everyone just called it the Dread Act. The law made it illegal to be a Dread, to support Dreads and even to wear dreadlocks. Anyone who killed or injured a Dread "found at any time of day or night inside a dwelling house" could not be prosecuted. Eugenia Charles went along with it, albeit reluctantly. All 160 soldiers and police officers went on full alert to enforce the law. They chased the roughly 300 Dreads through the steep mountain forests and got into shootouts with them. It was a small-scale guerrilla war.

The Dread leaders were Henry Esprit, whose nickname was Mal, which means *evil* in Creole, and Leroy Etienne, better known as

Pokosion, which means *danger*. Algie Maffei was Pokosion's right-hand man. "He was the type of fellow who didn't believe in law because he said the law men are legal criminals," Algie says. "And to a certain extent, I agreed with him."

Algie had been back in Dominica only a few months when he got into a shootout with police near his home in Fond Colé. Police seized a twelve-inch, sawed-off shotgun and ammunition. He was charged with receiving stolen guns and shooting at police. "I knew about him," Patrick John says of Algie Maffei. "All I know is he was one of the guys in the woods whom I hunted down during the operation of the Dread Act." Maffei didn't keep track of his ever-growing rap sheet. "Keeping a record of this in my head doesn't interest me."

Algie Maffei wanted to keep his dreadlocks, but his family told him he had to get rid of them. It was the law. So he cut off his *natties*. But he thought the Dread law was unjust. He called it worse than apartheid. He despised Patrick John, considering him a dictator.

The Dreads called the peaceful, natural world they sought Zion. The corrupt society they rejected was Babylon. There was a saying common among the Dreads. Some said it was just "rap talk," but others thought it betrayed a revolutionary agenda.

The saying was, "Babylon must burn."

INDEPENDENCE CAME on the 485th anniversary of Columbus' arrival. Princess Margaret represented the Queen at the ceremonies. Britain's gift to the new nation was $20 million, half of it an interest-free loan. The French promised to build an airport and improve the roads. Washington sent 250 reference volumes for the national library. The national flag was a yellow, black and white cross on a green background. At the center, a circle of green stars surrounded a Sisserou parrot, the national bird. The parrot was set on a red background. Some noted with concern that red was the color of socialism.

The national anthem was called "Isle of Beauty":

> *Isle of beauty, isle of splendor,*
> *Isle to all so sweet and fair.*

All must surely gaze in wonder,
At thy gifts so rich and rare.

Prime Minister Patrick John was forty years old, and spoke about steering Dominica towards socialism, although he was not averse to foreign capital. Foreign Minister Leo Austin was keen to put his country onto the world stage. "We will join the Organization of American States, the United Nations, World Bank, all of them," he said. It was one of Patrick John's proudest moments. But the journalist Parry Bellot says it was hardly an epic independence struggle. Britain was shedding its colonies as fast as they could come up with flag designs. Independence ceremonies were already scheduled for St. Lucia, St. Vincent, Antigua and St. Kitts-Nevis. "It wasn't a question of fighting for independence," Bellot says. "The British wanted to give us independence."

Statehood was no cure-all. The island's economy was feeble, reliant on a single crop vulnerable to bad weather. "A real banana republic," *Time* called it in a story about Dominica's independence. The headline was: *Poor Little Paradise.* The prime minister could not solve the economic puzzle, and became increasingly authoritarian as his policies faltered. Civil service strikes and the loss of the banana harvest to disease, blamed on the failure of the government-appointed banana board to provide the necessary sprays, only made things worse. Desperate, John and his entourage flirted with adventures that could only be described as ill advised.

Dominica had an uncanny knack for attracting offbeat investors, and in 1975, a Barbadian arms dealer named Sidney Burnett-Alleyne negotiated an agreement to build an airport, a hotel and a refinery that would supply South Africa, thus helping the apartheid regime evade sanctions. The agreement was met with outrage in Dominica and then faltered when French police seized a yacht off Martinique. It had been chartered by Burnett-Alleyne and it was full of weapons meant to help overthrow the government of Prime Minister Tom Adams of Barbados.

After serving prison time, Alleyne picked up where he had left off. He hired a British mercenary to draft an invasion plan for Barbados that involved 350 men who were to assemble in Dominica. Alleyne said he hoped to install Patrick John as prime minister of a united Barbados–

Dominica. Once again, the plot was discovered by the security services. Then the opposition revealed that John had secretly negotiated a pact with a Texas businessman named Don Pierson that would have given close to one-tenth of the island over to a foreign company for just $100 a year. "He wanted to set up a free port," says John. "That was a government decision."

As the government stumbled from one controversy to the next, the Dread problem continued. Police found a farmer named Augustus Ulysses buried in a shallow grave near a village on the island's east coast. The autopsy showed he had dirt in his lungs, indicating he had been buried alive. The police came to Algie Maffei's farm near La Plaine and found red stains on his banana leaves. Algie was arrested, along with Pokosion. They were taken to the Stock Farm Prison while the investigation continued.

ON MAY 29, 1979, it all came crashing down on Patrick John. A united front of his political opponents gathered outside the Government Headquarters. John had banned public gatherings in anticipation of the protest but they came anyway, by the thousands. It was Dominica's biggest demonstration ever. Already fed up with John, they were tipped over the edge by the prime minister's attempt to outlaw strikes and tighten press controls.

The crowd hurled rocks and the next thing anyone knew the Defence Force was marching down Hillsborough Street firing rifles. One of the bullets struck a nineteen-year-old in the stomach. He died. Ten others were wounded. The order to fire had come from Captain Malcolm "Marley" Reid, who personally discharged twenty-one rounds. A government commission would later call Reid's conduct that day improper and "directly responsible for the fatal shooting of Phillip Timothy," the youth who died in the street.

Inside parliament, Patrick John defiantly carried on with the business of government. Eugenia Charles stormed out. *Dominicans were shocked by the violence,* Parry Bellot wrote in his column. *It was on a scale they had never experienced. The shock turned to anger, then disgust. The people would take it no more.*

The killing united the opposition, which formed the Committee for National Salvation and shut down the country for twenty-eight days. One by one, members of Patrick John's government abandoned him. "They just crossed the floor," he says. "My majority collapsed." Oliver Seraphin became the interim prime minister. The crisis was over. The new regime warned the leftists that if the government was overthrown by force, the workers would strike.

WHATEVER STABILITY REMAINED in Dominica was washed away when David hit on August 29, 1979. Winds lashed the island for six straight hours. Algie Maffei was locked up at Stock Farm Prison, awaiting the outcome of the murder investigation, when he looked outside the security block and saw a coconut tree get sheared in half by a gust. The rain was coming down so hard he couldn't open his eyes. It felt like it was raining nails.

Hurricane David ripped the hilltop prison to shreds. The inmates couldn't believe their luck. Many of them just left. A dozen conscientious prisoners turned themselves in, but most just ran for it, like the Maroons of slave days. The prison guards rounded up whatever inmates they could find and walked them into town towards police headquarters.

Algie was handcuffed to Pokosion but when they got to Tarrish Pit, Leroy slipped out of his restraints and jumped. Algie kept walking, but when he reached J.C.'s Minimart he looked back and the guards were gone. So he walked home.

By the time people emerged from whatever shelter they had found, the streets were strewn with debris, upended telephone poles, window shutters and bodies. Thirty-seven were dead, and 5,000 injured. Three-quarters of the island's 75,000 inhabitants were homeless and the banana harvest was all but wiped out.

Looting was underway when a Royal Navy frigate reached the island the next day. British sailors worked to restore electricity and ferried the dead and injured out of remote settlements by helicopter. France, the United States and Canada joined the scramble to treat the casualties and provide emergency shelter and food. Coordinating the foreign military assistance was a burly senior officer of the Dominica Defence Force, Captain Reid.

The island had been badly beaten up, economically, politically and meteorologically. And it wasn't over yet. Satellite images showed a second hurricane, Frederick, trailing David.

Dominica needed help. Instead it was going to get mercenaries.

5

Aarne Polli doing reconnaissance in Dominica, October 1979

Houston, Texas
September 1979

MIKE PERDUE DROVE a 1977 Chevrolet Impala. It was a long, light blue sedan with Texas plates. It looked like an aircraft carrier on wheels. The hood, roof and trunk were flat and wide. You could almost land a helicopter on top.

With a V-6 behind the grill, the Chevy sailed the 350 miles of Interstate 10 from Houston to New Orleans, where Perdue was to meet Aarne Polli. The Canadian had just returned from a reconnaissance mission to Dominica. He'd phoned Perdue from Miami and they had agreed to meet in the Big Easy.

When they finally shook hands, Polli was disappointed. "He gave me the standard, 'We've got to get these commies,'" Polli says. "The guy was weird, but I thought, if he's a Vietnam vet, maybe he got fucked up over there and he's got post-traumatic stress."

Polli said he had the name of a Tennessee lawyer, J.W. Kirkpatrick. He might be willing to sink some money into a Caribbean coup. Perdue thought Polli was being very secretive about who gave him the name and address. But Polli was secretive about everything and Perdue needed financing for his coup, so they decided to take the Chevy north to Memphis to meet Kirkpatrick.

It was a 400-mile drive, straight up I-55. Along the way, Polli briefed Perdue on Dominica. Polli had arrived on the island only days after Hurricane David. He had rented a room at Vena's Guesthouse, the former home of Dominica's most famous novelist, Jean Rhys, the author of *Wide Sargasso Sea*. He had tried to look into business opportunities but, understandably enough, all anyone wanted to talk about was the hurricane. Foreign troops were arriving to help out and international aid was pouring in.

"There was money all over the place," he said.

But in the confusion after the storm, it was impossible to determine whether Don Andrews' plan to launch a front company that would conceal mercenary activities was going to fly, and Polli decided to leave.

Perdue liked what he heard. Politically unstable, economically devastated and all but blown into the sea by incessant hurricanes— Dominica sounded like a disaster. It was perfect. Mercenaries thrive in that kind of chaos. Perdue started to think that maybe he should forget Grenada and invade Dominica.

He was already having doubts about Grenada. It was too heavily defended. Since taking office, Maurice Bishop had rapidly steered the country into the communist sphere, confirming the worst fears of his critics. In his speeches, he denounced "imperialist domination" and spoke the Marxist jargon of the fashionable left. "Comrade President," he said in a speech before Fidel Castro in Cuba, "it is a changing world … We know that there is today being built a new Caribbean." But Bishop was haunted by the shadow of Eric Gairy. It was as if the former prime minister had put one of his spells on the young revolutionary. Bishop became infected by an almost hysterical paranoia, warning that Gairy was plotting a return to power. The New Jewel Movement began rounding up suspected subversives, accusing them of plotting the government's overthrow.

In a speech to mark the one-month anniversary of the Grenada revolution, Bishop complained that the American ambassador was "taking very lightly what we genuinely believe to be a real danger facing our country. Contrary to what anyone else may think, we know that the dictator Gairy is organizing mercenaries to attack Grenada in order to restore him to his throne." Bishop claimed that Gairy's "underworld friends" had written a letter "indicating how much and what kind of arms are available" for a counter-coup. The letter, combined with Gairy's public comments that he intended to return to office, "can only mean that he will use force in order to achieve these ends." At every opportunity, Bishop repeated his claims that a mercenary invasion was in the works. Only the handful of conspirators collaborating with Mike Perdue knew just how right he was. But the chances of a successful counter-coup seemed to diminish with every passing day. Cuba had already extended diplomatic recognition to the new revolutionary regime and sent a shipment of arms to help Bishop consolidate power. Cuban advisors had set up a People's Revolutionary Army training camp in the interior.

Taking the island was not going to be a cakewalk. It was going to require a major mercenary force to overthrow Maurice Bishop. And in all likelihood, it was going to be a bloody fight. On the highway to Tennessee, Perdue listened to Polli talk about the mayhem in Dominica and he began to wonder whether he should drop the Grenada project. He was still committed to a Caribbean invasion, but it was becoming clear he had neither the manpower nor the equipment or funds to take Grenada.

Dominica was another story. Everything he heard about the place made him think he was targeting the wrong island. He had only looked at Dominica as a staging area for the attack on Grenada. Maybe he had overlooked its potential as a primary target.

Politically, Dominica appeared to be drifting towards the same fate as Grenada. Even the CIA thought so. The agency noted the fall of Patrick John's *scandal-ridden government* in a secret intelligence report dated July 20, 1979. The authors of the report described the new Dominican prime minister, Oliver Seraphin, as *a young opportunist who has appointed to the Senate the leaders of the country's three previously peripheral leftist groups.* At the same time, the report said, a new regime *dominated by pro-Cuban leftists* had come to office in neighboring St. Lucia. And in St Kitts-Nevis, Premier Lee Moore, a *former Black Power activist* was expected to *follow a nonaligned foreign policy favorable to Cuba.*

No fewer than eight former British colonies were becoming independent during a period of economic downturn, disaffection among youth and *unprecedented* influence of left-wing radical groups. The CIA assessed that Cuba was moving quickly to exploit the regional trends. Most of the islands were thought to be cool to Cuban offers of assistance, but the report added a note of caution: *Cuban prospects have increased dramatically … because of the changes of government in Grenada, Dominica, Saint Lucia, and the Netherlands Antilles. Last weekend, the new leaders of Saint Lucia and Dominica ended their predecessors' official hostility toward Grenada and met there for a tripartite "microsummit" on regional affairs … a small Cuban delegation also participated.*

It made no difference to Perdue whether he invaded Grenada or Dominica. As far as he was concerned, they were both just Third World backwaters. But Dominica seemed more do-able. While the Cubans already had a lock on Grenada, they hadn't yet made it north to Dominica.

"Dominica," Perdue said, "would be so much easier."

THAT NIGHT IN MEMPHIS, Perdue and Polli stepped out of an elevator into a luxury penthouse suite to meet J.W. Kirkpatrick. The bar had an impressive stock of booze and a Confederate flag on the wall. It looked like a southern party pad. The lawyer introduced two of his friends, an accountant and a doctor. They had a few drinks, ogled the women in attendance and talked about how great it would be to have a casino in the Caribbean, a playground in the sun.

They talked about Grenada. Perdue told them it could not be done. "Too costly, too time-consuming and too bloody," he said. The communists were already on the ground in full force. But Perdue told them there was another island a few hundred miles to the north. With enough cash, Perdue said he could bring a team of mercenaries to Dominica and take over. Investors could open banks and casinos and make a pile of money. "I would be interested in seeing if a coup could be possible there," he told them.

He said he was willing to look into it if they'd put up some seed money.

All the discussion about mercenaries and invading islands was just beer talk as far as Polli was concerned. Polli was supposed to be looking into setting up a business in Dominica that Don Andrews could use as cover for the invasion of Grenada, but all he really wanted was to make enough money to retire somewhere warm. He thought the notion of invading islands was ludicrous.

"You couldn't invade Dominica. These guys would've got the snot kicked out of them by the toughs at the pool hall," he says. The British and Venezuelans had troops nearby, and then there were the French: Dominica is sandwiched between Martinique and Guadeloupe.

"You've got France on both sides—*hel-lo!*"

But the fantasy prevailed. The next morning, Kirkpatrick gave Perdue $10,000 in cash. The investment was to be reimbursed as soon as Perdue had taken control of Dominica. If the coup failed, the money was to be returned.

Perdue counted out $3,000 and gave it to Polli. He kept the rest for himself. "He gave me basically a plane ticket and hotel money," Polli recounts. "They gave me a couple of thousand dollars to go down and snoop around." Perdue got himself a new passport and met Polli in Miami on October 4 for the journey to Dominica. The purpose of their mission was, in Perdue's words, "To look at the situation and see if we could actually create a coup."

THE BRITISH WEST INDIES AIRLINES propeller plane aligned itself with a clearing hacked out of the jungle and touched down near a terminal with a yellow control tower sprouting red-and-white antennae. Mike Perdue stepped into the steamy tropical warmth and walked across the rough tarmac to the small terminal building. To the immigration police, Perdue and Polli were just a couple of traveling businessmen.

The road to Roseau followed Dominica's east coast to Marigot, to a long crescent of beach at Pagua Bay. A one-lane track cut inland and climbed into the hills on a series of tight switchbacks. The island was strewn with downed trees and collapsed buildings but it was still a place of awesome beauty. Twenty-nine miles long and sixteen wide, Dominica has the highest peaks in the Caribbean, a cluster of sharp volcanic towers that leap out of the sea and then plunge into lush valleys. "It's a mystical place, clouds and mountains, a haunting place," Polli says.

In the villages, chickens and jittery foot-long lizards clog the roads, and outdoor restaurants blast calypso songs. Every so often, a glimpse of a small church or the remnants of a rotting building appear through the greenery. Deep in the interior, the jungle is deafening, alive with the screeching of birds and the hum of insects.

It was more than an hour before the cab at last reached the hairpins that descend into Canefield, where the road turns south to the capital. The taxi crossed the narrow bridge over the mouth of the Roseau River, where old ladies wearing bright plaid sit behind market tables piled high with bananas, breadfruits and coconuts. The air smells of sweet tropical flowers, nutmeg and the sea. The scent of cooking spices wafts through the open doors of restaurants. High atop Jack's Hill, a silver Jesus looks over the city.

The seaside capital is no more than a few dozen blocks of shops, churches and two-level wooden houses on the river plain between the mountains and the bay. Women lean over railings on second-floor verandas, taking in the breeze and watching the street life in the beer houses and restaurants below, where people speak a musical language, a patois of English, French, West African and Carib.

The faces are overwhelmingly black. Of all the Caribbean islands, Dominica has the fewest whites or, as they are known in Creole, *béké*. The influence of colonial Europe seems to survive only in the street names—Victoria Street, King George V Street, Queen Mary Street. That and the churches. Half of Dominicans are Catholics.

The taxi rounded the traffic circle outside the Fort Young Hotel, owned by the family of Eugenia Charles, and dropped them a mile south of the capital at the Anchorage Hotel. Perdue got two rooms on the second floor, overlooking a swimming pool buckled by the hurricane. Once they had settled in, Perdue rented a Suzuki jeep from the hotel for $50 a day and drove north. They were far from Roseau when night fell. There were no hotels around so they drove to a Catholic mission school and the nuns put them up for the night.

"What do you do?" one of the nuns asked.

"We're here to look for business investments," Polli told her.

"Oh," she said, "you're here to take the place over."

Polli froze. Was it that obvious?

The island felt volatile to Perdue. Just a year after independence, Dominica was already preparing for its third government. "Ministers were coming and going," he says. "You could find a minister on one day and the next day it would be somebody else taking over." Perdue wanted to meet the former prime minister, Patrick John, but he could not find him. Instead, Perdue took pictures and observed, and what he saw convinced him that Dominica was ripe for the picking.

The generals who plan military invasions always look for the enemy's center of gravity, and that is where they focus their forces. Perdue quickly found Dominica's center of gravity. The Dominica Police Headquarters was a cement compound that occupied one half of a block at the edge of the capital. It was probably the most heavily fortified place on the island, but that wasn't saying much. There were several buildings within the compound. The Criminal Investigation Division (CID) was on the first floor of Block A. Two dozen officers worked there during the day but only a single officer remained on duty at night. The communications section was on the top floor of Block A. It was referred to as the Control Room, and the telephone and radio equipment was kept there. It was manned twenty-four hours a day.

There were two entrances into the police compound. The main gate was off Bath Road. A sentry was posted there day and night. Next to the gate was the charge office. It too was manned around the clock; there were always two officers at the desk, a duty non-commissioned officer and a guard, usually a police constable. The duty NCO worked an eight-hour shift, while the guard's shift was four hours. The only other way inside was through the gate off King George V Street. The gate was usually closed and it was guarded at night.

This was the sum total of Dominica's national defenses. Whoever controlled this one cluster of buildings would control the island. And it certainly did not look well guarded. Perdue figured that if a few mercs armed with heavy weapons were to burst in at night, it would all be over.

Using a small Instamatic, Perdue and Polli took photos of Government House, the Dominica Mining Company, the shanties, the harbor and the airport, a primitive landing strip with a DC-3 and a few Cessnas on the tarmac. They managed to get shots of an army barracks and ambled up beside a few soldiers gathered around a military helicopter that had put down in a grassy field beside a couple of army jeeps.

Perdue and Polli did not get along. They spent most of the trip arguing. Perdue thought Polli was wasteful and self-centered. Polli found Perdue annoying. He was always flexing in front of the mirror and talking about his bodybuilding gym. He was muscular, Polli thought, no question about that. But Polli never saw Perdue do a sit-up or a push-up, and he would get winded just walking up a hill. He preferred to get around by jeep.

"He was a puffed up little baby ape," Polli says.

The Memphis money disappeared quickly — the plane ticket, the car, the hotel, the $20 meals. And the rum.

At night, they sat at the open-air bar beside the pool, drinking while Perdue talked about Vietnam. One night, Polli devoured a bottle of rum and passed out. He had a dream that someone was kissing him, and when he opened his eyes, Perdue was leaning over him, very close. Too close.

"Wait a minute," Polli thought, "is this guy queer?"

They left after just over a week. Polli returned to Toronto and did not figure in the conspiracy again. "I went there with good intentions," he says. "I went there with the best of intentions and everybody around me, they had their own agenda."

Once he got back to Houston, Mike Perdue phoned Don Andrews and told him he didn't want to work with Polli anymore. Andrews said not to worry, he already had another man working on the project, Roger Dermée. The Belgian's task was to stay on the island and send reports back to Toronto concerning the political climate and the state of the military, Andrews explained. Perdue returned to Roseau on October 23 to meet Dermée.

After three days, he flew home to Texas to begin planning the invasion of Dominica.

6

Wolfgang Droege (right) in Malta

Toronto, Canada
November 1979

ALTHOUGH EVERYONE CALLED Don Andrews' place the Mansion, it was really just an old house south of Danforth Avenue, the center of Toronto's Greek Town. The kitchen was like a coffee house for the far right. People were always dropping in to listen to Andrews hold court.

This time the special guest was Mike Perdue. Andrews and Perdue had been speaking on the phone every day, sometimes three times a day. The calls were short. That was Andrews' nature. The two men had never met, though, and Perdue decided it was time. After returning from Dominica, he caught a plane to Toronto. "He was like the cigar-chomping American sergeant," Andrews recalled. "Gung ho was the best way to describe him."

The first thing they did was phone Roger Dermée, who updated them on the island scene. The country was still in disarray; the hurricane had really crushed the place. Andrews also put Perdue in touch with Martin Weiche. Weiche was the chairman of the Canadian National Socialist Party and he owned a twelve-acre property near London, Ontario. The Texan asked him for money. Weiche says he considered it but changed his mind after meeting Perdue. "I wasn't interested in his revolution," he says. Andrews also denies handing over $10,000, as Perdue later claimed. But he does admit he introduced Perdue to the man who would become his lieutenant in the invasion of Dominica—Wolfgang Droege.

Perdue and Wolfgang met for the first time at the Mansion and they hit it off. The big Texan and the squat Canadian with the German accent made an odd pair, but they soon found they had enough in common. Both were uneducated and from broken homes. Both had been drawn to the military in their teens and had been active in right-wing militancy. They were both in their early thirties, single and social outcasts in their own ways.

As he always did when he was trying to impress, Perdue introduced himself as a decorated soldier and talked about his mercenary work in South and Central America. Perdue never said outright that he was a covert government operator, but he gave the impression that he had official connections. Droege thought he might be working for the CIA.

Before long, they were talking about the Caribbean. Perdue explained his concerns about Cuba's expanding influence and how Dominica would make a good platform for an invasion of Grenada. Or it might make a good mercenary target on its own. "They said they were considering, instead of going to Grenada, going to Dominica," Droege recalled later. If they could make a deal with the deposed prime minister, Patrick John, if they could get him to agree to give them cash and favors in exchange for returning him to power in Dominica, they could do whatever they wanted. They could launch against Grenada or just sit back and soak up the sun on their own little piece of paradise. Perdue said he wanted Droege to find Patrick John and convince him to sign a mercenary contract.

Droege left for Dominica the next day.

DROEGE'S NICKNAME WAS "WOLF." He was barrel-chested and short, even in the thick-soled shoes he wore to gain a few extra inches. He had a big, round head with a sharp nose that jabbed out below small blue eyes. His hair was disheveled and he had a wispy beard. Sometimes he wore shirts with wolves stenciled on the front. Wolfgang was a German-Canadian. His family had owned a hotel in Bavaria and he spent his childhood listening to the war stories of German soldiers. He was five when his parents divorced. He spent a short time in a Catholic home until his grandparents took him in. He lived with them until 1963 when, at age thirteen, he moved to Canada to join his mother, who had remarried.

It was not easy being a kid with a German accent in post-war Canada. "I think that he never really felt like he fit in. He always felt like the proverbial outsider," says Grant Bristow, who befriended Droege while working undercover as an agent for the Canadian Security Intelligence Service. "So he was kind of a kid that was marginalized, a lot of it from his own doing, but also circumstances, you know, a kid coming off the boat from Germany essentially, not long after the war.... I think he felt like a foreigner in Canada. I don't know that he ever felt that Canada was his home. He gave that impression."

In his teens, Droege left for West Germany and flirted with neo-Nazi ideas. He tried to enlist in the German military but it didn't work out. He came back to Canada in 1967 and went north to Sudbury to work in the nickel mines before returning to Toronto. His mother Margot was embarrassed by her son's hardening views. She had lived through Hitler's reign and had seen first-hand the inhumanity and horror that occur when race and politics are mixed. But Droege became increasingly hard-line as he was drawn into the extreme right wing. The leadership of the far right knew how to recruit. They would give disaffected young sympathizers just enough attention to make them feel they were important. It worked because so many of them were self-loathing, psychologically beaten-up misfits.

Wolfgang and Don Andrews first met at Melanie's Tavern. Droege liked what Andrews had to say and joined the Western Guard. "Droege was made to feel that he was a somebody," Bristow says. At school, his German heritage and Nazi sympathies had made him a loner, but in the Guard they were accepted, even celebrated. "So like eighty-five or ninety percent of the people that get involved in the right wing, Droege finally found a port where he felt, 'I'm home, because it's everybody else in the world's fault for the shitty things that happen in my life; none of it's my fault.'" Droege seemed to believe in what the Guard stood for. Whatever was wrong in the world, Droege learned to blame on the government, Jews and multiculturalism. "I am not a white supremacist," Droege said. "We are racial nationalists whose eventual goal would be the creation of an exclusively white state for those wishing to live in an area among their own kind." Aarne Polli says, "He was on some Napoleon complex—maybe because of his height."

Droege was not an orator like Andrews. He was soft-spoken. "He wasn't a ranter, which I think was the most surprising thing that I found about him," says Bristow. "If it was just him and I hanging out, he would be very dismissive of blacks and Jews, but it wasn't in the form of a rant. It was just a simple statement."

His formal education was limited. He was a high school dropout, and his views were almost entirely cut-and-pasted from Andrews' fiery sermons, but he also found he was able to get people to rally behind him. He was a likeable Nazi. He was also "a diligent recruiter," according to James McQuirter, who headed the Canadian KKK, of which Droege was a founding member.

"He was a reactionary, basically," says Andrews. He was also arrogant, and contemptuous of those he considered weak, but mostly he was looking for action. When the Grenada mercenary plot emerged, Andrews immediately thought of Droege. "He was bored with life," is how Andrews summed up his former disciple. "He just wanted excitement. He was another guy hanging around, looking for adventure."

ONCE HE GOT TO DOMINICA, Droege tried to get a grasp of the island's political scene. "I met supporters of various parties and also met people who were communist inclined," he said. "And I had heard that even though communists only made up a small part of the population in Dominica, they were working on getting Rosie Douglas, who's a communist leader on the island, into power."

Douglas had been deported from Canada in 1976, after serving his prison sentence for his part in the Montreal student riot. Droege did not think Rosie the Red and his communists were a viable power, although he heard rumors they were seeking Cuban support. Nor did he believe the opposition leader, Eugenia Charles, was a communist. He saw her more as "a socialist type."

At a dinner party, a couple of Las Vegas businessmen sat down next to Droege. They introduced themselves as Carlton Van Gorder and Bob Goodman. Goodman was a Nevada Department of Tourism official. Van Gorder was in the gaming industry. Van Gorder explained that he was trying to open a casino on the north shore of the island but that he was having trouble getting the Dominican government to cooperate. Droege said he might have a solution. Perhaps the government would be more receptive if there was a change of leadership, he said. And change could be hastened by supporting the opposition, he said, or even staging a coup d'état. Van Gorder wasn't about to get involved in a military coup, but he did invite Droege to Las Vegas to meet some people.

It was dawning on Droege, as it already had on Perdue, that mounting a coup in Dominica could prove extremely profitable. The island was undeveloped and yet had huge economic potential, especially in the tourism and logging sectors. It was an unpolished diamond. The foreign businessmen he met were of the same view. They saw the place as an untapped tropical paradise.

Droege phoned Perdue and told him he hadn't been able to reach Patrick John. Then he left for Antigua, where he caught a plane to Puerto Rico, Miami and finally New Orleans. He got hold of David Duke and explained they were "switching plans," that the focus of the operation had shifted from Grenada to Dominica. "On a personal basis, I really liked Wolfgang," Duke said in an interview. "He had a good sense of humor, he was a kind guy, he was well-read. He was a friendly guy. He seemed honest to me and he was unselfish." Duke didn't like Mike Perdue, though, and he didn't like the way things were going. There just wasn't any ideological justification for a coup in Dominica.

From New Orleans, Droege flew to Houston, where he met Perdue and told him about the casino developers he had met on the island. "At this point, what we needed was financing," Droege said. The men from Nevada were their best lead. "So I contacted Perdue about meeting these people in Las Vegas who were saying that they may know someone in Las Vegas who would be interested in financing." Perdue called them up and told them he and Droege were coming to Vegas.

NOBODY TOLD DON ANDREWS what was going on. He still thought Grenada was the prize, and that Dominica was only a stopover on the way to overthrowing the Maurice Bishop communists. Andrews wanted to see Dominica for himself, so he bought a plane ticket to Antigua and caught the prop plane to Melville Hall airport.

"It was just like Africa," he says. "Giant jungle canopies, giant ferns you've never seen ... like King Kong's island."

At the airport, he hired a cab that climbed through the interior. Andrews was so terrified by the Transinsular Road that he tipped the driver to slow down. He checked into the hotel under the name Mr. Clarke.

Andrews had the gift of the gab, and he naturally drifted to the action. At the hotel bar, he overheard two men talking. He started up a conversation and found out they were on a reconnaissance mission, just like him. They said they worked for a California company that had a deal to sell Dominican passports to foreign nationals for a hefty sum. The company's principal shareholder was an Iranian, and his clients were Iranians who had been exiled by Ayatollah Khomeini's 1979 Islamic Revolution.

The revolt in Tehran had ousted the Iranian monarch, Shah Mohammad Reza Pahlavi, and members of his regime were looking for a new home. As far as Andrews could tell, the men he met (he thinks they were CIA agents) were looking at turning Dominica into an expat colony for "the Shah of Iran's entourage, all of his agents and torturers." The company was selling Dominican citizenship for $50,000, and there were tentative plans to build a settlement on the island's northern tip, which had the best beaches. "I thought that it was unconscionable and immoral what they were doing," he says. "I thought I'd tell it to the opposition."

Andrews went to the Dominica Freedom Party office and said he had important information. A party worker arranged for him to meet Eugenia Charles at Wallhouse at eight o'clock that night. Wallhouse had once been a cane plantation where close to 200 slaves had produced sugar, molasses and rum. J.B. Charles had bought it and now he lived there with his daughter, Eugenia.

It was like "a voodoo house," Andrews says. It was big and dark. Frogs croaked. A storm had knocked out the electricity, so they talked by candlelight. Andrews thought they were alone, so he was startled when he heard coughing somewhere in the darkness.

Don't worry, Eugenia said, that's my 100-year-old father.

She was intelligent and Andrews liked her. She was shocked to hear what Andrews had to say about the Iranians, although it was just the latest in a long list of dubious Dominican government schemes. She said she would raise it in Parliament.

"Just let me get off the island before you say anything," Andrews said.

The New Chronicle newspaper put the story on its front page. The headline was in big bold type: "Dominican Passports for Iranians: A National Scandal." The article accused the government of selling off the "sacred documents and symbols of our birthright."

WHEN HE STOPPED HEARING from Perdue and Droege, Andrews assumed the operation had been scrubbed. There was already a heavy Cuban presence in Grenada, and Eric Gairy was making unreasonable demands. Andrews thought Gairy should be present in Grenada during the coup. But Gairy was refusing to return until the mercenaries had safely recaptured the capital.

"You can't go on a black island with a bunch of white mercenaries without their leader there," Andrews says. "I thought the whole thing was off."

Perdue and Wolfgang were keeping him in the dark.

"The rule was, 'Don't tell Andrews,'" he says. "Dominica wasn't my target. They made it a target. I liked the place."

What had started out as a strike against communism had become a criminal enterprise whose main objective was to make a lot of money by exploiting the suffering of the poorest people in the Caribbean. "Everybody's looking for a fucking island," Polli sighs.

Mike Perdue and Wolfgang Droege were in charge now, and Grenada had taken a back seat, at least for the time being.

The target was Dominica. All they needed was some more money, a few guns and a ship to get them there.

7

The *Mañana*, 2007

New Orleans, Louisiana
May 1980

THE MAÑANA IS FIFTY-TWO FEET long with a trawler-shaped hull made of three-eighths-inch steel. She weighs fifty-three tons and has a two-ton crane, five double beds, two heads, a fully equipped galley and two generators. She is one tough ship.

In 1969, Hurricane Camille drove her ashore with its 200-mile-an-hour winds and twenty-five-foot storm surge. She ploughed through three houses before coming to rest on the levee. Two D-8 Caterpillars dragged her back down the street to the beach at Pass Christian and a tug pulled her into the water—and she still floated.

Captain Mike Howell made his living on the *Mañana*, mostly doing towing and salvage work. He'd do just about anything, as long as it didn't get him arrested. One of his favorite jobs was taking divers on charter trips to explore underwater archeological sites. He enjoyed taking documentary film crews along the Louisiana shoreline. After Vietnam, cruising the Gulf of Mexico was paradise. He lived aboard the ship. It wasn't easy making a living, but he had his Army pension to back him up. Mike was in his early thirties with a big smile and a football player's build. He was supposed to play at Louisiana State

University but Vietnam put an end to that. Running backs need two arms and Mike had left one in Vietnam.

On the lakefront, there was a breeze. The air was more forgiving than the still swamp country to the south. Across the lake, the long, low causeway disappeared into the hazy horizon, connecting the Bayou to the highways of America. Howell preferred the marine highway that flowed through the lakes and out into the Gulf.

Howell joined the U.S. Army on October 14, 1964. He was seventeen and enlisting was partly an escape from home and an abusive stepfather who owned a chain of first-run cinemas. He did his basic training at Fort Polk, Louisiana, and went to Jump School at Fort Benning, where he met a sergeant who told him about combat aviation. Helicopters crews were in heavy demand, and before long Private First Class Howell was in Vietnam, an expert machine gunner with the 334th Armed Helicopter Company.

He liked the military. Not the killing, but doing a job well. As the fighting intensified, Private Howell saw heavy combat from his perch in the attack chopper. At 11:45 p.m. on December 13, 1966, his fire fly team had just returned to base at Duc Hoa when mortars started raining down. Howell's team scrambled and got airborne just as the airfield began to shake with explosions. Howell's helicopter was a light ship. Its job was to illuminate the enemy in the jungle below so the gunners in the other choppers could take them out. It is one of the most vulnerable duties in combat because when the soldiers on the ground get lit up, the first thing they do is shoot at the light. Upon finding the source of the mortar fire, Howell and his team hovered overhead and beamed their spotlights on the gun positions, which were quickly hit, saving the American base from a pounding. For that, he was awarded the Air Medal, Fifth Oak Leaf Cluster with "V" Device.

On Boxing Day, near Gan Guioc, Howell's fire fly team came across Viet Cong soldiers crossing a river in sampans. As his pilot dodged ground fire, Howell beamed his light on the boats one by one and they were sunk. *He operated the light with great ability, never hesitating for a moment,* reads his citation for the Distinguished Flying Cross.

During the entire operation, PFC Howell's skill and determination contributed to the destruction of 111 sampans, numerous secondary explosions and the destruction of a large quantity of Viet Cong rice. Because of the extreme aggressiveness shown by PFC Howell, the transportation system of the Viet Cong was seriously impaired and the morale and effectiveness of a vicious enemy was dealt a severe blow. PFC Howell's actions were in keeping with the highest traditions of the military service and reflect great honor upon himself, his unit and the United States Army.

Four months later, on April 13, 1967, Howell was back at it. A light fire team made up of two helicopters was attacking a large gathering of North Vietnamese Army regulars across the border in Cambodia. The troops on the ground opened up on the U.S. choppers and Howell took a bullet in the left leg and then a rocket sailed into his helicopter and exploded. Howell's left arm was pulverized.

His crew chief was also wounded, but he reached over and pinched Howell's artery while the pilot tried to coax the damaged Huey UH-1C to the aid station with the exhaust gas temperature indicator pointing all the way in the red. They made it home in fifteen minutes but couldn't land because one side of the chopper was destroyed, so the pilot had to hover while the medics put Howell onto a stretcher. He was almost dead, and when the wind from the rotor blades knocked over the stretcher, he fell face down on the ground and stopped breathing.

"Don't waste blood on him," he remembers a voice saying.

"Bullshit!" a medic yelled. "Cut him down. I'll take his legs, you do his arm."

He lost his arm, but he survived. He returned to Louisiana and enrolled at Loyola University, the largest Catholic college in the South, which has a statue of the Lord with hands raised that students call "touchdown Jesus." He spent a few enjoyable years there, getting free tuition, room and board from the Army, and then he moved on.

AS A KID, HOWELL HAD OWNED a small rowboat, a gift from his stepdad, and he had escaped onto the waters of Lake Pontchartrain. He had always liked boats, and in 1973 he paid $1,200 for the *Mañana*. She was little more than scrap. The engine was frozen, the bow and stern were rusted. Howell began refitting her himself, a task that never really ended, and before long he put her to work.

Because he lived on his boat, Howell knew everyone along the lakefront and saw everything, so when a man from Alaska showed up with an automatic rifle in his boat, the captain called up the authorities. The Bureau of Alcohol, Tobacco and Firearms launched an investigation, which is how Howell came to meet two special agents from the ATF office in New Orleans named Paul Derby and John Osburg.

Howell particularly liked Osburg, a former New Orleans Police Department officer. After a few years as a cop, Osburg met a few ATF agents and decided to apply. "I saw more of a future with the federal agencies than I would have had with the New Orleans police, better pay, a chance to improve, the investigative part," he says. He passed the entrance test, got an interview and someone offered him a job. "I said what the hell," he says.

Tall and athletic, with straight blond hair and Nordic features, Osburg found he had a talent for undercover work. His slow southern drawl and easygoing manner concealed a sharp mind and a tenacious, inventive investigator. "You do the best you can," he says. "You grab at some straws, some ropes or whatever and sometimes it works out."

He spent a few years at the Oklahoma City ATF office and transferred to New Orleans in 1973 to work on cases involving illegal guns and explosives, and the underworld criminals that wanted them, like the notorious Dixie Mafia. As a field investigator, Osburg sometimes found himself in conflict with his manager, the SAC, or Special Agent in Charge. The bureaucracy of the ATF could be frustrating. The running joke in the office was "we're out of forms to order the forms." But Osburg found ways of getting things done.

His job was to enforce federal laws regarding the illicit trafficking of guns, booze and cigarettes. It was not an easy task, particularly in the American south, where some hold strong opinions about the right to bear arms. There was certainly no shortage of work for the New Orleans

ATF office. There seemed to be a never-ending parade of criminal schemes in the works at any time, although perhaps none as strange as the one that Mike Perdue and Wolfgang Droege were planning.

THE THREE CUBANS arrived at the New Orleans marina unannounced. They said they wanted to hire Mike Howell but not for a nature cruise. They wanted him to sail to Cuba and bring their loved ones to America. He heard them out and told them he'd do it, but he didn't want their money. If they covered his costs, he'd go. For Howell it was not a difficult decision to make.

"People needed help," he says. Mike loaded the *Mañana* with groceries and water, and stowed a couple of shotguns and rifles in the bow just in case. By the time he was out in the Gulf, a mass exodus of Cubans was underway.

The Mariel Boatlift started in April 1980 when five men drove a bus into the Peruvian embassy in Havana and asked for political asylum. They got it. But after Fidel Castro removed his guards from the embassy, ten thousand Cubans took refuge in the small diplomatic compound, all eager to escape the troubles of post-revolution Havana—the chronic job and housing shortages and Castro's crackdown on dissidents. The embassy was so crowded some had to cling to tree limbs. When Castro invited the asylum seekers to leave Cuba, ships streamed to the port of Mariel to pick them up.

Cuban-Americans began hiring every vessel they could find to make the journey across the Straits of Florida. The ships were too often overloaded and unseaworthy. Twenty-seven died, fourteen of them when a single boat capsized before reaching the refugee processing centers in Key West and Miami. The U.S. administration was unprepared for the boat people, and unsure how to respond. Ships were stopped in U.S. waters on their way to Mariel but after President Jimmy Carter gave a speech sympathetic to the asylum seekers, the mood changed. The U.S. Coast Guard called in ships and auxiliary volunteers from all over the Atlantic seaboard, and the Navy stepped up patrols to make sure the "freedom flotilla" made the crossing safely.

SEVEN HUNDRED AND FIFTY MILES after leaving Lake Pontchartrain, Mike Howell reached Mariel Harbor and anchored alongside the flotilla. He had the list of names the Cuban-Americans had given him in New Orleans, the loved ones he was to pick up and bring home.

Three days in Havana, however, made it crystal clear the Cubans were not going to make things easy. At first, they gave him a list of the passengers he was to take to the United States. It included those Mike had been sent to rescue but also three hundred others. Even the sturdy *Mañana* couldn't make it across the straits with that many passengers.

Mike had all but given up. A Cuban major finally told him he could leave—if he took along the passengers of a pathetic, disabled shrimp boat called the *Valley Chief*. He agreed, on one condition. Mike had heard rumors that the Cubans were releasing prison inmates and mental patients into the chaos of Mariel. Something about the look of the men on the *Valley Chief* made him suspicious. He told the major he would take the children, women and old people, but not the men. They could stay on the *Valley Chief*, and he would tow the seventy-foot hulk into U.S. waters, where the Coast Guard would take over.

In all, 124,000 Cubans made their way to the United States that year, among them over 2,000 criminals and mental patients released by Castro as a gesture to his northern neighbor.

Captain Mike Howell returned to his quiet life on the New Orleans lakefront and joined the Coast Guard Auxiliary. He was a war veteran and an idealist with a proven willingness to take risks to help those suffering under communism—just the kind of credentials that would bring him to the attention of someone putting together a team of mercenaries.

8

The Las Vegas strip

Las Vegas, Nevada
Summer 1980

IT COSTS MONEY TO MAKE WAR. You have to buy weapons and ammunition, hire mercenaries and pay their room and board and transportation expenses. Even in a country as small as Dominica, the bills pile up. Mike Perdue and Wolfgang Droege were not rich men. They were both jobless. They couldn't afford to finance a military expedition. They needed investors. They needed to find people who not only had money, but who would be willing to sink it into a country they had probably never heard of, for a mission that was clearly not above board and that might not even succeed.

So they went to Las Vegas.

It was a logical choice. Part of the evolving plan was to turn Dominica into a gambling haven. Once he secured the island, Perdue was going to build casinos and bring in foreign tourists. The profits would be split between the government, the mercenaries and their investors.

Carlton Van Gorder was a veteran in the gaming industry. He met Droege and Perdue at the Vegas airport and dropped them at a motel for the night. The next day, Van Gorder took them to meet a few men who had money to invest. "We probably spent four or five hours with them," Van Gorder recalled in an interview. The meeting did not go well. "We decided we wouldn't have anything to do with them. They were a little on the shady side," Van Gorder says. "I mean, anyone who talks about toppling a government, they aren't the type of people you go into business with." But a gaming executive named Tommy Thompson agreed to meet them in Memphis.

FOR ALL THEIR SIMILARITIES, Perdue and Droege were an unlikely partnership. Perdue was a hustler. The only thing that seemed to get him excited was money. Droege was dogmatic. He was deeply into white power. He cared about the money, but partly because he thought it would help advance his cause. To that extent, in Vegas, where it was all about money, Droege was just a prop. Perdue did the talking while Wolfgang, with his Klan credentials and David Duke connections, sanctified the invasion as a political act.

Perdue was trying to lure investors by promising big profits, but he was also appealing to their sense of patriotism. He talked about how the Cubans had tried to bring aid to the island after Hurricane David, and how the citizens of Dominica had flown American flags in a protest against the communists. Painting the island red helped Perdue sell his plot. Mercenaries often dress up their profiteering and adventurism in the language of politics, telling each other they are fighting corruption and dictatorship. Maybe it helps them sleep at night but, in the end, they are soldiers of fortune, like bank robbers or car thieves, only with more ambition. They steal entire countries.

The heist that Perdue was planning was going to be very profitable—if it all worked out. Dominica was by no means a wealthy place, but imagine the money you could make if you had the run of your own country? In exchange for staging a coup that would return Patrick John to power, Perdue and his band of mercenaries were going to *own* the prime minister and his island.

They could build casinos. They could cut down the trees and sell them off. They could sell drugs and guns. They could print themselves diplomatic passports and commit crimes around the world with immunity. Who was going to stop them? They would be their own sovereign, criminal nation, a crooks' paradise.

Following the meetings in Vegas, Wolfgang flew to New Orleans. A day later, Perdue came by in his Chevy and they hit the highway for Memphis, where they were scheduled to meet Tommy Thompson about financing the coup. Along the way, they stopped in Jackson, Mississippi to see one of Droege's friends, a former Klansman named Danny Joe Hawkins. Perdue and Droege spent the night there and continued on to Memphis, but Thompson never showed up for the meeting.

It was December 1979. Christmas was around the corner so they continued on to Kentucky. Droege caught a plane to Toronto and Perdue drove to the trailer park in Louisville to spend the holidays with his mother.

A FEW DAYS AFTER CHRISTMAS, Perdue called Wolfgang with instructions to meet him in Las Vegas. They stayed in a motel off Tropicana Street. Two weeks after they checked in, a man named Dick came by the motel and said he had heard about the coup and was interested in putting up some money. He just had to close a business deal first, he said, but then he could give them $25,000.

For five weeks, Perdue and Droege lived at the motel and hunted investors. Tommy Thompson paid their room and board, according to Perdue. The trip gave them a lot of time to talk things out. Perdue continued to drop hints that he was "connected." He talked about his contacts in the State Department and said that if they ran into any trouble, things would be taken care of. He said he had friends working on the Republican presidential campaign and that he would be a very influential man if Ronald Reagan won the White House.

Droege wasn't sure what to make of Perdue. Was he a spook? Was this all a covert CIA operation? Perdue never discouraged that impression.

No money ever came of their stay in Vegas. Perdue eventually returned to Houston empty handed. Droege stayed for a few more weeks before flying back to Toronto.

The march of communism had not slowed during their all-expenses paid business trip in the Nevada desert. If anything, it was gaining momentum. The Soviets had invaded Afghanistan, and the ideals of the Cuban revolution were spreading into Latin America, the Caribbean, Asia and Africa. "Cuba laid the basis for Grenada, Nicaragua, Vietnam, Cambodia, Laos, Guinea-Bissau, Angola and Mozambique," Maurice Bishop said in a speech on February 15, 1980. "The example and spirit of the Cuban revolution has therefore had international impact."

Bishop spoke about the West's "fear of Cuba. And the main fear of Cuba is that another Cuba may arise in the region … But it is fortunate that there was a Cuba," he said. "If there was no Cuba, we would not have been reminded that imperialist and reactionary forces, or their attempts at murder and sabotage, could never stop a people fighting for their freedom and liberation." To the far right, these were words of war.

FOR ALL THEIR SCHEMING, Perdue and Droege had little to show for their efforts to date. What money they had been able to scrounge from friends and contacts was long gone, spent on flights to the Caribbean and hotel rooms. Droege went back to his day job. Before Don Andrews had called him up and told him about the coup, Droege had been working in Victoria, British Columbia, making $23,000 a year as a manager at Capital Business Forms, plus a percentage of earnings that added another $6,000 to his paycheck.

He lived in a small house near the Gorge, the narrow tidal channel that snakes out to the sea. The provincial capital is a blessed city, set on the sparkling Pacific, with English-style gardens and pubs. It does not get the harsh winters that bury the rest of Canada for months at a time, nor the rains that darken nearby Vancouver. It was a good life.

Droege had nonetheless jumped at the chance to get in on a foreign adventure. He had thrown himself into the coup conspiracy, but organizing the overthrow of a country was proving tougher than he had thought, and when his boss asked him to come back to his old job, even just temporarily, to fill in while the manager was on vacation, he accepted.

Perdue was not ready to give up. He began to devote himself entirely to raising capital for the coup, but he got nowhere. Wolfgang finished his two-month contract and returned to Toronto, and Perdue flew up to see him. Droege was living with James Alexander McQuirter, who some called "Pretty Boy"—and who also happened to be the head of the Canadian Ku Klux Klan. The Klan had first emerged in Canada in the 1920s with chapters in Toronto, Ottawa, Montreal and on the Prairies, but it was all but dead by the Depression. McQuirter and Droege resurrected the Klan in Canada after meeting David Duke in Louisiana. McQuirter was the fresh face of the Canadian Knights of the KKK. He was "good looking, charismatic, able to win people over," says Grant Bristow. According to Bristow, some saw him as a northern David Duke, a "mini-Duke."

The headquarters of the Canadian Klan was a room with a desk and a phone in a rundown house on Dundas Street East. Its slogan was "racial purity for Canadian security." It even rhymed. Droege and McQuirter had business cards printed up and left them in public places. When Perdue came to town, Droege introduced him to McQuirter and before long the Canadian Klan boss had agreed to take part in the coup. McQuirter was to serve as a communications link between Droege and Perdue. "In case anything worked out in Dominica, he was to supply me with information through Perdue—Perdue was to supply him with information and he was to pass it on to me," Droege explained.

The trouble with McQuirter was that he liked to talk. His newly minted role as Canada's Klan chief had put him in the media spotlight. He had been doing his best to attract a following by getting himself in newspapers and on the radio and TV. He was talking to reporters. And that kind of profile could be a liability on a mission that depended on a high level of secrecy.

JOHNSTON COUNTY IS a mix of farms and forests south of Raleigh, North Carolina, which prides itself as the most military friendly state in the nation. There are eight active bases there, including the Fort Bragg Army base and the Camp Lejeune Marine Corps base.

There's also Miller's Farm. Frazier Glenn Miller was a former Green Beret who owned a twenty-five-acre farm in Johnston County where he operated what some called a paramilitary training camp. Miller had been a lieutenant to the American neo-Nazi Harold Covington and, after leaving the U.S. Army in 1979, he threw himself into the extreme right wing. Five months after he retired, the Communist Workers' Party held a protest in Greensboro, North Carolina. Miller took part in a counter-demonstration organized by the Klan and American Nazis. The groups clashed and gunfire erupted. Within a few seconds, five of the communists were dead. Despite two trials, nobody was ever convicted. One Klansman explained it like this: if it's okay to kill communists in Vietnam, why not right here in America?

Bob Prichard spent a lot of time at Miller's farm. "He used to come out on the weekend, play Nazi music, wide open out there on the farm and just enjoy ourselves," Miller says. "We'd get together and have a firing competition with .22 rifles, have bull's-eye targets set up and then we'd give away a new shotgun or .22 rifle or something to the winner."

A native of Illinois, Prichard had joined the United States Army at seventeen. It was July 1966 and he figured he was going to be drafted anyway. Eleven months later, he was in Vietnam, a Recon and Scout Specialist with the 34th Armor. He got there just as the war was entering some of its toughest months.

The first time he was shot, the bullet lodged in his right shin. He figures it must have been a ricochet. The second time, the bullet hit his left thigh and went out the other side without doing much damage. Then he was riding in an APC, eating his rations, when the vehicle took a hit from a rocket-propelled grenade. The next thing he knew he was lying in the bushes at the roadside. The can of rations was still in his hand. He was peppered with shrapnel. "That was all the fun I could stand," he says.

He left Vietnam in the summer of 1968 with a Purple Heart, Bronze Star, National Defence Service Medal, Combat Infantry Badge, the Republic of Vietnam Campaign Medal and the Republic of Vietnam Gallantry Cross and Good Conduct Medal. His next assignment was at Fort Hood, Texas, where he served as a tank gunnery instructor. "That's the biggest reason I can't hear shit nowadays," he explains.

Bob left the Army in 1972. He had come home from Vietnam angry and volatile, and he soon fell in with a bad crowd. After returning to Chicago, he began hanging around at the headquarters of the

National Socialist Party of America, a pro-Nazi group that tried to stop blacks from moving into white neighborhoods.

Prichard drove a truck for a while and, after a breakup with a girlfriend, moved to Raleigh, where he met Miller. White supremacists from across the country used to meet at Miller's farm. Shooting contests, rallies and cross burnings were a regular occurrence, and Prichard was right in the middle of it.

"I was mixed up with the right-wing whackos," Prichard recalls, "and a bunch of them came down from Canada."

A FEW HUNDRED PEOPLE showed up for a rally at Miller's farm in August 1980. They came from as far as Detroit and Nebraska. A few came from Toronto—Wolfgang Droege and Steve Hammond.

Better known as the Limey, Hammond was a former British soldier who had joined the National Front, the British far right organization, in 1977 before moving to Canada to find his father. Once he got to Toronto, he called up the Western Guard and asked where he could find a bed. "Call this number," he was told. He dialed and Don Andrews answered. Before long, Hammond was living at one of Andrews' rooming houses. He became one of the Androids.

He knew nothing about the coup in Dominica, but he had been in on the discussions about invading Grenada. In the fall of 1979, he says he traveled to England to ask the leaders of Britain's far-right movement whether they wanted to participate, although he was under instructions not to reveal the name of the island that was being targeted.

"They were very unsure," Hammond says, "but very kind of willing to listen. You've got to understand that back then, the world was not so international and to talk about America and the Caribbean to nationalists [in Britain] was kind of like a different planet."

Hammond spent three weeks at the North Carolina Nazi headquarters in the summer of 1980. He even gave a speech, standing on a podium surrounded by swastikas. He doesn't remember exactly what he said but he does recall the last two words were *Seig Heil*.

The summertime rally at Miller's farm was a big hit. "We had two big crosses wrapped up in burlap and the one in the middle was a swastika," Prichard recalls. "It looked right impressive when it was lit up at night. Johnston County's about as flat as shit; you can see a hundred miles in either direction."

Bob Prichard and Wolfgang Droege met for the first time at the rally. "He seemed like an all right guy," Prichard says. "We weren't close or nothing. To start with, he's hard to understand. He couldn't shoot worth shit."

Miller's farm had a pond that was overrun with snapping turtles. In the afternoons, when they were sunning themselves on a log, the Nazis would pick them off with their handguns. Target practice.

Miller was accused of running a paramilitary training camp on his farm, but Steve Hammond says that wasn't quite true. "That's a very unfair accusation. He had a target range. I actually had a few beers, went down and won the prize." Hammond hadn't forgotten the rifle skills he'd learned at basic training in Britain.

Wolfgang also spent time at the firing range. "He tried to learn how to shoot there," Prichard says. "He got so he was passable, but he was by no means a designated marksman."

Wolfgang was preparing himself for the coup. He said nothing to Prichard about it; that could come later. Droege would soon be recruiting mercenaries, and Prichard was exactly what he needed.

ON SEPTEMBER 3, Mike Perdue drove to Jackson, Mississippi to see Wolfgang's friend Danny Hawkins.

"I'm kind of low on funds," Perdue said. "I'm trying to raise some more money."

Hawkins went to a longtime family friend named L.E. Matthews and the three of them met at a motel. Matthews was a Mississippi businessman, an electrical contractor who had struggled with the bottle until joining Alcoholics Anonymous. If a friend was having household wiring troubles, he'd come right over and fix it, no charge. The FBI believes he also put his skills to more deadly use. The agency considered him the Klan's bomb maker, responsible for the timing devices on the explosives used to terrorize Jews in Mississippi. He had also been Imperial Wizard of the KKK.

"Hi, my name is Mike, Mr. Matthews," Perdue said.

The months he had spent meeting with potential investors was finally beginning to pay off. Perdue says Matthews gave him a check for $3,000. It was enough to get started.

9

Patrick John

Captain Malcolm Marley Reid

Roseau, Dominica
September 1980

WHEN YOU SEE PATRICK JOHN for the first time, it is difficult not to stare. Technically he is not a dwarf, but he is a very short man. Somehow, you just don't expect a former Third World strongman and commander-in-chief of a country's armed forces to inhabit a boy's body. But once you get over his stature, you quickly realize that "Long John" is warm and intelligent, and it is easy to understand why his political supporters worship him and once put their young nation's hopes in his hands.

Patrick John and Mike Perdue met for the first time on September 19, 1980, at the Anchorage Hotel, in a district called Castle Comfort on the seaside one mile south of the capital. From the small balconies that hang over the hotel swimming pool, you can see the Roseau waterfront, where Patrick John was born, where he was raised by a huckster woman who sold fresh produce by the roadside and on the nearby islands. He attended the Roseau Boys School, taught for four years at St. Mary's Academy, worked as a shipping clerk and founded the Waterfront and Allied Workers Union before launching his storybook political career as a member of the town council and then mayor, colonial premier and, finally, prime minister of an independent Dominica.

Roseau was also the city where he had fallen, forced to walk away from his position because of Eugenia Charles. *She* had led the opposition and the stone-throwing protests that had made it impossible for him to continue governing, and now she was sitting in his seat at Government House. On July 21, 1980, Charles had led the Dominica Freedom Party to victory in general elections. The party won seventeen of twenty-one seats. After twelve years in opposition, Charles was not only prime minister but also the Caribbean's first female head of state. The island was hers to govern now. She was also the de facto head of the Dominica Defence Force.

Caribbean leaders sometimes served decades in office: Eric Gairy, Fidel Castro, Errol Walton Barrow, Vere Bird, Francois Duvalier. John's predecessor, Edward Oliver LeBlanc, was premier for thirteen years. John had lasted less than a year.

And because he had departed under the cloud of scandal, he might not even get the basic perk afforded to almost every other leader who had led his country to independence: having an airport named after him. There would be no Patrick R. John Stadium, no Patrick Roland John Boulevard. He could end up as nothing but an historical footnote, remembered more for the accusations that brought him down than for his service to the nation.

In the four months since the uprising against him, he had tumbled from prime minister to pig farmer. He built a pen outside his house and bought three sows and a boar. A friend brought him old bananas to feed the animals. He was going into the pork business. He also ran a gas station. PJ had not given up on politics, though. He was reorganizing the Dominica Labour Party, focusing on its youth wing. He hoped to merge the party with Oliver Seraphin's Democratic Labour Party. He was planning his comeback.

THEY ARRANGED THEIR MEETING by telegram, and upon arrival at Melville Hall airport, Perdue lined up at the immigration desk and handed the officer a landing card that identified him as an American "exporter." An exporter of what, he did not explain but the immigration officer waved him through and he hired a taxi to take him across the island to Roseau.

Deception was second nature to Perdue. His unseemly profession required it. If this was going to work, to the outside world it had to look like nothing more than an internal revolt. He would supply the arms and lead the raid, but by morning he and the other mercenaries had better be out of sight, their camouflage ditched in favor of Bermuda shorts or business suits. Some might wonder what they had done to gain the favor of the prime minister, as these foreigners seemed to get all the island's business concessions, but the deal would have to remain a secret because if anyone found out that a bunch of white mercenaries were behind the coup, the new regime would collapse for lack of legitimacy.

Every mercenary force needs a puppet—a credible, local leader who becomes the public face of the artificial revolution. Mike Perdue hoped that man would be Colonel Patrick John.

When Perdue had at last convinced an American investor to put some money on the table to finance the coup, he had phoned Droege in Toronto and told him he was flying back to Dominica to meet PJ. He told Droege to sit tight and that he would be in touch after he had spoken to the ex-prime minister.

They met in Perdue's hotel room. "I'd be interested in financing, you know, a coup for the island," Perdue told John.

The next morning, Perdue was packing to leave when John's friend Julian David dropped by with a Letter of Intent:

> *I, Patrick John, do hereby agree in principle with the general provisions of the proposed agreement, subject to further discussions and amendments.*
>
> *I further agree to meet with you and your colleagues in order to finalize figures and plans as discussed, at your earliest possible convenience.*
>
> *Patrick John.*

It was not a formal contract, but to Perdue it at least showed that John was willing to talk.

When he got back to Houston, Perdue called L.E. Matthews and told him the news. They met a week later and Perdue said he needed more money. Perdue returned to Houston with a $4,800 check and phoned some of the potential investors he had met in Las Vegas. They told him to come back to Nevada and they would see about contributing.

SAM'S TOWN CASINO is the kind of success story that Las Vegas loves. Sam Boyd had arrived in Nevada with eighty dollars in his pocket. He worked as a dealer and pit boss, saving enough to buy a share of the Sahara Hotel. He built Sam's Town on thirteen acres of desert.

Ted Thorp brought three businessmen with him to Sam's Town to meet Mike Perdue. One of them was Jim Kingsbury, a casino operator newly married to one of Dr. Thorp's nurses, Cherie.

Perdue had decided to take a business-like approach to the coup. He hoped it would help convince wary investors to put up the cash he desperately needed to finance the invasion.

This is how it worked. He created a company called Nortic Enterprises. The fee that Perdue was going to receive for overthrowing the government of Dominica would go to Nortic. So would all the revenues derived from the development of the island, the logging of the rainforests, agriculture, the airport, banks, casinos and tourist facilities. Perdue was going to make Patrick John agree to give Nortic the rights to it all, tax free. To raise capital for the coup, Perdue was going to sell shares in Nortic. The mercenaries who participated in the attack would also be offered Nortic shares as a form of payment. Perdue told the four men gathered at Sam's Town he was selling shares for $6,000 each. He guaranteed a twenty-five-to-one return on the investment. He said he had already sold seven shares but that there were two or three left.

There was one catch: the business plan required him to invade the island, oust the current government and install the former prime minister. He passed around the letter signed by Patrick John and said the CIA was backing the whole thing.

There were no takers. Kingsbury didn't feel comfortable about what he heard. He said no. So did Thorp.

"Look, I'm not buying shares in anything,'" Thorp said. "You know, after you've got everything settled down, I'll come down and, you know, help get things organized, but I'm not interested in coups. Call me after it's done, and I'll come down and help you get the economy going again."

Perdue left Vegas the next day with empty pockets.

A MESSAGE WAS WAITING for Perdue when he got back to Houston. It was from Dominica.

Patrick John's supporters wanted him to return to the island at once. There were some people he needed to meet. He arrived on December 13. This time, on his landing card, he wrote that his occupation was Importer. On the line marked Purpose of Visit, he wrote: "Bussiness".

He drove across the island to the Anchorage Hotel, where another cab picked him up. "I was taken to the interior and walked to a house that was in the mountains," Perdue recalls, "and there I met with Patrick John, the ex-prime minister; Major Frederick Newton, head of the military; Captain Malcolm Reid, second in command of the military; Ronnie Roberts ... and I met with a couple of Rastafarian leaders."

Captain Reid and Major Newton were the leaders of the Dominica Defence Force. Officially, Reid was on leave. He had applied for a temporary absence until April 14. Major Newton had signed it. Reid and Newton were like brothers. They had been friends for so long that Reid's mother, who lived in a house on the hill above Mahaut overlooking the sea, referred to them both as her sons. They even wore each other's clothes. "We got into the military together and it remained that way. Best friends. And I mean really best friends. And over the years it got so we could depend on one another," says Reid. They had one more thing in common: an unwavering loyalty to Patrick John.

The Dreads were also at the meeting in the hills. They had been the sworn enemies of Patrick John and the DDF since the days of the Dread Act. But an odd alliance was emerging. They both wanted Eugenia Charles out. Captain Reid and the Dread leader Henry "Mal" Esprit had known each other for years. They had grown up together in Mahaut, and now they were talking about the future of the country.

The key to the coup was Mike Perdue. Neither the DDF nor the Dreads could do it alone. They needed weapons and professional soldiers if they hoped to overtake the police headquarters, so they met Perdue in a house in the mountains behind Roseau. They deliberately picked a remote location for their session, and for good reason: The topic of discussion was treason.

The Defence Force officers briefed their American guest on the military logistics of the island. All the arms had been confiscated by the police and taken to the central police station, they said. If Perdue could get them enough firepower, they could mount the coup themselves, with the mercenaries as backup; the mercenary force would be present for the coup, and they would fire if they had to, but they would only step in when absolutely necessary.

Perdue agreed to the terms.

There was some debate over the fate of the old regime. The military chiefs thought Eugenia Charles and her ministers should be deported, but the Dreads wanted to kill all the politicians and policemen. They wanted Babylon to burn. Perdue feared a slaughter of opposition figures would not go over well in the Western capitals he intended to tap after the coup for diplomatic recognition and economic aid. He said that would be a bad PR move; they were not going to make any friends by killing the prime minister. Why not just put her on the first plane out and send her into exile along with her ministers?

The DDF gave Perdue permission to recruit mercenaries and solicit funds and guns for the takeover. They sealed their bond by making Perdue an honorary member of the Defence Force. He was given the rank of captain. "He sort of came across like, 'I have the resources; I have the contacts,'" Reid says. "The soldier of fortune aspect, he spoke like he had guys lined up to come in here tomorrow."

The next evening, Captain Reid dropped by the Anchorage Hotel and joined Perdue on the balcony of his room. Night comes early in the Eastern Caribbean. The sun burns hot through the late afternoon and melts into the seas off Nicaragua and Honduras. The air cools and the neon flickers on, lighting up the rum shops that line the narrow streets. By seven in the evening, the sea and sky are black, except for the stars and the lanterns on the wooden skiffs.

Dominicans say *soley kouché*: the sun sleeps.

Mike Perdue and Captain Reid faced the darkened sea and talked. Perdue presented himself as the answer to Dominica's problems.

"He spoke about Vietnam, Special Forces, but he also spoke about having some business connections, access to funds," says Reid. "He spoke an impressive line. What the gentleman did, he sort of gave the military-type aura. He wanted to portray himself as an individual with all the contacts, the right people in the right places, access to funds, the ability to provide, almost without limit."

There was a lot of talk on the island about a coup but Reid said that as far as he knew, there was no formal plan. Not yet. "In retrospect," he says, "there were a lot of threads hanging and no connection, no nucleus, no connecting thing." He had the impression something was going on. "There was more happening than I knew. There must be someone pulling the strings and calling the shots because Mike appeared to know something. He was a mover and a shaker. Patrick appeared to know something.... Every other person seemed to think, 'Hey, there's something coming down.'"

The two men—black and white, a soldier of his country and a soldier for hire, men whose ambitions had converged around a single military objective—talked until well after dark. The hotel night security guard, Rollins Laurent, saw them sitting together on the balcony. Just a few weeks remained until they hoped to seize this little nation of shanties, volcanic peaks and old colonial plantations. Reid stayed until one in the morning. At five, Perdue left for Houston to make it all happen.

Perdue had forged some odd alliances. His coup had united right-wing North Americans and Caribbean leftists; white nationalists and black revolutionaries; First World capitalists and Third World socialists. Only one type of man could have managed such a political juggling act: one who believed in nothing at all.

10

The revolutionary: Algie Maffei

St. John's, Antigua
January 1981

THE HIGHWAY THAT SNAKES UP Dominica's west coast from Roseau passes through Goodwill, Canefield and Massacre, where British troops wiped out a tribe of Caribs in 1674.

The next village is Mahaut, in the parish of St. Paul. The homes and shops, some no bigger than garden sheds, are built on a narrow plateau above the beach. The buildings are so close to the road that anyone stepping out their front door risks getting mowed down by the minivan taxis that rush through, their horns beeping to warn pedestrians and oncoming traffic. Uphill and right at the pink house, then along a road as steep as a goat trail, there is a wooden shack at the curve, the home of Captain Malcolm "Marley" Walter Reid. It isn't much, but Reid's mother lives just up the hill, and what do you expect on a soldier's pay?

Algie Maffei climbed the hill to Captain Reid's house, past the small garden plots and front stoops where old men sat on folding lawn chairs talking about the cricket scores. Accompanying Algie was the Dread leader Henry "Mal" Esprit. The captain wasn't home when they got there so they waited on the porch until he arrived forty-five minutes later; then they went inside.

"This is the guy I was telling you about," Mal said, introducing Algie. "He will represent the Dreads during the coup."

The first time Algie had heard about the plans for a coup he was at the Dread encampment in Giraudel. They told him about the foreign mercenaries and the DDF. The Dreads were no friends of either, but they felt they would be better off without Eugenia Charles as prime minister. If they helped get rid of her, the new revolutionary regime would owe them and the Dreads would at last be able to live close to nature and *Ja* without government harassment.

"There's nothing to be afraid of," Captain Reid said to Algie. "We have backers. We'll be getting help from the outside."

"From which place?" Algie asked.

"The U.S.A."

"What sort of help?"

"Finance, arms and ammunition."

"And what," Algie pressed on, "would be the purpose of these arms and ammunition?"

"To take over the police force and overthrow the government," said Reid.

"Have any plans been drawn up?"

"Yes, you must study the plans."

"Before I make any decision," Algie said, "I want to study these plans."

Sixteen months had passed since Algie had walked out of *gaol*, freed not by an act of justice but by an act of nature, the hurricane that had obliterated Stock Farm Prison. Although he was still wanted for the murder of the farmer found dead near his banana plantation, Algie remained on the loose. The police had not taken him back into state custody.

Algie had reason enough to hate the *polis*. He had been arrested so many times he had lost count. He says he thinks he has nine convictions but he isn't sure; it could be more. This time he was really in trouble. The maximum sentence for murder was the most severe imaginable: the judge could make him a *pandi*, a hanged man. But the people of Dominica say a sunken ship does not prevent another from sailing. Maybe the coup was a ship that Algie could board to freedom, to escape the police investigation that weighed on him.

A few days after the meeting at Reid's house, the captain came to Algie's place high above Fond Colé, overlooking the electrical generating station and, across the valley, the utilitarian buildings that make up Stock Farm Prison.

"I'm still thinking about it," Algie told him.

"Can I use your *telifonn?*"

"If it's an overseas call, make sure to call collect."

Algie heard the captain ask the operator to place a collect call to Mr. Michael Perdue in Houston, Texas.

ON SUNDAY, ALGIE WENT BACK to Captain Reid's house and two men walked in—Julian David and Colonel Patrick John.

They talked numbers. They said they needed locals to take part in the coup. Most of them would be drawn from the Dominica Defence Force, but they needed about twenty Dreads to participate. Together with the twenty mercenaries they were hiring, that should be sufficient for the task.

"Sixty to eighty men would be good enough to handle the operation," Patrick John said.

"What about if we meet stiff resistance?"

"We will have no choice but to use two hundred mercenaries."

Captain Reid asked Algie if he could recruit at least twenty Dreads.

"I can try," Algie said.

"You must work on that immediately."

"Okay."

Mobilizing the Dreads was not going to be easy. They lived all over the island, in the most inaccessible places, growing *ganja*, living off the land and terrorizing the farmers. Algie was going to need a jeep. He asked if they could get him a Suzuki, but they did not think they could raise that kind of money. Not a Suzuki, but maybe a second-hand Land Rover or Volkswagen.

"I think we have that kind of bread," Julian David said.

Patrick John and Julian David left and Algie was about to leave as well when Captain Reid called him back.

"He gave me a small slip of paper with a phone number and a name, Michael Perdue and Houston, Texas written on the paper. He told me to try and get in touch with Michael Perdue on my telephone, I can call him collect. He told me what to say to Michael Perdue."

Algie made the collect call and uttered the pre-arranged code greeting: "Walter said hello."

Perdue wanted to meet. He suggested Texas. Algie said he would need a visa to travel to the United States. Perdue suggested Montreal or Toronto, but Algie explained he had a deportation order in Canada.

Perdue was reluctant to return to Dominica. He had been there too many times and made too many phone calls. He thought the U.S. State Department might be on to him. Maybe the agency didn't care. Maybe it supported him. Perdue told himself he was worrying too much. "Paranoia, probably," he said. But just to be careful, he decided to stay clear of Dominica.

He also had some money to throw around. After returning to Houston, he had shown Patrick John's Letter of Intent to a Texas investor who had forked over $10,000 cash and two checks, one for $12,000 and the other for $20,000. Now he could start buying gear and hiring mercs. And he could afford a few nights at a Caribbean resort.

"What about Antigua?" Perdue said.

"That will suit me fine," Algie replied.

They agreed to meet at the Castle Harbour Hotel on January 30. Perdue said he would send money to Julian David through the Royal Bank of Canada to pay for the flights and other expenses. Algie told Captain Reid about the meeting in Antigua the next day.

"Why the date was fixed so low down?" Reid asked.

"This was the guy's suggestion," Algie said.

Four days before he was to leave for Antigua, Algie got a call from Julian David, telling him to meet Captain Reid in Mahaut. Reid wasn't home when Algie got there, but he came by Algie's place later in the afternoon.

Reid said he was glad the date of the trip was so "low down" because now he would be able to go along.

Algie went to Julian David's office the next day, but the money hadn't yet arrived from Perdue. He returned the next day, but still no money. On the 29th, he went back again and David called the bank. The money was in—$400. Reid went by Algie's house in the afternoon with cash and two tickets on the next day's LIAT flight to Antigua. He told him to be at the airport at 1:30 p.m. at the latest.

Algie was still loyal to Rosie Douglas. Of all the politicians on the island, Rosie was the only one he trusted. They had forged a bond in Montreal and now they were back in Dominica, Canadian deportees trying to implement the radical social and political revolution they had talked about in furnace heated apartments while the snow fell outside. "I used to keep nothing from him," Algie says. Algie confided in Rosie, told him everything he had learned about what Patrick John and Malcolm Reid were up to. Before he left for Antigua, Algie asked for Rosie's advice. Should he go? This was getting serious. They were planning revolution. But Rosie encouraged him to make the trip. Otherwise, how would they know what was really going on?

ALGIE PACKED HIS TRAVEL BAG and waited by the Fond Colé fisheries depot at 10:15 a.m. Howell Piper pulled up in his jeep. Julian David was in the passenger seat. Algie got in and they climbed the switchbacks above Canefield to Patrick John's house.

By 11:45, Captain Reid still hadn't arrived. Algie was about to go looking for him when Patrick John summoned him into a room.

"In entering the room, I observed Mr. John fitting on a pair of rubber gloves, the color was pink, and then he handed an envelope to me," Algie said. "When I was about taking it with my hand, he told me, don't allow my fingerprints to get on this envelope."

The envelope was sealed and stapled. Using the tip of his shirt as a glove, Algie dropped it into his overnight bag. Algie says Patrick John told him to give the envelope to Captain Reid, who was to deliver it to Mike Perdue.

Algie walked down to the flats at Canefield and waited until Captain Reid arrived in a jeep. Again using his shirt tail, Algie handed the envelope to Reid. They made a quick stop at Reid's house to pick up his bag and passport, and then they drove across the island to catch their flight.

They knew they were late. They called ahead and asked the airline to hold back the flight. The LIAT pilots waited ten minutes but when the passengers didn't show, they left. The plane was already in the air when Reid and Maffei reached Melville Hall Airport. There was another flight in the morning so they drove to Concord. They knew a man who worked at a restaurant there called the Stop and Go, a musician named Hemple Bertrand. They spent the night in the restaurant, then returned to Melville Hall in the morning and caught the early flight.

The plane climbed north over the tiny island of Marie Galante, past the eastern shore of Guadeloupe. Forty minutes later, they descended over the turquoise bays and white sands of Saint John's. Antigua and Dominica were like twins. Dominica was bigger and more mountainous, but both islands shared similar histories, having shifted between the colonial orbits of Spain, France and Britain. Both were named by Christopher Columbus (in the case of Antigua, after a church in Seville). Both had roughly the same number of inhabitants, and English was their official language. But while Dominica struggled, Antigua prospered.

That was mostly because of the tourists who arrived at the airport and took taxis to the resorts. Antigua had been blessed with a gentle topography and sandy coves, whereas Dominica's shoreline consisted of rock or slivers of black volcanic sand. Antigua was a land of bays and beaches; Dominica was all mountains and rivers. Before Columbus had named it after the Christian holy day, its name was *Waitikubuli*, which means *tall is her body*. Legend has it that when Columbus returned to Spain and was asked to describe Dominica, he crumpled a sheet of paper and threw it on the table.

To the explorers and colonists, Dominica may have been a discarded hunk of paper, but it was much more than that. While the rest of the islands were transforming themselves into a playground for tourists, Dominica remained authentically Caribbean, a place for West Indians, not just a destination for sun-seeking vacationers. Perhaps Dominicans could one day achieve the wealth and stature of Antiguans, but as it stood, most people outside the Caribbean had never heard of Dominica, or they confused it with the Dominican Republic. Most couldn't even pronounce the country's name. Eugenia Charles' foes were convinced that Dominica needed change—revolutionary change.

ON JANUARY 30, Patrick John typed a letter to a fellow Labour Party official named Nugent Thomas, who was in Antigua. It described John's efforts to revitalize the party and pull it out of debt following its defeat at the hands of Eugenia Charles and her Freedom Party. The letter ended with a request.

> *Bearer of this note M. Reid should be returning to*
> *Dominica, so give him a gallon bottle—Johnny Walker*
> *for me.*
> *Thanks.*
> *Yours In The Struggle,*
> *Patrick R. John*

The former prime minister got on a plane to Miami, but he said it was only a shopping trip. He did not meet Mike Perdue during his brief holiday in Florida.

THE CASTLE HARBOUR HOTEL sits on a hill overlooking Saint John's. Mike Perdue arrived on British West Indies Flight 409 from Miami, this time listing his occupation as "Import-Export." The immigration officer on duty, Sergeant Winston Nathaniel, recognized Perdue as a regular visitor.

Upon their arrival, Captain Reid and Algie took a taxi to the hotel and asked for Perdue. The receptionist said he was out, but that he had left a message and he would be back soon. Perdue had reserved a single room for Reid and Algie to share, but they insisted on having separate rooms and the hotel desk accommodated them. All the rooms were billed to Perdue.

The bellboy took Algie to room 29. He was resting when there was a knock at the door. Reid told him Perdue had returned and was waiting in room 31.

"This is Maffei," Reid said, introducing his colleague.

Captain Reid gave Perdue the envelope he had carried from Dominica. Perdue opened it and took out two smaller envelopes. One was marked "Michael Perdue." The other said "Copy." Perdue handed the copy to Reid and kept the one addressed to himself.

It was a contract. It was much more detailed than the two-paragraph letter of a few months ago. In five pages, it spelled out the terms of an agreement between the Black Revolutionary Council, represented by acting chairman Colonel Patrick John, and Nortic Enterprises, represented by Mike Perdue.

The first section dealt with improvements to the Defence Force that would be needed to keep Patrick John in power once the coup was over. It said the council would add 200 soldiers to the militia within ten days *for the purpose of national security and the maintenance of the government.* The Defence Force would *assume full and all military functions for the internal and external security of Dominica.* The revolutionary council also agreed to *make financial provisions for the purchase of equipment, other military items and supplies and proper accommodation for the national defence force in order to maintain complete national security and protection of Dominica.*

Perdue was offered a senior post in the militia: *The Council shall employ Michael E. Perdue who shall be responsible for the supervision and training of the national defence force.* The terms and conditions of his employment were to be negotiated and spelled out in a separate contract. *Michael E. Perdue shall be allotted duties and responsibilities by the Chairman of the Council on behalf of the Council and shall report directly the chairman.* A senior officer was to be assigned to work with Perdue.

The rest of the contract explained the rewards that Nortic Enterprises would receive for "installing" Patrick John as prime minister: *The Company shall be paid an amount of $50,000 U.S. for its participation in the installation of the Council,* it said. The money was to be paid within four months. In addition, Perdue would get to keep 2.5 percent of an $80-million development loan the country expected from foreign donors.

The contract continued:

> *The Council accepts and agrees that the Company should operate businesses in the state of Dominica. The Council agrees to give the Company fiscal incentives as follows: (a) Tax exemption for 20 years. This concession can be reviewed at the end of the twentieth year. (b) During the*

> tax exemption period, the Company shall not pay income
> tax and shall also be exempted from taxes, duties and levies
> on equipment and articles imported solely for the operation
> of the commercial and/or industrial enterprise of the
> Company. (c) Persons of Nortic Enterprises are allowed to
> repatriate funds without restrictions.

In exchange, Perdue would return Patrick John to power within one month:

> The Company shall undertake to install the Council
> by February 28, 1981. The Company shall supply the
> Council with all the necessary equipment and supplies for
> the successful operation and ultimate installation of the
> Council.

THE DEAL WAS WORTH MILLIONS, both for Mike Perdue and Patrick John. Three percent of the profits of Nortic Enterprises were to be funneled to the Black Revolutionary Council leader, in addition to 2 percent to each of the principal officers and 1 percent for the Council itself. Nortic was also obliged to train and employ Dominicans and invest 30 percent of its profits in the agricultural development and agro industries, construction of an international airport, tourism and *other related development projects.* Nortic could do what it wanted, as long as it acted *in the interest of national security and national development.*

While Algie flipped through a *Penthouse* magazine, Perdue talked guns with Captain Reid. The Texan opened a book with the title *Democracy* and showed Reid the selection of firearms he could provide for the coup. The M-16 was a good weapon but it couldn't handle mud or water, Perdue said. The Bushmaster, on the other hand, was "a very simple, semi-automatic rifle, a high-powered rifle." It was made for any weather. Ideal for jungle warfare.

Perdue said he could get his hands on a few, although he wasn't sure exactly how many. He went to his briefcase and took out fifteen $100 bills and handed them to Captain Reid. "For expenses in Dominica," he said.

They ate lunch at The Golden Peanut. Algie was pleasantly surprised when he met the owner and recognized her as a Dominican he knew from his days with Rosie Douglas. Over lunch, they discussed the police headquarters in Roseau and its various entry points. Perdue said he had been invited to a barbeque and asked Algie and Captain Reid if they wanted to come along, but they said they wanted to go back to the hotel to rest.

"While I was in my room," Algie recalls, "Reid brought in the envelope marked 'Copy.' He gave it to me; he told me to study it, for this is a contract which we will have to dispute on the return of Perdue tonight." Algie looked it over for the first time. He recognized the name Black Revolutionary Council. He had heard it discussed in Dominica, at meetings he attended with Patrick John, Reid, David, and Dennis Joseph, and he understood its purpose was to replace the government of Eugenia Charles.

That evening, Perdue knocked on the hotel room door and said he would be at the bar. They sat with a young American woman, a middle-aged couple and a Canadian naval officer. Then they all went upstairs to the balcony that overlooked the drive-in theater. When the others had left, the three conspirators met in Perdue's hotel room to discuss the contract.

Perdue said there was a big problem with the wording of the document. "The first thing we have got to change on this paper is the name, Black Revolutionary Council," he said.

"Why?"

"The word 'black' will prejudice the minds of the financiers and investors," he said.

Perdue underlined the term *Black Revolutionary Council* and wrote above it: *must be changed.*

Perdue also said the money wasn't good enough. The contract offered $50,000. He said he needed more. He scribbled his demand in pen: *Must have $200,000.* He elaborated in a note on the back of the page: *I must have at least $150,000 within two weeks to complete imediate* [sic] *security. The $50,000 can come later. This money will go completely* *to pay my people and national defense. No personal payment. But must be independent to secure counsel. M.E. Perdue.*

Captain Reid agreed but said the Council would have the final say. Perdue made a few other changes, adding "bank charter" and "lumber export" to the list of business activities that Nortic Enterprises was permitted to undertake. Where the contract said that a senior military officer would be assigned to work with him, Perdue specified that it must be Malcolm Reid.

It was after midnight and Algie was dozing off. Perdue told him to get some rest. Algie went to his room to lie down.

IN THE MORNING, after breakfast, Reid said he wasn't feeling well and stayed in his room. Perdue wanted to get out of the hotel. He knocked on Algie's door. "Let's go for a walk," he said.

They took a cab to the port and started walking. "He tried to create an impression on me as if he was a big military man," Algie says. "He started calling me lieutenant, as if I'm part of his army."

Perdue made a deal with Algie, one he must have known would win over the Dreads. Following the coup, Perdue said he would finance and build a *ganja* depot that would buy marijuana from the Dreads and ship it to foreign markets. The Dreads farmed their own marijuana; it was part of their way of life and their social outlook. It was a spiritual act for Rastafarians; they believed it brought them closer to God. They also claimed that *ganja* originated in Africa, and that smoking it was a way of returning to their roots. Perdue was promising them not only an income for doing what they did anyway, but also the chance to export their dogma.

Algie accepted the offer.

Perdue also offered to let the Dreads grow coca, which would be processed into cocaine and exported, but Algie said that went against the culture of the Dread movement.

The two men strolled downtown to the docks. When they got back it was already midday. Captain Reid phoned the airport to check on their flight and then they all went down to the bar.

Before returning to his room to pack, Captain Reid stopped at the hotel boutique and bought a bottle of skin cream.

"Why you bought that?" Algie asked.

"You'll find out later," Reid said.

Algie was packing when he saw Captain Reid fold his copy of the contract and fold it again and again until it was very small. He wrapped it in plastic, sealed it with tape and slipped it inside the bottle of skin cream. He poured the cream back into the bottle, screwed on the lid and placed the bottle in his bag.

Perdue accompanied them in the taxi to the airport. If all went smoothly, their next meeting would be in just a few weeks, on the beach north of Roseau, during the first stage of the coup d'état.

TWO DAYS LATER, Algie and Reid took a motorcycle into the hills above Canefield to Patrick John's house. According to Algie, Patrick John was there, as well as Julian David and Dennis Joseph, a guitar player and a member of one of Dominica's most popular calypso bands, The Gaylords, which worked the Caribbean hotel and carnival circuit. He wrote some of their greatest hits, like "Pray for the Black Man." The band's biggest single was "Hit Me with Music," but the group was best known for its singer Greg Breaker Bannis, who went on to join the British pop sensation Hot Chocolate, best known for "You Sexy Thing," "Disco Queen" and "You Could Have Been a Lady." Later, Joseph ran the Dominica Broadcasting Service and served in Patrick John's Labour Party.

Joseph says he was not there. He believes he was wrongly implicated in the plot because he had been an effective Labour Party campaign manager and therefore Eugenia Charles did not like him. "She had a problem with me," he says. "This is how she was getting back at me."

The meeting at John's house was meant as a debriefing to discuss Perdue's response to the contract. They passed around the agreement and read Perdue's scribbled notations. They agreed to take out the name Black Revolutionary Council; they would just describe themselves as the Council. Perdue's monetary demands were another matter. Patrick John didn't know how he could come up with $200,000. But they had no choice. They agreed to send a message to Perdue telling him to go ahead. A new contract would be typed up, with all the amendments.

The following weekend, the five of them met again, this time at another home in Canefield, to go over the assault plan. The mercenaries were to land at the Dominica Mining Company at Rockaway Beach at 2 a.m. The Dreads and DDF troops would be waiting for them at the beach. That would give everyone an hour to get into position for the attack on the police headquarters, which was to begin at 3 a.m.

There were still a few tasks to take care of. They wanted to find out who controlled the HAM radio sets on the island, and they needed to organize vehicles to carry the mercenaries from the beach to the police compound. And Perdue had to let them know how soon he could reach the island with his men and guns.

Confident their operation would be successful and that they would soon form the government of Dominica, the men discussed the positions they would hold in the new regime. According to Algie, Dennis Joseph was to be in charge of Radio and Communications; Julian David was to be Treasurer; Reid would lead the Defence Force, and Algie would be his second-in-command.

Patrick John would hold the most prestigious titles: Chairman of the Revolutionary Council, Minister of Foreign Affairs, Minister of Defence and Prime Minister. And he would hold those titles because of a contract that, stripped of its formal-sounding business language, proposed a simple but crude exchange: You put us in power; we make you rich.

"They were using Patrick as a stepping stone to go after their goals in the Caribbean," Algie says of the mercenaries. "He would be like a puppet on a string. He would have to do whatever he was told."

Algie went to see Rosie Douglas and told him what had happened in Antigua.

Rosie thought the coup would probably succeed. The Dominican police were poorly armed; the mercenaries had them outgunned. Algie explained that he wanted the invasion to go ahead, but only because he was planning to betray the mercenaries. "My plan was to allow them to land because I had all the plans, where they would be landing, and my plan was to deal them a blow," he says. "Just like Bay of Pigs."

Part II

Operation Red Dog

Lost causes and losers go with the job.

—Manual of the Mercenary Soldier

11

Dominica, West Indies, 2007

Houston, Texas
February 1981

IN FOOTBALL, THERE IS A PLAY called a "Red Dog." A defensive back drives through the line and tries to sack the quarterback. Mike Perdue never played football in high school. It was too much work, and he didn't have the discipline. He was too busy with his gang, getting into trouble. But his brother Bill was a quarterback and Mike recognized the parallel between the play and the invasion of Dominica. The mercenaries were going to blitz the island and take out the prime minister. They were going to Red Dog her, and he named his invasion accordingly. He called it Operation Red Dog.

The invasion plan was a ripoff of *The Dogs of War*. The movie opened in theaters on the second Friday in February. Christopher Walken starred as Shannon, an American hired by shady businessmen to overthrow a vile African dictator. Tom Berenger was cast as his right-hand man, Drew. The battle scenes were vivid but what caught the critics' attention was Walken's dark portrayal of a sullen mercenary committed to nothing but the success of his operation.

The MGM production was based on Frederick Forsyth's 1974 novel about a British company that hires a veteran mercenary named

Cat Shannon to install a puppet president in Zangaro in order to exploit a platinum deposit worth $10 billion. In the book, Shannon signs a generous contract and criss-crosses Europe buying weapons and recruiting men of dubious character. He hires a ship to ferry them to the waters off Zangaro, and they use light rafts to land on the beach near the capital in the early morning. They storm the presidential palace, the armory and the radio station and are gone before dawn, leaving a new regime in power.

Mike Perdue's plan copied the story step by step. He was to travel by sea, come ashore in inflatable dinghies, neutralize the local defenses, seize the radio station and armory, and depose the prime minister. Even the name Perdue picked for his invasion sounds plagiarized. Perdue worked out the details at home in Houston. Wolfgang Droege helped. They started by dividing the invasion force into three teams, which they named Red Dog One, Red Dog Two and Red Dog Three. Each was a mix of foreign mercenaries and locals, the Dominica Defence Force, and the Dreads.

Red Dog One consisted of five men. Once ashore, they were to drive a single vehicle to downtown Roseau. They would stop on King George Street, proceed on foot to Bath Street and overrun the charge office of police headquarters.

The eighteen mercenaries of Red Dog Two would take four vehicles to Bath Street and enter the police compound through the main vehicle gate, where they would meet up with the seventeen members of Red Dog Three, who had left their five cars at the corner of Bath Street and Cork Street.

Red Dog Two and Red Dog Three would then advance together. Once inside the police compound, they would break into three smaller units. One unit would raid the communications building, while the second would hit the armory, where all the Defence Force weapons were locked up. The third would storm the barracks at two separate entrances, catching the Dominican police dozing.

After Perdue returned from his meeting in Antigua, he sketched it all out in a diagram, with arrows showing how the three teams would capture the police station and, by extension, the island. It would all be over in a couple of hours.

MIKE PERDUE HAD a lot of work to do. He needed to start recruiting, but first he had to finalize his contract with the Dominican revolutionaries. He ironed out the details by telephone from his home. A week later he had a final draft that was agreeable to both parties.

The Black Revolutionary Council had granted Perdue the concessions he had asked for in Antigua: $150,000 to be paid within two weeks of the coup, plus another $50,000 within four months. There were a few more incentives. The deal promised him 3 percent of the $80-million development loan, rather than the 2.5 percent initially offered (a $400,000 increase) and broadened the range of business activities that Nortic Enterprises could pursue, adding gambling, banking and the harvest and export of timber. Perdue would also get Dominican citizenship and, as improbable as it seemed, a senior position in the Black Revolutionary Council.

Perdue's end of the bargain was unchanged: "The company shall reinstate the Council as the government of Dominica."

He put the final draft in his briefcase. He would take it with him on the invasion, and once the coup was completed, he would sign it. Perdue was putting a lot of faith in his contract. It never seemed to cross his mind that the Council might have agreed to his demands because it had no intention of honoring them.

The contract did not mention everything. It made no reference to the marijuana export business that Perdue had promised the Dreads, nor the plans to sell passports and armaments internationally, nor Droege's scheme to build cocaine factories.

The months that Wolfgang had spent with his new friend from Texas had an impact on him. He was getting right into the spirit of Third World exploitation. He was thinking about big money. And why not? Nobody could stop them. They were going to own the country, even though to the outside world it would look like just another backwater revolt. In a way, it was. How many other coups have been quietly orchestrated, not in rebel camps in the jungles, but in the world's financial and political capitals?

Under the terms of the contract, Perdue was supposed to recruit up to thirty "specialists" who would serve as advisors to the Dominica Defence Force. But how? The memoirs of Colonel "Mad

Mike" Hoare, the hero of mercenaries everywhere, were blunt about recruitment. Mercenaries were motivated by one thing: "the desire to make big money quickly, all risks accepted." Of course, idealists and adventurers also came out, but Hoare found they were rare. In the end, it was just a job.

Perdue decided he would offer his recruits $3,000 each. As an added incentive, he would give them a share of Nortic Enterprises. For those who were more principled, or not motivated by money, he would have to appeal to their sense of patriotism, and in 1981, the best way to do that was to raise the threat of communism.

A lot of Americans were worried about communism, and with good reason. The Soviets were a determined enemy. They were arming and financing Western democracy's foes around the world, from Afghanistan and Mozambique to Cuba and Grenada. President Ronald Reagan took office on January 20, 1981, warning in his inaugural address "there are those in the world who scorn our vision of human dignity and freedom. One nation, the Soviet Union, has conducted the greatest military buildup in the history of man, building arsenals of awesome offensive weapons. We have made progress in restoring our defense capability. But much remains to be done. There must be no wavering by us, nor any doubts by others, that America will meet her responsibilities to remain free, secure, and at peace."

The Soviets were aggressively expanding their military strength as part of a strategy to export communist revolution. They had invaded Afghanistan and were trying to suppress an anti-communist uprising in Poland. At the same time, the Kremlin was trying to prevent Western ideas from slipping under the Iron Curtain. The Soviets even placed strict curbs on the use of fax machines which, along with the Sony Walkman, were the biggest technological innovations of the day. At his first White House cabinet meeting, Reagan set the tone of his presidency by announcing that he hated taxes and communism.

Invading Dominica, Perdue would tell his recruits, was exactly what the president wanted. There was just one problem: Prime Minister Eugenia Charles was not a communist. In her first speech after coming to office, she declared herself an *enemy* of communism. She was on good terms with Washington. If anyone was leaning left, it was Patrick

John. Even the name *Black Revolutionary Council* sounded like the kind of thing the Soviets could get behind.

To convince his recruits they were fighting communism, Perdue was going to have to rebrand Dominica. He would have to turn the island's politics upside down. But the kind of men he hoped to hire were not likely to know the difference.

Perdue wanted to know what caliber of recruits he could attract with the money he was offering, so he placed a classified ad in a newsletter called *Le Mercenaire*. It read, *Security personnel interested Caribbean work 5-year term $10,000–$15,000 bonus, $250 a month.*

The ad made no direct mention of a coup but any idiot could read between the lines. Applicants were asked to write to a post office box in Longview, Texas.

"WHEN ONE GOES INTO the market for soldiers, what is the response likely to be?" Colonel Mike Hoare wrote in his memoir, *Congo Mercenary*. "Is there a reserve of would-be soldiers lying dormant in the community at any one time waiting for just such an opportunity as this? And what type of men are they likely to be?" Mad Mike Hoare was an Irishman who had served in India and Burma. Following the Second World War, he led a force of hired guns into the Congo to fight a communist insurgency. Hoare made no apologies for being a soldier of fortune and came to believe that mercenaries might be the only hope for stopping what he called "the communist invasion of Africa." When Congo fell into chaos in 1960, Moise Tshombe, president of the resource-rich province of Katanga, declared independence and sent an advisor to South Africa to hire foreign mercenaries. Colonel Hoare answered the recruiting call and assembled a force he called 4 Commando. Tshombe was eventually ousted and exiled to Spain, but in 1964 he was invited to return as Congo's prime minister. Once again, he turned to foreign mercenaries and contracted Hoare to suppress a communist rebellion.

Mike Perdue was not an educated man. He couldn't write a shopping list without misspelling a word or two. But he read books and almost every would-be mercenary had read *Congo Mercenary*. What Perdue did not learn from *The Dogs of War*, he seems to have picked up from Hoare's memoirs. Like Hoare, Perdue had been contracted by a returning prime minister to supplement a weak national army. Hoare also gave his mercenary jobs formal names, like Operation White Giant and Operation Watch Chain. And like Hoare, Perdue had to contend with contract negotiations and the recruitment of fighting men. Hoare was able to hire 300 recruits, although they were a ragtag crew. Those who answered his calls to arms were often drunks and "layabouts" who couldn't find work anywhere else and were only looking for easy money, he lamented. He was horrified by all the "dagga-smokers and dope addicts" who reported for duty. "Perhaps the greatest surprise of all, and it was to remain so right through the three six-month contracts we served, was the incidence of homosexuals," he wrote. "Of all places to find these highly sensitive and usually very intelligent gentry, I would have thought a mercenary outfit to have been the last."

Danny Joe Hawkins was Operation Red Dog's first recruit. Danny Joe was a thirty-seven-year-old father of three from Smith County, Mississippi. He was five-foot-ten, with a cool, unimpressed look on his face. He had a mustache, sideburns and sandy hair. "He was a tough guy," says Reverend Kenneth Dean, a civil rights worker who tried to deal with the Klan by getting to know its key players, Hawkins included. "Somebody mess with him and they had a fight on their hands."

Hawkins had no military experience. He was a soldier of the Ku Klux Klan. "He's been a longstanding Klansman and his father was too," says Jim Ingram, a retired FBI agent who worked on Mississippi civil rights cases in the 1960s. Adds Dean: "Danny was not a fringe player. You can put him at the center of things and you won't be wrong."

His father, Joe Denver, was a construction contractor and his mother was a Sunday school teacher at the Baptist church in Sullivan's Hollow, known as one of the toughest places in the state. "You had to work hard, scratch to make a living and use everything that you could think of to survive," says Ingram. "Anyone that came out of there was a survivor." Working class and tough, Hawkins traces his zeal, according to the reverend, to a 1962 incident in Oxford, Mississippi. That fall, James Meredith tried to become the first black student to enroll at the University of Mississippi. United States Marshals had to accompany him to campus to help him register, but the governor refused to allow it, and hundreds of segregationist protestors descended on Ole Miss, piling wood and bricks into roadblocks and firing birdshot at federal troops amid the swirl of tear gas. Two died and dozens were wounded. "This is really where he got his baptism," says Reverend Dean. "He talked about it all the time."

A Bureau of Alcohol, Tobacco and Firearms bulletin describes Hawkins as a "convicted felon and known member of the KKK." In truth, Hawkins had only ever been convicted of a single crime: He had used a fake name to buy a Heckler and Koch rifle. He thought the firearms law was bogus because it conflicted with the Second Amendment of the Constitution. "People have the right to own and bear arms without any government involvement," he says. But Hawkins had been arrested more than a dozen times—for firearms violations, assault, marijuana possession and several racially motivated attacks.

The Mississippi Klan waged a reign of terror around Jackson in the late 1960s. It began on March 7, 1967 when a bomb gutted the offices of Blackwell Real Estate, following rumors the company was selling homes to blacks in white neighborhoods. It was the first of a dozen attacks that targeted homes, offices and synagogues. At 10:40 p.m. on September 18, 1967, a bomb made out of an estimated half case of dynamite exploded at the Temple Beth Israel synagogue in North Jackson. Hours later, FBI agents arrested Hawkins and his father. They were charged with assaulting the FBI officers but not for the bombing. Joe Denver was sentenced to sixty days in Hinds County Jail. Danny Joe, then twenty-three, was released.

Hawkins was later arrested following a bank robbery in Memphis. The FBI searched his car and found two rifles, a .45-calibre pistol, ammunition, two billy clubs and a hangman's noose. He was arrested once again for his alleged role in the real estate office bombing but an all-white jury acquitted him. Three months later, he was charged over an attempted bombing at the home of Meyer Davidson, a Jewish businessman in Meridian. Hawkins was not present at the attempted bombing but had been seen beforehand with the man behind the plot, Tom Tarrants. Once again, the charges against Hawkins did not stick. "He shied away from certain things," Ingram says. "The FBI was never able to pin anything on him." The same went for his father and his friend L.E. Matthews.

The wave of attacks stemmed from a change in Klan thinking. Communism was the new enemy, and the Klansmen viewed Jews and civil rights workers as agents of communist influence. "There was a point at which this state made a shift and the focus was not on blacks at all," says Reverend Dean. "The focus was on communism. These guys were all convinced that there was a real move to create a beachhead for communism in the Southern states, and it would come about through invasion of the Southern states through these islands down in the Caribbean. And of course the lynchpin was Castro and Cuba, and the Klan thought that there would be attacks made from the Caribbean. So in their minds, if they could take over an island, they would be establishing a foothold and a beachhead."

Since getting out of prison early in 1979, Hawkins hadn't been able to find a job so his wife, Sue, worked and he stayed at home. He took care of the boys, Danny, Eric and Wes, and kept the house clean and repaired the family cars. "I'm a house husband," he said. Danny knew Wolfgang Droege through the far right. "Wolfgang and Danny Joe, they were almost twins," says Dean, who knew both men. "Both of them had abilities beyond their supposed education level and both of them were fearless. Both of them had this idealization of the German racial myth."

Droege took Mike Perdue to Danny Joe's house. Mike told Hawkins he was starting a movement that was organizing an incursion to put a stop to the advance of communism in the West Indies. Perdue would later say he wasn't sure the word "coup" was ever uttered, but he says he made it clear he was planning to get rid of the regime that was in power. "The only way to do that was through a military coup," Perdue said. "I certainly didn't mention anything about elections." No particular island was identified—at first. "It was just touched on ... that this might be a good place to go in and stop some of the incursion," Hawkins says. "It was just real vague." Hawkins realized Perdue was feeling him out to see if he was interested in joining the mercenary force. He was.

"Well, I'm a pretty strong anti-communist," Hawkins said.

A few weeks later, Perdue phoned Hawkins and explained their target was Dominica. The communists had taken over Grenada and now Dominica was at risk, he said. Prime Minister Eugenia Charles, he added, was talking with the Cubans.

Perdue said the Dominica Defence Force was trying to save the island from communism. The military chiefs wanted to put an anti-communist named Patrick John back in power, but the military needed help. Perdue said he was a captain in the Defence Force and that he had been commissioned to recruit fighting men ready to take a stand against communism.

"Well," Danny replied, "does the island belong to anybody, like the French or the English and all of that?"

Perdue explained that Dominica was an independent nation. Danny Joe wanted to know more before making a decision, so he went to the library and checked out a book on the Caribbean. He was soon convinced.

"I mean, it was coming up for grabs there," he says. "It was whoever was going to come out the strongest on that deal, either the communists or the good guys. I was going to side with the good guys."

Perdue said the job paid $3,000. Hawkins says he would have done it for free.

"Money means absolutely nothing to me on this particular type of thing, absolutely nothing. All they had to do was pay my way to go. Just give me a rifle down there; I would be glad to help. That's how strong I feel about it."

He felt so strongly that he asked two friends to come along.

BILL WALDROP WAS an industrial painter at the Grand Gulf Nuclear Power Station in Port Gibson, Mississippi's third oldest town, which General Ulysses S. Grant had declared "too beautiful to burn." He was thirty-three, with a wife and a child, and he had known Danny Joe Hawkins for fifteen years. They went to school together and had been close ever since. They even got arrested together in 1971; Waldrop was fined for carrying a concealed weapon.

Waldrop was at the Hawkins' house in Jackson when Danny Joe told him about Dominica. He explained that he had met someone who was planning to overthrow the government and install Patrick John. "He told me that Mr. John was a staunch anti-communist, that he had been a popular prime minister and that he was no longer in office," Waldrop says. Danny asked Waldrop if he wanted in.

Bill Waldrop had no military training. He had been a member of Youth for Christ at Province High School in Jackson, and he had served as president of the Hinds County chapter of the Patriotic American Youth Organization. At college in Brookhaven, he was president of the Freshman Class and Class Senator.

He was moved by what Hawkins told him and went to his boss to ask for a six-week leave of absence. It wasn't about the money, he says. He would have made just as much if he'd stayed home and painted. He says he joined the mercenary force for one reason: "To fight communism."

Waldrop was "pretty sure" the U.S. government was behind the invasion of Dominica: "Oh, with all the publicity and whatever about the communist activities in the Caribbean, I thought in all probability the United States government might want to establish a base of operations down there."

DANNY JOE HAWKINS brought in one more recruit. George Taylor Malvaney loved the outdoors. He was always out in the woods. But even his mother had to admit he had his problems. At Murrah High School, "Home of the Mustangs," he earned a reputation as a troublemaker. "We have taught ourselves over the last ten years not to say 'nigger,'" one teacher told *The Jackson Daily News.* "He'd walk into a class and say, 'This class is full of niggers.'" He dropped out but later completed his GED and joined the United States Navy on October 3, 1977. Seaman Malvaney was a gunner's mate. From the Naval Training Center in Orlando, Florida, he was assigned to the combat shore ship USS *Concord* and then the USS *Detroit*, a supply oiler. Malvaney had a good service record, but his involvement in the Ku Klux Klan concerned his superiors. After organizing a Klan event in Virginia Beach, he was transferred to the Naval Air Station at Brunswick, Maine. He left the service shortly after that. "I mean, it's obvious you're going to have some potential issues with the military and Klan activities," he says. "It was becoming problematic and I requested a discharge and they agreed. I was honorably discharged. We shook hands and had a mutual parting and everybody was happy."

Malvaney returned home to Jackson and went to work in construction. He was soon convicted of assaulting two black police officers, although he said he never touched them. He said he was pulled over for a traffic violation and his dog went after them, "but I didn't sic the dog on them or anything. It was a misdemeanor conviction."

Racial tensions were high in Jackson. A white police officer had shot a black woman and a civil rights protest march was scheduled for the morning of October 4, 1980. The Klan scheduled a rally for the same time and place. Klansmen in robes and combat fatigues turned up at Smith Park in the afternoon, along with about 200 supporters. They walked to the Hinds County Courthouse, where a Klan leader talked about race war. The *Clarion-Ledger* newspaper reported that Malvaney had obtained the parade permit for the Klan event, but he said that is not true. In early 1981, Malvaney left the Klan. "It just kinda wasn't for me," he says. "I wasn't ever kicked out or anything like that."

George Malvaney was at Danny Joe Hawkins' house when the phone rang. Danny took the call and then said to George, "You might be interested in meeting this guy." So they drove to the Howard Johnson's restaurant. Mike Perdue was waiting for them. He explained that he was recruiting and went over the operation, briefly. He didn't name the island but said it was in the Caribbean and that the CIA was probably going to finance the whole thing.

He told Malvaney that if he came along, he'd get $3,000 for thirty days of work. George signed on.

"Well, of course you know, money was a motivating factor," he says. "That was one of the things. There were different motivating factors. I would say the main motivating factor was Perdue had led us to believe that the present prime minister of Dominica had communist leanings and that the former prime minister was a staunch anti-communist and that we would be going down there against communism and a way to fight communism. That was probably one of the main motivating factors. I was going down there to fight communism."

12

Mike Perdue (right) and brother Bill in Indiana

Merrillville, Indiana
February 1981

BILL PERDUE WORKED at the Ford plant and lived across the
street from the First Presbyterian Church off US-30 in Merrillville,
Indiana. He was a decade older than his youngest brother, Mike,
but they were close. Even though Mike Perdue was estranged from
most of his family, which did not approve of his lifestyle, Bill stayed
in touch. Bill was the oldest of the brothers and he accepted Mike for
what he was.

Whenever Mike came to town, he'd stay with Bill and his wife
Lenore on West 79th Avenue. Bill had been laid off at the auto plant
when Mike dropped by to ask if he wanted to join his mercenary team.
Mike explained the deal he'd worked out with the ex-prime minister
and the plans for casinos. Bill had served in the United States armed
forces; he had skills to offer, and Mike trusted him.

Bill thought about it but he is more cautious than Mike and it
sounded too risky. There were too many ways to get caught. He tried
to talk Mike out of it.

"I don't see how you can really protect yourself," Bill said. "You
might go in and take over, but how're you going to maintain anything?
Even the guys underneath you, you know? They're all soldiers of

fortune. They want to move up too. It's very possible you're going to end up in some dark hole in Dominica and never get out."

Bill told his brother he was "fucking nuts" to march into Dominica like that. "How are you going to sleep at night?"

It was Lenore who posed the most obvious question: "Mike, why would you want to go down there with all these black people? You were a big shot in the KKK."

"It's going to be different down there." Mike replied. "It's going to be like having a bunch of slaves. I'm going to own them."

As Mike was leaving, Bill took him aside again. "You're still going to go through with it, right?"

"Yup," Mike replied. "I'll find somebody to guard my back."

"God help ya," Bill said.

WOLFGANG WAS HAVING BETTER LUCK at recruiting. Because of his involvement in the far right, he knew a lot of people of militant character. Ever since his first trip to the United States in 1975 to meet David Duke, he had returned year after year, making new friends each time. In 1976, he drove to New Orleans for Duke's International Patriotic Congress, where he met Don Black. He went to Buffalo in 1977 to watch Duke and Black speak at a Klan rally and afterwards, invited them both to Toronto. They stayed at Andrews' house. Duke returned to Canada in 1978 to open the West Coast chapter of the Canadian Klan, which Droege had set up. Some of Droege's contacts were true believers, some were thugs and some were the kind of men who, for the right price and with a little convincing, might be talked into taking part in the violent overthrow of a country they could not even find on a map.

Droege was in Toronto when Perdue phoned from Houston to tell him about his deal with Patrick John.

"Start preparing the manpower up," Perdue said.

Perdue wanted to focus on raising money and leave the rest of the recruiting to Droege. It was a division of labor that suited their personalities. Perdue was the scammer who knew how to talk men out of their money. Droege was the ideologue who could manipulate his way into the hearts of outcasts. "Droege had some skills when it came to organizing people," Grant Bristow says. "They liked him. They felt they could trust him."

IN EARLY FEBRUARY, Perdue called Wolfgang and Danny Joe Hawkins and told them to meet him at the Holiday Inn in New Orleans. Hawkins got there first and Perdue went over the Operation Red Dog invasion plan with him. Perdue explained how they were going to arm and back up the Dominican Defence Force.

"If we're needed, then we will step in," he said. "If not, then we stay out of it."

Perdue had received a check for $5,000 from an investor. He gave $1,600 to Hawkins to buy ammunition—.223s for the Bush Master AR-15s and AR-18s he was planning to pick up right before the coup, and 12-gauge shells for the shotguns.

Perdue and Hawkins were having Sunday dinner at the hotel restaurant when Wolfgang arrived and told Mike there was someone outside he should meet. Don Black was in town to pick up an organizational mailing list from David Duke. Wolfgang just happened to run into him. Droege thought Black was "an adventurist type person" who might be interested in joining the invasion force. Black had military training, a definite asset given the overall inexperience of the crew so far.

Private First Class Stephen Don Black had served in the U.S. Army Reserves from February 13, 1974 until June 20, 1975, when he entered the U.S. Army Alabama National Guard. He served for one year in the 87th USA Maneuver Area Command in Birmingham. He had strong views about communism. He had strong views about pretty much everything.

"I believe in America," he said. "I believe in a strong national defense. I believe in the principles upon which this country was founded. I believe in the Constitution of the United States. I believe in freedom."

He also believed in the Ku Klux Klan. Black had been involved in the far right since his teens. In the 1970s, he became Grand Dragon of the Alabama Knights of the Ku Klux Klan and led robed Klansmen on marches through Birmingham to protest what he claimed was rising crime caused by blacks.

An enterprising newspaper reporter who infiltrated the Alabama Klan described in a series of articles in the *Nashville Tennessean* how Black had inducted him into the organization at a secret ceremony at his apartment. "At the end of the ceremony," wrote Jerry Thompson, "Don Black sprinkled me with water and sonorously decreed: 'By the authority vested in me, I now declare and proclaim you a citizen of the Knights of the Ku Klux Klan and invest you with the title Klansman, the most honorable title among men.' Somehow," Thompson wrote, "having just gone through a forty-minute racist ritual in which I had dedicated my life to white supremacy, I didn't feel all that honorable. In fact, there was nothing about the title Klansman that made it honorable to me." To Thompson, the Klan seemed to have few members, although it had a network of prominent, wealthy supporters.

The Klan was all but dead by then, a shadow of a shadowy organization. Founded by Confederate veterans who wore white robes they thought would intimidate blacks, the KKK used brutality to restore white supremacy to the South. The early KKK did not last long but, in the 1950s, a reborn Klan added Jews, Catholics, immigrants, union activists and civil rights campaigners to its list of targets. The violence continued through the 1970s, but membership numbers tanked. A Klan resurgence began in the late 1970s, though all that remained of the once mighty Klan by 1981 were a few thousand holdouts who, while the rest of the Western world had moved on, were still fixated on race and the notion that America was for whites only. The new Klan was more geographically dispersed than it had ever been, but its stronghold remained the states of the Old South, notably Alabama, Mississippi and Louisiana.

Mike Perdue followed Wolfgang out to the hotel parking lot beside the New Orleans causeway strip, where Don Black was waiting. They all sat in the car and Perdue dug out his maps.

Black had never heard of Dominica, but Perdue laid out the political dynamics in simple terms: Grenada had just fallen to the communists and Dominica was about to meet the same fate. The only stabilizing influence, Perdue went on, was the military, which was loyal to Patrick John, whom he described as "pro-American and very anti-communist."

The military was going to put John back in office, he said. Dominica would then become a staunch ally of the United States. Perdue said he was a commissioned officer in the Dominica Defence Force and that he was looking to hire military advisors. If Black came along, he would get $3,000 and if he stayed on for more than a month after the coup he would receive a 1-percent share of Nortic Enterprises. It wouldn't be much at first, Perdue said, but within three years it might be worth $30,000 to $60,000 a year.

Black found the proposition a bit unusual. He also had the impression that this was a secret government operation. "He ... gave me a very definite impression that the United States government was backing this," Black says. "He did mention his friends in the State Department and he told me ... part of this was in conformance with the Reagan Administration's policies on containing communism throughout the world, but particularly the Caribbean."

Black had followed the presidential election closely. He supported Reagan and agreed with what he said about the need for strong national defense. Even after Reagan had made his distaste for the Klan known, condemning Jimmy Carter for speaking "in the city that gave birth" to the KKK, Black supported him during the three-way presidential race. "If I vote for any of the three, it will be Reagan," he said at a 1980 rally. He was tired of watching one country after another get swallowed up by the communists, and the Caribbean was so close to home.

One of Reagan's first official acts as president concerned the Caribbean. He hosted Jamaican prime minister Edward Philip George Seaga, who had replaced the pro-Cuba Michael Manley, in the White House Dining Room and spoke about Seaga's "struggles to remain free of foreign interference." He called the Jamaican's actions "an inspiration to the world," and offered America's support. "I pledge to you the goodwill, the cooperation, and the moral and material assistance of the United States as you are to meet the many challenges that you will face in the months ahead."

Don Black shared the President's concerns about the Caribbean, but he wasn't sure he was ready to take up arms. It was an odd proposal.

"I don't know," Black said.

He told Perdue he'd think about it.

"If there's anyone else you know who wants to come, let me know," Perdue said.

Black said he couldn't think of anyone with a military background who'd be interested.

"That's not important," Perdue said. "They just have to be solid people, solid stable personalities."

"Okay," Black said.

Perdue and Wolfgang went back to the Holiday Inn and reviewed the contract signed by Patrick John. Perdue explained the arrangement with the Dominican Defence Force, and the financial setup involving Nortic Enterprises. It was the first time Droege had heard about it in detail. Perdue said Wolfgang would get 5 percent of the company, in addition to his $3,000 fee.

That night, Wolfgang and Danny Joe Hawkins went out to the French Quarter. It was Carnival season in New Orleans, the buildup to Mardi Gras, when everyone puts on masks and costumes and takes to the streets. Dressing outrageously in purple, green and gold and long feather boas is a way to escape. That is the magic of carnival season. Everyone gets to step out of their skin and become someone else, if only for the day.

And in a way Mike Perdue, Wolfgang Droege and their band of mercenaries were doing the very same thing. None of them had great jobs. They were misfits, every one of them, rejected by society because of their outdated views on race. They had money troubles, troubles with the law. What Dominica offered them was a chance to get away from all that, to live a fantasy. They weren't liberating Dominica from communists. They were liberating themselves.

DON BLACK THOUGHT CAREFULLY about Perdue's offer. He talked it over with Wolfgang on the phone. Droege assured him Perdue was on the level and that this was not a set-up, that they were not going to end up like the Cuban exiles who took part in the failed Bay of Pigs invasion.

Black was low on cash. He could use the money. He wanted to do it, but he needed to know more so he went to the University of Alabama library to do some research. There weren't many books on Dominica, but he did find a couple of magazines that mentioned the island. In a *National Geographic*, he found an article, "The Caribbean: Sun, Sea and Seething," about the political turmoil in the world's favorite sun destination. The color photographs alternated between shots of slothful, sunburned vacationers stretched on lounge chairs and scenes of abject poverty and political upheaval. There was some basic Caribbean history, describing the islands as "creations of European colonists" who used them as "commercial factories" for gold, tobacco and sugarcane. The article said the indigenous Arawak Indians and Caribs had been wiped out and that three-quarters of the population were descended, at least in part, from African slaves, with the rest being Europeans, East Indians and Chinese.

Dominica was barely mentioned in the lengthy spread, but the author visited Jamaica and wrote about the fears of its drift towards Cuba and communism, and interviewed Maurice Bishop of Grenada about the arms he had received from Cuba and the airport the Cubans were building on the island. The article pointed out that almost half the oil exported from the United States passed through the Caribbean.

"The Caribbean's restlessness has brought changes to governments and economic systems that hint at new alliances, capturing the attention of the world's superpowers and thrusting these once quiet islands onto the world political stage," its author, Noel Grove, wrote. Grove also addressed the Soviet Union's role in the region. The USSR was propping up the Cuban economy, he wrote, although he quoted an economist as denying estimates that Moscow pumped $10 million a day into the country. Soviet military equipment, he added, was supplied free of charge, and was turning up, along with Cuban soldiers, elsewhere in the Caribbean as well as in Central America and Africa.

The articles that Don Black read at the library left him with little doubt that Dominica was an unstable country. Undeveloped, newly independent and devastated by hurricanes, the island seemed vulnerable to the aggressive expansionism of Moscow and its puppet in Havana. One of the articles said that, after Hurricane David, Cuba had sent an expedition to the island but that the Dominican people had draped American flags all over the island in protest.

Black had never been to Dominica, or anywhere else in the Caribbean. He didn't even have a passport. But between his research and what Mike Perdue had told him, he concluded the island was on the verge of a communist takeover. He didn't like that.

"I see one-third of the world controlled by communists," he said. "I consider that a very serious threat." Sure, Eugenia Charles had been democratically elected, but "every commie country in the world has elections."

He felt if he were to join Perdue and Wolfgang, he would be helping rid the world of an oppressive regime. "Everything I could see about it was in the best interest, and I still see it that way, it was in the best interest of the United States government, militarily and strategically, because this whole area is vital to the security of this country.

"And furthermore, it was also in the policy of the new administration. I mean, it had been very strongly stated that Mr. Reagan didn't want to see any more communist takeovers, particularly in this hemisphere. And that was exactly what I could see happening in Dominica, particularly after Grenada. And I'm more than familiar with the fact that the State Department and the CIA use all kinds of people for their operations. In the Bay of Pigs, for instance."

A week after meeting Mike Perdue at the Holiday Inn parking lot, Don Black got a call from Wolfgang.

Black told him he'd do it.

"Certainly it was a sense of adventure involved here. Certainly it was a romantic thing to do, and I guess it was a little exciting," Black says.

He wasn't sure how long he would stick around after the coup, but he decided he would give it a month and take it from there. "I was in an adventurous mood and I also needed the money," he explained. There was no firm departure date yet, but Wolfgang said they would probably be leaving for the island in about six weeks.

MIKE NORRIS WAS a security guard at Cottondale Wood Products in Tuscaloosa, Alabama. He was twenty-one and lived in half of a duplex with his wife of two years. His parents lived in the other half. "I wouldn't say we were poverty stricken, you know," he said. "We had a hard time paying our bills, you know, but I guess everybody does."

Don Black knew Norris through the Alabama KKK and told him about a job opportunity in a "military-related" field. The entire Caribbean was threatened by communism, Black explained. Dominica was particularly at risk. It was an impoverished nation where few people had jobs. The communists were building their strength there, he said. The government was also unstable because of an internal dispute. On the one side of this struggle was the right wing, which was pro-American and anti-communist, and was represented by the military, Black explained. And on the other side was the left wing, which was pro-communist and represented primarily by the prime minister of Dominica, who was trying to bring the Cubans to the island and establish a Marxist regime. Prime Minister Charles was using her police to suppress the anti-communist opposition through beatings and other violent means, said Black. Her government was not allowing the army to mop up the communist terrorists and guerrillas. The political right wing and the military wanted action, Norris was told. They wanted to arrest the prime minister and disarm her state police.

"Then he said there was some people here in the United States who were interested in going down there and helping the Dominica Defence Force," Norris recounted afterwards. "He said they were going to help out in this power struggle and help establish pro-American right-wing influence within the government.... They were going to put this prime minister, apparently, out of power."

Black explained that a company was involved. The company was hiring men to go down and back up the Dominican military. If he were to join, Norris was told, he would get $3,000 and a share of the company.

"What exactly are we going to be doing down there?" he asked.

Black wasn't sure how to answer.

Norris got the impression the U.S. government was backing the operation. He was convinced of it. Norris had no military experience whatsoever, but he figured someone would show him what to do. And he had read about people serving in foreign countries. Some of them had been hired despite their lack of experience and trained on the job, so he was not concerned about that.

The money was tempting. It was a lot more than the $3.50 an hour he was making as a security guard.

"Yeah," Norris said. "I would go even if it weren't for the money."

Norris went to Woods and Water Sports in Northport, Alabama and bought a 9mm Browning automatic. He also borrowed a Remington 12-gauge from his father, Stanley. The next day, Black bought himself a .45 at Southern Gun Warehouse in Irondale, Alabama.

"The purpose in carrying weapons was to defend the Dominican island against communist incursion," Black says. "That was our purpose."

13

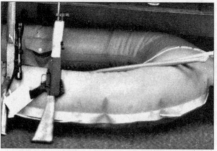

The mercenaries were to land at Rockaway Beach in inflatable dinghies.

Houston, Texas
February 1981

ONCE THE MERCENARIES LANDED at Rockaway Beach, Mike Perdue wanted a strong soldier at his side, someone who had done this before. When he looked at his roster of recruits, he wasn't sure he had one yet. And then a letter arrived in the mail from Oklahoma City. Christopher Billy Anderson had served briefly in the U.S. Air Force and had later worked as a sheriff's deputy in Kansas and Oklahoma before becoming chief of police in Kiowa, Kansas. "A nice little town," he called it.

A bad decision had ended his law enforcement career. Chief Anderson caught a convicted child molester on a parole violation. The man was supposed to stay outside the Kiowa city limits, but someone spotted him at the local 7-11. Anderson told the convict to get out of town but he refused to leave without a police escort. The father of one of the girls he molested had a shotgun and the convict was afraid. He wanted the chief to ride with him, so Anderson got into the man's car and they drove off together with a beat officer following in a patrol car.

At the city limits, Chief Anderson told the man to pull over. He refused. He wouldn't stop the car. He just kept on going. Anderson didn't have a gun so he punched him in the chin, yanked the keys out of the ignition and threw them out the window. The man ran for it. The other officer threw his gun to Anderson, who fired a warning shot over the man's head. The police chief later pleaded guilty to aggravated assault. Kidnapping charges were dropped. He resigned.

Six years later, Anderson was forty-one, with a wife, Rebecca, a twenty-year-old son and two daughters, ten and thirteen. He earned $4.90 an hour driving a yellow school bus and swabbing the hallways at Western Heights High School in Oklahoma City. To make extra money, he did contract security work on the side. He'd been hired to break people out of jails in Mexico. He'd rescued a man's daughter from a commune. He also did personal security work, bodyguarding. He says he did a bit of work for friends in the CIA as well, but he won't talk about that. Anderson subscribed to the newsletter *Le Mercenaire*. He always checked the classified section, and when his latest issue arrived, he read about a job that was offering good money for security work in the Caribbean. The ad was vague, but he figured it would only cost him the price of a postage stamp to find out more.

When Mike Perdue got Anderson's letter, he called him up and invited him on an all-expenses paid trip to Texas. They met at the airport and went to Perdue's house. "He had a fairly nice house in Houston," Anderson recalls. "I don't know if he rented it or owned it, but he had a guy living there with him." After meeting Mike's roommate, Ron Cox, Anderson wondered if Perdue might be homosexual. The house was in a part of Houston known for its gay community. Anderson noticed the zebra skin rug in the living room. Perdue said he'd brought it back from the Bush War in Rhodesia. "He told me he'd been a mercenary in Africa," Anderson says. "One thing that sticks in my mind, he said, 'Well, I do like my comforts.'"

They went to a motel and Perdue paid for a room. Perdue introduced himself as a former sergeant in the Marine Corps and a Vietnam vet. He listed off his medals. And then he started the mercenary sales pitch: "He told me that the north end of the island was literally infested with communism," Anderson says. "He left me with the impression that Mrs. Charles' government was kind of leaning pro-communist." There was going to be a coup, Perdue said, and he was hiring advisors. There would be minor resistance, he warned.

"I would like to have a bloodless coup," Perdue told him, but, "who is to know what will happen in a situation like this?"

Although Perdue never said outright that it was a CIA-backed operation, he dropped hints. He mentioned his military experience and his "friends" in the State Department. "He planted in me in a roundabout way the seed of suspicion," Anderson says, "where I suspicioned possibly that the CIA might be involved in this." Perdue chose his words carefully. He said the U.S. Navy wanted to build a submarine base on the island. He said the CIA would be "interested" in what they were doing. Anderson realized that could mean any number of things, but one interpretation was that the CIA was somehow involved, which meant that this was a U.S. government-sanctioned coup d'état.

"You'll get $3,000 for going in," Mike said. "About a month or so afterwards, you'll get your $15,000 for staying with me."

If Anderson agreed to stay on for the full five years as a First Sergeant in the Dominica Defence Force, he would also get one-sixth of Nortic Enterprises, the company that was going to develop the island's economy.

"I've got a five-year contract," Perdue said. "We'll be in an advisory position. This is their country, so we respect their laws."

Anderson said he was interested, so they went over the photocopied maps and the hand-drawn assault diagram of the police station. Perdue said he wanted Anderson to be his wingman in Red Dog One. Together, the two of them would capture the charge office at police headquarters.

"If you're in it for the money, the adventure, and to fight communism, to prevent expansion of communism in the Caribbean," Perdue told him, "you're in."

Anderson wasn't an ideologue. He had nothing to do with the Klan or anything like it. For him, this was a chance to make money. He thought Perdue was businesslike; he seemed like he knew what he was doing, like he had done this before.

Anderson said he wanted $30,000 upfront and another $30,000 upon completion of the mission. "That's the way I work," he said.

"Okay," Perdue said. "When you leave to come down here for the operation, when you report in here, I'll have $30,000 transferred to your account."

Anderson spent the night at the motel in Houston at Perdue's expense and flew back to Oklahoma in the morning to quit his job at the school and get ready for the mission.

One thing bothered him, though. Prime Minister Charles was going to be killed. She and her staff were going to be rounded up, stood against a wall and shot. "That's exactly what he was going to do," Anderson said in an interview. "He was going to kill that old lady down there."

WITH RED DOG ONE READY TO GO, Perdue began assigning recruits to the other two mercenary teams. He contacted James McQuirter in Toronto and told the former Canadian soldier he would be leading Red Dog Three. *You will lead the reinforcements into the police station and your men will secure the fire station,* Perdue wrote in a letter. *Know who you will be working with and have knowledge of the fire station.*

The Canadian Klan leader was to fly to the island in advance of the invasion and sit tight until the others arrived with the guns. While he waited, McQuirter was to make contact with Patrick John's people.

> *Tell them also that our business people feel they can arrange a $8,000,000 loan within a few months. If I am light on merc's then his locals will have to fill in. But I don't expect this. Check out any potential landing by sea and air. Check out the airport at night, any personnel, etc. See if it's possible to get about 10 to 11 men in and then land the equipment. These are items I need to know.*

McQuirter's reward: he would become Dominica's Minister of Information.

GEORGE MALVANEY WENT TO a gun show in Jackson and bought some boxes of ammo. A few weeks later, he drove to another gun show in Birmingham. Between the two of them, using Perdue's money, Malvaney quietly purchased 3,000 rounds of .223, .30, 12-gauge and 30-30 ammunition.

"I'd rather have it and not need it than need it and not have it," he said.

It was all coming together. They had money, a contract and a small band of mercenaries. The guns would be no problem. The one thing that concerned Perdue was explosives. He didn't have any, but Wolfgang had heard about a guy in the Toronto underworld. He might be able to help.

They also needed transportation. As it stood, the mercenaries had no way of getting themselves and all their military gear to Dominica to mount their assault. They had approached a businessman in Miami about a boat. They never said they were going to take over a country. They just told him they needed to get to Dominica. "I never knew what these characters were doing," says the businessman. He wanted $50,000 for the job but that was beyond Perdue's budget. Their only other lead was a man Perdue had met at a New Year's Eve party in the French Quarter. His name was Shelton Udell and he thought he could help. David Duke was at the same party but says he had nothing to do with the discussions. "Apparently there was a conversation, that I wasn't even a part of, about a boat," Duke says.

The mercenaries in *The Dogs of War* advised against chartering a boat. The crew might be unreliable, the captain might have second thoughts and any vessel that would accept a mercenary job could already be well known to the authorities. In Cat Shannon's view, it was worth spending the extra money to buy a small freighter and hire a handpicked crew. "Apart from the arms," Shannon wrote in a report to his bosses, "the acquisition of the ship will be the most difficult part."

Mike Perdue didn't have enough money to buy a ship. He was going to have to charter one, but he thought he could at least minimize the risk by using his contacts to refer him to seamen who could be trusted.

Perdue told Wolfgang to find Shelton Udell. They met and Perdue spoke to him about fighting communism and defending America. In Droege's words, "He was trying to appeal to his patriotic patriotism."

Udell said he would check around. On February 22, Perdue called on Udell again and the two of them drove north to the New Orleans lakefront to meet a man who owned a marine brokerage. His name was Peewee.

14

John Osburg (right) in Dominica

New Orleans, Louisiana
February 1981

CAPTAIN MIKE HOWELL was on board the *Mañana*, taking off his Coast Guard Auxiliary uniform, when the phone rang. It was Peewee. He said he had met someone who wanted to charter a boat.

Mike Perdue came on the line and said he needed to get to Dominica, so Captain Howell invited him over. Twenty minutes later, Perdue arrived at the yacht club in the West End, off Robert E. Lee Boulevard on Lake Pontchartrain. It just so happened that Captain Mike had the charts for the Eastern Caribbean so he laid them out in the wheelhouse—as best he could given that his left arm was a prosthetic—and they looked at the tide, winds and currents.

By Howell's calculations, the island was roughly 2,000 nautical miles from New Orleans. He was excited about the job. He had always wanted to see the Windward Islands.

They talked money—how much to get down, how much per day to hang around. Howell asked Perdue the purpose of the trip.

"Marina research," Perdue replied.

The captain was immediately suspicious.

The *Mañana* was indeed a research vessel. She was built in 1946 as a government conservation ship called the *Vieux Carré*, after the old

French Quarter of New Orleans. John Santos owned her until she was purchased by John Smith of Gulfport, Mississippi, and rechristened the *Mañana*. Smith donated her to the Sea Scouts, who sold her to Howell. By 1981, Captain Mike had chartered out the *Mañana* for dozens of marine research expeditions, working with Louisiana State University in Baton Rouge, the University of New Orleans and the National Oceanic and Atmospheric Administration.

But Perdue wasn't asking about marine research. Howell knew a lot of researchers, and it was clear to him that Perdue was an unlikely one. He didn't even have his terminology straight. He was trying to pass himself off as a marine researcher, yet he was talking about researching marinas. It was ridiculous.

The charter boat operators who work the Louisiana waterfront were regularly approached by drug smugglers looking for someone to help them retrieve bundles of cocaine and dope from offshore dumps and bring them to land. They were all wary of it, and Captain Mike's first thought was that Perdue was working for a drug cartel.

Howell decided to confront the Texan. "What do you *really* want to do?" he asked.

Perdue was quiet for a moment, and then he admitted he hadn't been truthful. The real reason he needed a boat, he said, was to transport a dozen mercenaries and sixty military assault rifles to Dominica, where they were going to overthrow the communist government and install a pro-American regime.

Howell was shocked, all the more so because he got the impression that Perdue was actually telling the truth. Perdue went on to explain that he was working for the CIA and the State Department. Howell was skeptical. The CIA does not walk up to Mike Howell on a Sunday afternoon and ask for a ride to Dominica to topple a government, he thought. If this is a government operation, he said, then have someone from the government come down and talk to me. Perdue quickly "crawdadded" about the government's involvement, but Howell still felt he was being honest about the invasion.

There was no way Mike Howell was going to help a bunch of mercenaries take over a foreign country. He needed money, but not that badly. He also knew that he would be an expendable part of Perdue's operation; were he to do it, he would likely be killed once he'd completed his part and was no longer useful to the mission.

He knew right away how he was going to handle this. What he was going to do was call his law enforcement friends and tell them what was going on. But he didn't let Perdue know that. He decided to just play along for the time being, and let the officers do their thing. He would handle it like any other charter.

Howell chose his words carefully. "The boat is capable of this," he said.

SPECIAL AGENT JOHN OSBURG had a wife and three kids. He worked hard but he tried to keep a healthy balance between his job and his family. It isn't easy. Many undercover agents can't do it. Being a pretend crook for the bureau and a parent and husband for your family can be confusing. The duplicity of it all can be disorienting and it eats away at you.

Osburg played flag football and racquetball. He coached his kids at baseball, track and basketball. And he kept his undercover operations to himself. He would rather get to the office early or stay late than bring it home.

"You can't bring it back and forth," he says. "You don't want to let your family know what you're doing because it tends to upset people if they've got an idea, even if you're not concerned with your safety."

As soon as Perdue left the *Mañana*, Howell called the Bureau of Alcohol, Tobacco and Firearms and asked for Osburg. But it was a Sunday and Osburg wasn't on shift. He was home with his kids. The duty agent put him in touch with another agent named Paul Darby instead.

Darby thought it was a joke. "Osburg put you up to this, didn't he?" he said.

Howell had to convince Agent Darby he was not kidding. Howell was concerned because he had played along with Perdue. He wanted to make it crystal clear that he was not interested in getting involved in the coup, so he made Darby write out a note indicating that Howell had called to report that he had been approached for a mercenary job. He wanted it on the record that he was not part of the conspiracy.

Darby asked if he thought anything else was going to happen that day.

"No," Howell said.

"Well, we'll call you Monday morning."

In the morning, Howell had a cup of coffee and phoned the New Orleans ATF office again but nobody was there, so he called the federal government information line and asked for the number of the State Department in Washington, D.C. He dialed the number and asked for the Dominica desk. He didn't even know if one existed, but he was given another number to call and ended up speaking to a man named Fred Exton.

Howell explained how Perdue had told him he was working for the U.S. government and that he was part of a CIA mission to overthrown the communists in Dominica. If this is really a government job, Howell said, then come down and talk to me. Exton said it was not a government job and Dominica was not even a communist country.

The FBI called Howell later in the day and said they wanted to talk to him. Then Agent Osburg called. Howell told him the FBI was on the way. Osburg rushed to the marina and got there first, and Howell quickly told him the story. The FBI agents arrived minutes later and said they were taking over the investigation, but Howell told them he knew Osburg and trusted him and he wanted to work with the ATF.

Special Agent Osburg wasn't quite sure what to make of it. He asked Howell if he wanted to take part in an undercover operation. All he had to do was keep playing along. The ATF would take care of the rest. Howell agreed to do it. He asked not to be called a Confidential Informant because he didn't want to look dirty, but Osburg needed to assign him a CI number on the warrant applications, so he became Confidential Informant 4302-30.

Howell wasn't afraid of Perdue. He'd been a helicopter gunner in Vietnam; his only fear was that he might bungle the investigation because of his lack of experience, but Osburg assured him the ATF would manage everything. They would brief him before every contact with Perdue and tell him what to do.

Osburg told Howell to stay in touch with Perdue. If they talked again, Howell should try to arrange another meeting, he said. Osburg would be there undercover. He said Howell should introduce him as his business partner.

Special Agent Osburg returned to the ATF office and began the paperwork that preceded every investigation. He requested authorization for "use of a tape recorder with telephone induction coil to record consensual telephone conversations." A few days later he filled out a second request for authorization to use "non-telephone electronic or related devices to monitor and/or record verbal communications." Permission was granted.

The ATF wired a superscope tape recorder to Mike Howell's phone, so all his conversations with Perdue could be used as evidence. "The purpose," Osburg says, "was to infiltrate his group, gather evidence and intelligence and sufficient information regarding his involvement and others in this attempt to overthrow the government and the illegal exportation of weapons and ammunition from the United States."

THREE DAYS LATER, Captain Howell phoned Mike Perdue's house in Houston. Perdue seemed to be trying to reassure Howell, to make him feel comfortable about skippering the mercenaries and their guns to Dominica. He mentioned the names of a few southern powerbrokers like John Connoly, Congressman Ron Paul and Judge John Lindsay, and insinuated they were aware of the coup and supported it.

"These are friends of mine," Perdue said.

They weren't really Perdue's friends. Perdue knew Judge Lindsay's executive assistant, Ron Deer. They worked out at the same health club. Perdue had approached Deer for financing, telling him he was raising money for an operation in the Caribbean. Deer had stopped him cold and said he didn't want any part of it. But Perdue needed a ship, and he thought the name-dropping might work with Howell.

Ever the scammer, Perdue awkwardly tried to tell Howell not to expect payment until after the coup.

"I was thinking," Perdue told Howell over the phone, "about, you know, I got enough front money and afterwards I'm going to have enough money to, uh, you know, I got like one hundred fifty thousand dollars. What I do is my business. People here, uh, unless you need it all right there, you know, and when you come back they could pay you."

Howell said he wanted $18,000 for the job, up front.

"Don't worry," Perdue said, "nobody knows about the coup except my mercenaries and financial backers."

They talked on the phone several more times. All the calls were recorded. Osburg typed up transcripts and deposited the tapes in the ATF evidence vault on Carondelet Street.

Mike Howell was enjoying his undercover work. He grew his hair out so that he'd look the part. But his inexperience showed. In his phone calls with Perdue, he was talking too much. Special Agent Osburg noticed it when he was transcribing the tapes and he had to coach his CI to shut up and let Perdue do the talking. Let Perdue hang himself with his own words. There was little value in recording conversations in which the suspect said nothing but, "Ya" and "Uh-huh."

MIKE PERDUE WAS STAYING at the Holiday Inn beside the I-10 highway, in a bleak part of town that had none of the charm of old Louisiana. On March 5, two days after Mardi Gras, Howell called the hotel at just after 9 p.m. and Perdue said he would be over soon.

At 10:15 p.m., Perdue climbed aboard the *Mañana* and shook hands with Howell and another man he had never met, a tall blond southerner with a mustache. Howell introduced him as his business partner John. Perdue didn't seem rattled by Osburg's presence.

Perdue explained that he had been working on the coup for two years and had money, manpower and the cooperation of Patrick John. He said he had made arrangements to buy guns—Bushmaster rifles, Winchester 50/50 shotguns and Uzis fitted with silencers. He opened his briefcase and took out a handful of photos of Dominica and diagrams showing the police station and government buildings in Roseau. He pointed out the location of the armory, the barracks and the communications center. The diagrams had arrows showing where each of his three Red Dog teams would attack. All he needed was a ship to take his mercs and their gear to Dominica.

"My men are ready, the equipment is ready," Perdue said. "The situation down there is at prime, you know, and so I have to go ahead and move."

He explained that the ship would drop the men close to Roseau at between one and three o'clock in the morning and the invasion force would go ashore in rubber rafts. He said the Dominica Defence Force was going to meet them on the beach to collect the shotguns. Perdue said he was going to keep the big guns for his own men. The mercenaries would storm police headquarters, gain control of the island and then slip quietly into the wilderness before dawn, leaving the impression Patrick John and his men had staged the coup.

Captain Howell and Agent Osburg asked Perdue about the defenses on the island, but Perdue said there was no reason for concern. The police were barely armed and the country's navy consisted of a wooden patrol boat that was currently in dry dock. The biggest risk was going to be getting past the U.S. Coast Guard, Perdue said. If the *Mañana* was approached en route to Dominica, they were to dump all the guns and army gear overboard. It was all carefully planned. Howell thought Perdue was methodical and gave a good briefing.

"Most of my men, uh, three of my men have been down there before," Perdue said. "Two of them I worked with before, in Nicaragua and Uruguay ... I know nine of them personally. The other three are just boys that my men know and want to bring ... They span from Canada, Mississippi, Germany. For my executives, I've worked as far as Germany."

Perdue never used their real names; he referred to the mercenaries only as "his men," although he did mention Droege but only by his first name. He said Wolfgang would be glad to hear about the boat.

Perdue portrayed Eugenia Charles as an illegitimate ruler, claiming she had been elected by only 5 percent of voters. And he used his communist expansion theory to justify the operation, branding her an anti-American leftist who was about to fall into the Soviet orbit.

"She has really made some ties with communist Cuba," he said. She had already taken money from Castro's regime, he added.

"You see, Cuba's really tied up in Latin America now, and that's where the buffs are right now. They've got Grenada. Well, Grenada is expanding politically all right."

Howell felt sick. Even though Perdue tried to make it sound like he was doing something noble, the captain understood that what the mercenaries were committing was nothing less than the rape of a country, and he thought that did not seem like a very nice thing to do to a nation of 80,000 poor people.

Perdue opened his black briefcase and took out five stacks of $100 bills and laid them on the table. The $5,000 was a down payment, he said. He'd give Howell another $10,000 prior to departure. Perdue said he would also give Howell the ownership to his 1977 Chevrolet. Once Howell returned from the mission, Perdue's business manager would pay the outstanding $3,000 and take back the car. The voyage would take twelve to fifteen days. Perdue said he would send another $600 in money orders to pay for groceries to feed his men.

Until that moment, everyone at the ATF office in New Orleans had been skeptical. Maybe Perdue was just a talker. The ATF was always getting tips that went nowhere. They had to check them out anyway, just in case. But all that money that Perdue was waving around convinced them this was for real.

Special Agent Osburg saw something else that night that made him decide it was time to take the case seriously. When Perdue took the money out of his briefcase, Osburg spotted it laying beside the pile of charts and photos, a .45-caliber pistol.

Perdue stayed aboard the *Mañana* for almost two hours. He left at just before midnight and walked past an ordinary-looking van. Inside sat Special Agent Nick Fratta, the ATF's electronic surveillance expert, who had recorded the entire conversation from a miniature transmitter hidden among the marine radios in the wheelhouse.

15

Prime Minister Eugenia Charles

Roseau, Dominica
March 5, 1981

ASSISTANT SUPERINTENDENT Desmond Blanchard was head of the Special Branch, the division of the Dominica Police responsible for national security. The guerrillas were his biggest concern, the Dreads who had taken Rastafarianism to new heights of militancy. But he was also hearing about a new threat.

In a radio address to the nation on February 19, Prime Minister Eugenia Charles said a "second group" was trying to destabilize the island. She said this group consisted of "rejected politicians and their hangers-on." She did not name them but described them as motivated by "destructive jealousy."

"The authorities are therefore monitoring both of these groups. The information and evidence is coming in and is being pieced together," she said.

To assist police, the government declared a state of emergency. Among those picked up for questioning under emergency powers were two senior Dominica Defence Force officers, Captain Malcolm Reid and Ronnie Roberts. The Special Branch had heard that something was going on. They didn't have any solid evidence, it was just talk, but Carnival was approaching and they didn't want any trouble. "So they could have a proper Carnival season, they decided there were some people who should be locked up for safe keeping," Reid says.

The two detainees were held at police headquarters. The cellblock consisted of three rooms, each eight by ten feet with concrete walls on three sides and a metal gate at the front.

Constable Bernard Pacquette, a traffic officer, was walking past the cells on the afternoon of March 5 when Ronnie Roberts handed him a sealed envelope that was to be delivered to Major Fred Newton, the Defence Force chief.

The constable delivered it instead to the sergeant in the Criminal Investigations Department, who opened it and took out a piece of white ruled paper.

The letter read:

> Fred,
>
> Somebody will give you a number to call Mike Perdue in Texas (collect call).
>
> Complete all instruction arrangements for any day next week if possible not necessarily Saturday.
>
> You will have to set up both trucks, the van and probably your car. Pipers' jeep and Jno Charles' van. I have already settled payment.
>
> Contact Pat and keep him informed.
>
> I will let Piper put everybody else on standby and he will report to you.
>
> The main strike should be the P.S. and all other moves will be made from there.
>
> You should come and see me.
>
> DON'T PANIC We must make it.

Despite the clumsy effort to disguise the message, the picture was clear to Police Commissioner Oliver Phillip: the police station was about to be attacked. The names were all familiar—Fred Newton, Howell Piper, Hubert Jno Charles and Pat, whom he reasoned had to be the former prime minister, Patrick John.

The only name he had not heard before was Mike Perdue. Although Roberts had passed along the note, the police did not believe he had written it. They thought they recognized the handwriting as that of Captain Reid.

"Unbelievable," Assistant Superintendent Blanchard said. But not entirely unexpected. The disaffection of the Defence Force was widely known. "It was a pretty volatile situation. The Defence Force was in the process of disbanding. They were all going to lose their jobs, lose their livelihoods," he says.

WITH HER ELECTION VICTORY, Prime Minister Eugenia Charles had inherited a beautiful, wretched island—a tropical paradise burdened by poverty, violent crime, political upheaval and the lingering damage of Hurricane David. A month after she was sworn in, Hurricane Allen hit, destroying the banana crop yet again. Her biggest challenge, however, was the military. The DDF was costing the government $1 million Eastern Caribbean dollars a year, and yet it openly scorned the prime minister, its commander in chief. "She and us, we've always been at loggerheads," Captain Reid says. The militia was Patrick John's creation and its officers remained loyal to him after he left office. Some even called it Patrick's Army.

The troubles began the day Eugenia Charles moved into government headquarters. Among the papers left behind by the departing government was a report by a Guyanese military consultant, Colonel C.E. Martindale, who had been brought in to investigate the DDF. His study portrayed the Defence Force as undisciplined and poorly led. It documented incidents of sexual harassment and marijuana use in the ranks, and singled out the two top officers, Major Newton and Captain Reid, for criticism. The hostile relationship between the government and the militia worsened after Prime Minister Charles was advised that her soldiers were trading guns to the Dreads in exchange for drugs. She ordered police to disarm the DDF and suspended its senior officers. Sergeant Truman Howe was assigned to collect Major Newton's self-loading rifles and submachine guns. But the sergeant could not find one of the rifles.

"It will take care of itself," Major Newton shrugged.

The seized military weapons were locked away in the armory at police headquarters. Rumors fueled by the opposition began to circulate that the DDF's days were numbered. The troops feared losing their jobs, but they also felt their military traditions were at risk under the new prime minister. "She had no respect," Captain Reid says. The soldiers did not hide their disdain for their new political chief. They sent the prime minister letters of protest and demonstrated outside the legislature. Worse, they began to talk about taking action. "They were not happy," Patrick John recounts. "For over ten, fifteen years, I mean, their lives were in the army ... and I think that grievance grew, and from that grew the animosity towards her."

Dennis Joseph, who was accused of involvement in the coup plot but later acquitted, says, "I think they were getting back at her. They couldn't get jobs, she had blacklisted them."

The New Chronicle published a front-page editorial warning that "as long as those malcontents remain in the Force, they will be constantly scheming with their discredited and disgraced members.... The spate of military coups in Third World countries over the last two decades has given sustenance to the view that the true locus of political power is the barrel of a gun, no matter who holds it."

PRIME MINISTER CHARLES and Patrick John remained bitter enemies. "She was a good prime minister," John says, "but there was a heavy rivalry between Eugenia and myself. She had a problem that I am the only politician that beat her in an election. I personally believe Eugenia Charles hated me."

He quickly added, "I don't believe she hated me. I believe she feared my politics, vis-à-vis hers." John claims she thought she was above him because she was the daughter of the wealthy J.B. Charles and he was the son of a huckster woman. "She couldn't see someone from 'down there' being her leader."

Two revolutionary currents were merging. The Defence Force was preparing for a military coup. At the same time, Mike Perdue, for his own reasons, was bringing in weapons and fighting men to accomplish the same task.

The man who united both conspiracies was Captain Malcolm Marley Reid. "I happened to have, so to speak, a leg in both camps," Reid said in an interview.

The captain says he was the only direct link between the DDF and Perdue's mercenaries, although he said he kept Major Newton in the loop. "Most everything I did, I told Fred." But the major had not yet consented to do anything. As for the ex-prime minister, he said, "Patrick is the kind of guy, when he's on your side, he's on your side and he doesn't have to know what you're doing to support you. Two people were protected from knowing too much, and that was Patrick and Fred. They had to appear to be above board. So Patrick wasn't given too much information." Nobody had any idea the mercenaries were being recruited from the American and Canadian white supremacist movements.

In addition to rumors of a coup, the government was hearing reports the DDF was arming and training the Dreads at camps in the forests. When Ted Honychurch, the head of one of Dominica's oldest white families and the father of Eugenia Charles' press secretary, Lennox Honychurch, was kidnapped, the prime minister redoubled her efforts to defeat the Dreads.

Captain Reid had been held at the police station without charge for a week when he began to get a bad feeling. The new government was coming down hard on the Defence Force, and he felt things would only get worse for him.

"It wasn't looking good," he remembers.

He wrote the letter to Major Newton thinking the time had come to act, but it was a serious mistake. Anyone could read between the lines. The police quickly rounded up Patrick John, Major Newton, Howell Piper, Dennis Joseph and five others. The warrants alleged the men "did traitorously conspire together and with other persons known and unknown, inside and outside the Commonwealth of Dominica to traitorously overthrow the lawfully constituted government of the Commonwealth of Dominica by force of arms."

Police Commissioner Oliver Phillip asked Major Newton to explain the letter. The military chief said he didn't know Mike Perdue and had no idea what Captain Reid was talking about, although he said a week ago someone had told him to "Be on the lookout. Something is going to happen and you must be very careful."

Locked up in a cell at police headquarters, Patrick John asked for writing materials and a policeman brought him a pen and a pad of lined paper. He wrote night and day until he had filled thirty-two pages. He called his treatise, "Political Life and Social Change." It concerned "the effective use of power in order to attain goals for society." It also discussed the revolutionary ideology that was sweeping the post-colonial world.

"Revolutionaries," he wrote, "seek rapid, radical and intensive changes in the basic beliefs, structures, individuals and policies. They affirm the need for greater equality of economic conditions, of opportunities for the masses to participate in politics and of social sharing of the nation's wealth."

He sent his thesis to a university and, a little while later, received a Doctorate in Metaphysics in the mail.

THE HEADLINE IN THAT WEEK's edition of *The New Chronicle* read "High Treason" in big bold type. The newspaper printed a copy of Captain Reid's letter above a photo of Prince Charles and his fiancée, Lady Diana Spencer, and reported that the coup plot was supported from overseas.

"Arms and equipment were already paid from a Mike Perdue in Texas, U.S.A., who was in constant contact with Patrick John and his henchmen," the front-page story read.

The prime minister went on the radio. "The time has come for us to tell you all that we know," she declared.

She described her dealings with the DDF since taking office and, while she named Captain Reid as one of the "troublemakers" in the force, she laid the blame at the feet of her longtime political foe.

"You will recall that Patrick John got on the radio and spoke of the volcano that was about to erupt and he spoke of revolution. Those were not idle words. He knew what he was plotting."

She read Captain Reid's letter and explained how the conspirators had met Mike Perdue on "a neighboring island" to finalize plans for a coup to install Patrick John (although she erred by claiming that John, Dennis Joseph and Julian David were present at the meetings in Antigua). She said one more man was implicated. She did not name him, but said Dominicans would be shocked when they found out.

The attack was scheduled for Carnival night, she said. The conspirators thought the police would be too preoccupied with the celebrations to put up an effective resistance. A businessman had paid a calypso band "to keep playing on after dark to provoke the trouble," she said. Howell Piper was supposed to "round up the other soldiers." She said he had been detained and that she had ordered Defence Force vehicles locked up, "away from malicious hands," since they were to have been used in the attack.

"It is unfortunate that the politician Patrick John sees himself in the role of a revolutionary," she continued. "We cannot help but recall his plot to use Dominica as a training ground for mercenaries with the intention of invasion of Barbados and placing himself as head of the Commonwealth of Dominica and Barbados. Now he has hatched another plot to bring in foreign soldiers to take down the Government of Dominica, which you elected so overwhelmingly last July, and put himself at the head of the government. Significantly, the plot was set for March 14—close to the date of the Grenada Revolution.

"But, fellow Dominicans, we the people of Dominica must show to Patrick John and his band of malcontents, some of whom are still at large, that we will not let the safety and security of our country be invaded, that we want and insist on having the peace and tranquility which is the only atmosphere which is conducive to development in this country. It is the success that we have had in the past seven months in putting government forward on the road to development that has caused these disgruntled politicians to act in this manner.

"To maintain this peace, which we love so dearly, will be the duty of every man, woman and child to make of themselves soldiers of the country. We must be vigilant, we must guard our interests. In particular, we must man the shores and bays to repel the entry of any vessel, ship or launch which comes to our shores illicitly.

"This is our country and we must fight for it."

The Iron Lady of the Caribbean, having discredited and disarmed the Defence Force and arrested its senior officers, then went to parliament and dealt it one final blow. She ordered the government to disband the militia once and for all.

The troops were sent home. Those not "tainted with disloyalty" would be offered jobs in the police. The Commonwealth of Dominica Police Force was now the island's only security.

The police had no illusions that the threat was over. The mercenaries were still out there, somewhere. The police went on high alert, positioning men along Rockaway Beach north of Roseau, the expected landing site. The senior police officers couldn't wait for the fight to begin. They knew this band of foreigners planned to attack their headquarters, kill members of their police force and take over their island. If these hired guns thought capturing Dominica would be easy, they were in for a surprise.

The defensive strategy was basic and brutal: when the mercenaries landed on the beach, the policemen would step out of the shadows and wipe them out.

16

The mobster who lived guns: Charles Yanover

Toronto, Canada
March 10, 1981

MIKE PERDUE READ ABOUT the arrests in the Houston newspaper. The headline above the brief item in the world news column was, "PM of Dominica arrests predecessor." It said Patrick John, Fred Newton, Julian David, Dennis Joseph and Howell Piper were in police custody "for plotting a coup." He clipped the story from the paper and put it in his file.

The arrests spooked Perdue. If the authorities in Dominica found the contracts or if Patrick John or any of the conspirators on the island talked, they would know Perdue was involved. The Dominicans would tell the Americans and before long he would be arrested. He felt certain federal agents were on to him. He was too frightened to leave his house. He called Wolfgang and told him what had happened. Droege immediately called Don Black.

"It looks like it's off," Droege said. "People have been arrested."

Perdue phoned the *Mañana* and left a message for Mike Howell, saying the trip was postponed. Howell called back and Perdue told him there had been arrests on the island and he was trying to find out what was going on.

On March 10, Perdue went to the First City Bank of Houston and transferred $1,800 in U.S currency to the Royal Bank of Canada in Roseau along with a telexed message: *Please pay to Julian David, Number 2 Lower Murphy Lane, Goodwill, Dominica, West Indies.* Julian David was locked up in the police cells at the time so his brother picked up the cash. Perdue hoped it would be enough to help his friends make bail.

Perdue stayed at the house in Houston for a couple of days and then drove to Jackson to talk to Danny Joe Hawkins. Perdue told him he didn't know if he could still pull it off. Without the Dominican Defence Force, it was a completely different playing field, and he did not have the manpower to do it alone.

Everything was on hold. He left Hawkins, drove to Kentucky and stayed with his mother. From there, he made his way to Toronto to see Droege.

"As far as I was concerned it couldn't be done, not with what I had gathered up. We needed the Defence Force to do it," Perdue said.

But after all the time and money Perdue had spent on this, he was not ready to give up. There had to be some way to salvage the coup. He talked it over with Wolfgang and they came up with an idea: They would send someone down to look things over. They needed to know where Patrick John was being held, if a state of emergency was still in effect, if the military was on a heightened state of alert and if the police were armed. Ultimately, they wanted to know if they could spring PJ from jail and help him take over the government. It wasn't the original strategy, but it wasn't far off.

"Let's continue with it," Perdue said.

WOLFGANG DROEGE HAD A FRIEND named Marion McGuire, an Irish Catholic beauty with long, dark hair who was raised in County Derry in Northern Ireland, the daughter of Irish Republican Army sympathizers. In Canada, she worked as a secretary for the government employment office but she hoped to become a nurse and was enrolled at Humber College. She was a hard-drinking woman. She just couldn't stop. Late in 1980, she was admitted to Lakeshore Psychiatric Hospital, where she met a fellow named Mark at an alcoholics' support group.

They were soon married at City Hall, but upon her release she went back to her drinking and they separated after three months.

Marion met Wolfgang at a bar and before long she was hanging around with the Western Guard and attending Don Andrews' lectures. She moved into one of Andrews' rooming houses and Droege introduced her to James McQuirter, who told her about the Dominica plot. It all sounded very carefully planned; she had the impression the coup was going to be easy. Newly divorced and struggling with alcohol, she was going through a personal crisis. She had even contemplated suicide, so when Droege asked her to fly to Dominica and send back reports on the island's security situation, she jumped at the chance. "If they'd asked me to go to the Arctic to count polar bears, I would have done it," she says.

Droege figured that as a woman, she wouldn't look suspicious. "We wanted to make sure that everything was okay on the island, and because we weren't quite aware of exactly what was going on, just in case, we thought we better send someone down there and that's when McGuire came into the picture and she went down to Dominica to give us any last-minute reports."

All you have to do, he told her, is sit in the sun and wait for us to get there. Mike Perdue gave her $2,000 and a credit card. He called her his "recon agent." She left on April 15. "All she saw was a free Caribbean hotel and booze," says her friend Steve Hammond. Perdue gave McQuirter $800 and told him to get to the island as well, to prepare a fleet of vehicles.

Before returning to Houston, Perdue met someone else Wolfgang had suggested might be worth talking to. His name was Charles Yanover. "Originally, the reason I went to Chuck Yanover was to try to get explosives because Wolfgang said that he, you know, knew a man in the underworld that could furnish the explosives," Perdue says.

Yanover was indeed a firearms expert and businessman. He was also a mobster.

CHARLES YANOVER HAD A NIGHTCLUB on Yonge Street in Toronto called Cooper's. He was known to some as Chuck the Bike, because he once owned City Custom Cycle and sold motorcycles to outlaw bikers.

But guns were his specialty. He knew all about them, how they worked, how to get them, how to smuggle them. He would sell them to anyone, even American white supremacists. Some say he was obsessed with guns. He also knew a thing or two about explosives. They were skills he put to use as an enforcer for mob boss Paul Volpe.

Yanover was a *capo*. As the head of a branch of the mob, he had his own soldiers but reported to Volpe. By his own admission, he was reckless. He had been in an out of prisons since the age of twenty-five. A prison shrink called him opportunistic and egocentric. His police file identified him as an international arms dealer and mercenary.

He was accused of attempting to control construction unions and orchestrated the January 9, 1980 bombing of the Arviv Disco on Bloor Street, Toronto's most popular disco.

Yanover was just out of prison when Don Andrews, whom he had met through a mafia acquaintance, introduced him to Wolfgang. "Yanover and Wolf hit it off because they were both gun nuts," Andrews recalls.

Later, Droege came by Yanover's club and told him about the Dominica coup.

"You know who I am?" Yanover asked.

"Ya."

"You know what you're asking me to do?

"Ya."

"Are you prepared to pay me?"

Yanover had just sunk $50,000 into his nightclub and bought a second Cadillac, a brand new 1981 Coupe de Ville. He was hard up for cash but he knew all about Droege's Nazi inclinations.

"You know I'm Jewish?" Yanover said. "If I catch you putting swastikas on synagogues, I'll come after you."

It was not Yanover's first foray into the mercenary world. In 1977, he had trained a team of British mercenaries preparing to assassinate the president of Togo. He spent months on the project before it was scuttled when the president was warned of the plot. Upon his return to Canada, Yanover was questioned about his involvement but claimed he had only visited Togo as a tourist and consultant. He was never charged.

Yanover was a big man; he could bench press 315 pounds. He could be very persuasive. He was a consummate con artist. "He's one of the best, or he'd like to think he's one of the best," Kingsley Graham, the Toronto lawyer who represented Yanover's wife on gun charges, said at her sentencing. "I wouldn't believe Mr. Yanover if he came in here today and said it was Friday."

It *was* Friday.

Despite the arrests in Dominica, Yanover thought the coup should proceed. Droege said he needed guns, explosives and reconnaissance photos. Yanover said he'd do it if the money was right. "If you think I'm going to put any of my own money into this, you're crazy," he said.

Yanover talked about setting up an arms depot on the island and asked Andrews to write him a letter of introduction so he could meet Eugenia Charles to discuss it with her. But Yanover was first and foremost a con man. He went along with the coup planning, but his intention may well have been to participate for only as long as it took to separate Droege and the mercenaries from their money. He took Wolfgang into a back room and showed him some photos of guns, TNT and plastic explosives. Following the meeting, Yanover went straight to the Volpe "family" and told them about it.

Volpe had long dreamed of opening another Caribbean casino. He had warm memories of a Haitian casino he had bought in 1963, when he was feeling the heat from police and needed to get out of town for a while. The International Casino was in a hotel in Port-au-Prince and it was a perfect mob front. No tax collectors, no police and a corrupt regime was running the country. Volpe used the casino to launder the proceeds of his Canadian criminal operations. And when a gambler lost big, he had another debtor in need of a high-interest loan. The Haitian government was in on it. Volpe bought off Papa Doc Duvalier, formally known as President for Life, Maximum Chief of the Revolution, Apostle of National Unity, Benefactor of the Poor, Patron of Commerce and Industry and Electrifier of Souls. The dictator got a tenth of the nightly profits. In return, Haiti's secret police turned a blind eye to the mob casino. Volpe was even used to promote tourism on the island; his photo was featured in a Haitian travel brochure. Volpe left in 1965 and sold his stake in the casino three years later but he always thought about doing it again.

Maybe Dominica was the place.

CHUCK YANOVER'S FIRST IMPRESSION of Mike Perdue was that he was physically strong but not too bright. Perdue explained the details of Operation Red Dog, and said he was stockpiling military assault rifles and had already bought 5,000 rounds of ammunition.

"That's enough for me," Yanover said. "How about everybody else?"

Perdue asked Yanover if he would fly to the island to see whether he thought the coup was feasible following the arrests of Patrick John and his men. He wanted Yanover to assess the readiness of the local forces and check out the government installations. Perdue wanted the benefit of the mobster's observations and firearms expertise.

Yanover said if the coup succeeded he wanted to be minister of defence, or at least a major in the Dominica Defence Force. Perdue said the best he could offer was colonel. Yanover accepted but he insisted on having his uniform tailor-made in Paris by Pierre Cardin. He wanted one with gold epaulettes.

WOLFGANG DROVE YANOVER to the Toronto airport. The mobster had decided to bring his girlfriend, Chris, and his partner, Mikey. They flew to Antigua and took the British West Indies Airways turbo-prop plane to Dominica, where they were picked up by a driver they had hired for the week. "This is the land that God forgot," he said as the cab made its way through the lush mountains to the capital. On the drive to Roseau, Yanover studied the roads, looking for infiltration and exfiltration routes and sizing up the state security forces. They got rooms at the Sisserou Hotel, named after the Amazona parrot with green wings that is Dominica's national bird. It was a small motel on the rocky shoreline south of the capital, a short walk from Pointe Michel, the village where Eugenia Charles was born.

In the morning, Yanover unpacked his camera, a Nikon with a powerful 1000-millimeter lens he had "inherited" from a photographer who owed him money. They got in the car and headed out to spy on the island. It had been almost a year since the last big hurricane but from the look of the place it could have been two weeks ago. The banana trees had bounced back, offering their first crop since the storm, but the roads remained treacherous and sometimes impassible. A third of the phone lines were still down. Disaster relief had poured in, but not nearly enough to repair all the damage. Yanover took photos of the harbor, the airstrip and Government House, and at night he returned repeatedly to the police headquarters. It was a rectangular compound with a courtyard in the middle. Not that defensible, he thought. Being a gun fanatic, he took note of the firearms he saw in the hands of the police officers: .38s and 9-mm handguns, .303 rifles, SLRs and SMGs. The police force numbered around 130 personnel.

It was a week of wasting time in paradise. Yanover found Roseau a bit slow. There weren't a lot of places to go out for a meal and a drink. He bought souvenirs, placemats with brightly colored parrots on them. He was just fulfilling his end of the deal. Of all the Caribbean islands, Dominica had the fewest who claimed European ancestry. Now that he saw the place, he thought it was ridiculous that a bunch of white supremacist mercenaries believed they could take over. At the same time, he believed a coup was militarily feasible. Most of the police were unarmed. Yanover was confident that he and Mikey could have taken police headquarters on their own with a couple of handguns. The problem was, what next? How could you possibly rule the country, short of state terror and brute force? It made no difference to Yanover. Even if it all fell apart—which, in his estimation, was the most likely outcome—at least he got a tropical vacation out of it. On the off chance the coup was successful, he thought he might open a casino. Or he could always pull a double-cross. If Mike Perdue and Wolfgang Droege actually managed to seize power, Yanover could throw together a bunch of gangsters and storm the island for himself. Then the mob would own it instead of these Nazis. It had not occurred to him that, while the mercenaries needed his firearms expertise, they didn't trust him. He was not one of them, and they were already talking about killing him once he got to the island.

17

Tough guy Lloyd Grafton

New Orleans, Louisiana
April 10, 1981

THE BUREAU OF Alcohol, Tobacco and Firearms office was at 546 Carondelet Street, on the third floor, just below the U.S. Secret Service. It had high ceilings and big wooden cased windows that rattled in the wind.

The agency operated on a shoestring budget. The desks were made of metal, hand-me-downs from the U.S. Navy, which had used them during World War Two. The wooden chairs also came from the Navy and the Internal Revenue Service.

The electronic surveillance equipment was almost as primitive, bulky Nagra tape recorders. At eight inches by four inches and an inch thick, they were not easy to conceal. The office also had a couple of transmitters the size of pagers but "a lot of times the antennae wire, if you didn't have it right, it would shock you or heat up," Special Agent Osburg says. They could only look with envy at the fancy gear used by the Drug Enforcement Agency.

Investigation F-4381-2 was going well in some respects. Osburg had managed to infiltrate the plotters by gaining Perdue's confidence, but he did not know the identities of the other mercenaries. All he had was a single name that Perdue had mentioned: Wolfgang. Osburg did his best to elicit more names. In his phone conversations with Perdue, he asked probing questions like, "What number should I call if I can't reach you at home?" It didn't work; the only number he ever got was Perdue's home phone in Houston.

The FBI also tried to identify Perdue's associates. The Bureau had launched its own investigation at the request of the U.S. State Department. The letter that Dominican police had seized mentioned a "Mike Perdue in Texas," and on March 10, 1981, the Director of the State Department's Office of Caribbean Affairs asked the FBI to look into it. FBI agents in Texas pulled Perdue's phone records to find out who he'd been talking to. The agents made pretext calls to some of the numbers and ran background checks on the names they came up with. The Dallas, Houston, New Orleans and San Juan field offices all got involved.

The telephone traces led to Las Vegas and then Detroit, where the field office was asked to investigate a local businessman who'd been contacted by Perdue about financing the operation, although the FBI doubted he knew the true purpose of the mission. The Legal Attaché at the U.S. Embassy in Ottawa was informed. On March 23, the FBI sent a synopsis of the investigation to the director of the CIA. A phone number that the Buffalo field office checked out turned up a link to Don Andrews' Western Guard, which an FBI bulletin noted "has had connections with alleged members of the KKK." Eugenia Charles gave the FBI the names of three Americans she thought might be involved in the coup. FBI headquarters asked its field offices to check them out and determine the nature of their relationship to Perdue.

The investigation had to be discreet, however. Nobody wanted to blow the ATF undercover operation. Osburg's case, and possibly his life, depended on it. Even as the list of FBI field offices involved grew to twenty, headquarters told its agents they were not to conduct any interviews. "We do not wish to alert any of the individuals involved by showing interest in their activities," the memo read.

The FBI thought Perdue's motives were "at best hazy." The Bureau was not even convinced Perdue intended to carry on with his paramilitary expedition. A confidential memo sent to the San Juan field office said "the coup plot may have been defused." But the FBI eventually came to believe that Perdue was going ahead with it.

A memo noted that, despite the arrests in Dominica, "Perdue now indicates however that he will do this with his own men and will not depend on unreliable Dominicans."

In undercover operations, law enforcement agents try to slide their confidential informants out of the picture as fast as possible. It's always safer to leave it to the professionals. Captain Mike Howell was still very much involved. The *Mañana* was his boat, but Osburg had been gradually inserting himself into the planning with Perdue, and phoning him directly instead of getting Howell to do it.

In early April, Osburg called Perdue and suggested they charter a second boat. The invasion force was growing and the *Mañana* would only hold so many men, he said. Perdue said he would have to run it by his people, but the truth was he didn't have the money, not yet. On April 10, Perdue told Osburg his men would be carrying twenty-one firearms in total, rather than the sixty they had initially talked about. The plan was to sail from New Orleans by the end of the month. Perdue promised to send money for groceries. A letter arrived at the Municipal Yacht Harbor six days later addressed to Captain Mike Howell. Howell delivered it to Agent Osburg. Inside he found four money orders from the Tyler Bank and Trust Company totaling $600. There was also a brief note:

> *Dear Mike,*
>
> *Sorry for the delay but here is $600 on the food. If it goes over I will settle once I meet you. See you Saturday evening of the 25th.*
>
> *Thank you, sincerely,*
>
> *Mike Perdue*

Four days later, Perdue phoned Captain Howell and said he was leaving for Canada. Osburg wanted to know what was going on, so he called Perdue and left a message asking him to call before he left. Perdue phoned back and said he needed to meet a few people in Toronto.

ALGIE MAFFEI WAS IN SOUTH AMERICA when Patrick John and Captain Reid were taken into police custody. He was studying at the Kuru Kuru Cooperative College in Georgetown, Guyana. Rosie Douglas had made a few calls and got him a six-month scholarship. He needed to get out of Dominica. He was wanted for murder and mixed up in the coup. Algie stayed with a woman he knew in Georgetown. Her name was June. They had met in Canada. In Guyana, Algie was known as Ras Abdul Shaka. Guyana was friendly to revolutionaries. Under President Forbes Burnham, the former British colony had developed ties with Cuba and the Soviet Union. Following the arrests in Dominica, Algie sent a letter to Mike Perdue:

> Dear Mike,
>
> I was sorry to hear what went on with this whole thing. The reason for all this [is] our friend don't follow instructions ... I decided to cool out here for a while but I would like to meet you somewhere to talk in order to reconcile our position. I am quite concerned about the men in the lock-up. It would be good to meet to talk. But I am stranded [and] I can't make the movements I want.
>
> I [hope] you are well and don't break down yet. We can still work together to achieve what we set out for. My friend is young in mind. He need some more technique in his movements.
>
> My boys are still strong and willing. They also have the farmer. This is why we can still make it. I know the place good enough. If you are still willing to help contact me by mail. I am afraid of the phone. If you can help send me some bread to make movements I am financially depressed.
>
> Awaiting,
>
> Algie
>
> Remember we can't use Antigua anymore, it's dangerous.

Algie got a reply from Perdue a few weeks later:

Dear Algie,

It was very good to hear from you. I too am sorry for what has happened.

Call me collect as soon as possible and we can discuss matters over.

Write a registered letter to me also as soon as possible I need to know a few things.

I need to know exactly where they are being held and I need to know who tipped off the opposition. Write me immediately and inform me.

Here is some money not much but later I can send more.

We need to meet somewhere to talk.

Sincerely your friend,

M. Perdue

He enclosed a $50 bill.

THE ATF INVESTIGATION had gone into high gear since the meeting aboard Mike Howell's boat. It became a monitored investigation, meaning the supervisors were now managing it, and headquarters in Washington, D.C. wanted regular field reports. To identify the other mercenaries, Agent Osburg tried following the money. He took Perdue's $5,000, the down payment for the boat, to the New Orleans Police Department, where a lab technician sprayed the bills with ninhydrin to raise fingerprints, but there were none, so he put the cash in a safety deposit box at the Bank of New Orleans at Poydras and St. Charles. The money led nowhere.

Osburg traced Perdue's phone number through Southwest Bell and found it was listed to Ronald Cox at 1609 Marshall Street in

Houston. He ran the license plate on Perdue's Chevrolet Impala through the Texas Department of Public Safety and it too was registered to Ron Cox at the same address. Agents in Houston began a surveillance operation targeting Perdue. They took pictures of his house, searched his trash and followed him wherever he went but still, the identities of the other mercenaries remained a mystery. The undercover operation was their best hope for finding out who was involved.

Osburg wanted a second agent to go undercover as a crewman on the *Mañana*, and he knew just the man for the job. Wally Lloyd Grafton was the undercover guru at the New Orleans district ATF office. Broad shouldered with a grimace to rival Charles Bronson's, he could easily pass himself off as an underworld thug. He had posed as a drug dealer, a hit man and a gunrunner, using the tricks he'd learned through trial and error to gain the confidence of crooks. Grafton could infiltrate any group, and he enjoyed it. He was a bit of an actor. And he was obsessive about things. When he was on a case, he lived and breathed it. He would sit down at night with his headphones on, going over his surveillance tapes while his wife tucked the kids into bed at their home in Slidell, across the lake from New Orleans. At trials, he would testify in his farm boy drawl about the incriminating conversations he'd recorded using a hidden wire. Every one of his cases resulted in convictions.

He started out in the military, serving sixteen months in Korea with the U.S. Army Infantry's 7th Cavalry Brigade before enrolling at Louisiana Tech University. Upon graduation, he went to work for the Federal Bureau of Prisons and then the Bureau of Narcotics and Dangerous Drugs. He was working on an undercover case in Wichita Falls, Texas when he met an ATF supervisor who asked if he'd like to join the agency. For a year, Grafton went undercover on a case in Tulsa, Oklahoma. The target was a black-market abortionist with no medical training. He hired Grafton to kill his business partner, whom he suspected was stealing from him. Following his transfer to the New Orleans ATF office, Grafton heard agents complaining about their lack of informants inside the Ku Klux Klan. They were building a case against the Grand Wizard in Baton Rouge, the Klan stronghold, but they were not happy with their coverage. Grafton said why not get an undercover agent to infiltrate the Klan? The others thought it was impossible because the KKK was notoriously security conscious. Grafton decided to do it, just to show it could be done.

Grafton had grown up in Klan country. Union Parish, Louisiana was one of the biggest Klan centers in the United States. So he knew a thing or two about the kind of people that joined the KKK, and he had read volumes about the organization. One night he went to a warehouse in Metairie, where a Klan initiation was taking place. He gave his name as Floyd Griffin and asked to join. The white hoods gave their ritual warning: if you are an informant or police officer, this is your chance to leave.

"I'm neither," he replied.

Afterwards, a man approached him about a uniform.

"Do you have your sheet?" he asked.

"No."

"Well, I have the concession on sheets."

"What kind you got?" Grafton asked.

"Regular cotton and polished cotton," the man said.

"How much?"

"Regular cotton $20, polished cotton $25."

"I want to look nice," Grafton said, "so I'll take the $25 polished cotton."

He took the uniform back to the ATF office, where one of the black agents put it on and walked around in the pointy white hood, puffing on a cigar.

Grafton knew there was a split in the Klan between those who liked David Duke and those who despised him, so he played on it. He started openly putting Duke down, and before long he was asked to join the rival faction in Livingston Parish. He became a security officer for the very man the ATF agents in New Orleans were after and was able to get enough evidence to convict him on a firearms charge.

OSBURG AND GRAFTON made a good team. They were both good at their jobs and they got along. Together they started planning the arrest of Mike Perdue and his mercenaries. Safety was the priority. They didn't want to start a war in downtown New Orleans. The arrests would have to take place somewhere out of the way, where there were no innocent bystanders who might get killed by a stray bullet. Ideally, Osburg and Grafton wanted to somehow separate the mercenaries from their weapons and then move in.

Osburg came up with a brilliant scenario. He would tell Perdue to gather his men somewhere on the outskirts of town. Osburg would tell the mercenaries to load their guns into a truck that was going to take them to the *Mañana*. Then he would tell the men to get into the back of a second truck. Once the mercenaries were all inside, he'd lock the door and deliver them unarmed to the FBI. He decided he would do this at Fort Pike State Park. There were few homes around and only one road in and out, so the State Police could close it off to traffic and the Coast Guard could keep marine vessels away.

There was just one catch. It could only work if Perdue agreed to put all his men in the back of a single truck without their guns. Was he really that stupid? Osburg had arrested a lot of people in his career, and if they had one thing in common it was that they were not exactly rocket scientists.

Osburg mapped out the arrest in detail, trying to predict every little thing that might possibly go wrong. He took aerial photos of the marina where he planned to make the arrests. He sketched it all out in diagrams. Every level of law enforcement was involved, from the FBI down to the local sheriffs. Such inter-agency cooperation was unprecedented. It was cumbersome working with so many different organizations. Osburg would draft his arrest plan and hand it to the Special Agent in Charge, who would send it back a few days later because one agency wanted to change this and another wanted to change that.

Osburg's policy was "anticipate the worst and hope for the best." He was, after all, dealing with a formidable load of military-grade firearms and a band of men intent on invading a country. The FBI New Orleans SWAT Team started rehearsing the arrest. After disarming the mercenaries, the SWAT officers would hand them over to two processing teams made up of ATF, U.S. Customs and FBI officers, who would take the fingerprints and mug shots. There were still a lot of unknowns. They expected at least ten mercenaries but possibly fifteen, and nobody was sure how many guns they'd be packing. On April 15 the ATF, FBI and

Customs met in New Orleans with Lindsay Larson, the Assistant U.S. Attorney. The date of the arrest was set for April 27.

"This is like the Bay of Pigs," one of the ATF agents said during an operational planning meeting.

"More like the Bayou of Pigs," another agent cracked.

The name stuck. Even in the classified criminal enforcement reports that Osburg had to type up, the case was from then on referred to as "the Bayou of Pigs investigation."

18

Dominica Police Headquarters, main gate

Toronto, Canada
April 18, 1981

THE ROOM AT the Ramada Inn was a mess of maps and photographs. They were scattered all over the floor. There were dozens of views of the port, police station and Government House. Chuck Yanover and his partner Mikey were showing Mike Perdue the reconnaissance photos they had taken on the island. One of Yanover's pictures showed a lone guard, asleep on a bench outside police headquarters. They had a good laugh over that. Capturing the station was going to be easy, they said, especially with the backing of Patrick John's DDF and the unkempt but violent Dreads.

"It was such a simple operation," Droege said. "All you had to do was take over the police station. When we were to arrive, you know, we already would have had people in place like McQuirter and also Rastafarians and others who were going to pick us up at the beach or near a landing spot and we would have, of course, come in late at night when the city is totally shut down and just gone over to the police station and taken out the police station."

Wolfgang didn't even expect any shots to be fired.

"They would have been totally overpowered, because their forces didn't even know how to use FNs. They weren't even trained in using them. All they were trained to use was Lee-Enfields, which are World War One issue."

MIKE PERDUE HAD ARRIVED in Toronto on April 20 to make the final plans for the coup d'état. It was sunny and cold outside but they stayed hunkered in their hotel. Perdue ordered food to the room, but there was no booze. There was too much work to do.

The first thing Perdue did was go over the coded messages that Marion McGuire had sent from Dominica. The first was a postcard Marion mailed to the home of a Toronto journalist named Gordon Sivell, who had been covering the Canadian Klan for his radio station, CFTR. It simply said that she had arrived and was working as a nurse at the hospital in Roseau. Sivell didn't know what to do with the postcard so he called McQuirter.

"I got this thing from Dominica. What's it all about?" he said. "What does this mean?"

"Well, just don't worry about it. Just bring it down here."

So Sivell dropped it off at Klan headquarters on Dundas Street. McQuirter knew the police might be intercepting his mail. He was, after all, the head of the Canadian KKK. Unbeknownst to Sivell, the coup conspirators had arranged to use his address to avoid drawing the attention of police.

Marion talked to Wolfgang over the phone a couple of times after that, passing on her observations about the island. Patrick John was still imprisoned. They were going to have to break him out.

Because of the changed circumstances on the island, Perdue came up with a new ten-point assault plan. It was a modified version of the original: In addition to raiding the police headquarters, they were going to have to storm the prison and free Patrick John and his men.

Perdue wrote it out in longhand:

Operation Red Dog

I. *Eight mercs will be in Roseau doing Recon and once clearance is given Red Dog will leave the States for Dominica.*

II. Red Dog will arrive off the coast of Dominica and an officer will meet with the Recon at the Dominica Mining Co. It is unguarded and we can group force. It is 3 miles outside of Roseau.

III. Once clearance is given Red Dog will harbor off the jetty at the mining co. and all the mercs will group and mount in autos that Recon has made available.

IV. Red Dog will Group into 2 units.
Red Dog I—14 merc.
Red Dog II—7 merc.

V. Red Dog I will lead the convoy into Roseau where Red Dog II will cut off and approach the Dominican Prison. Red Dog I will proceed across Roseau River up Queen Mary St. to Cork. St. turning East towards Bath Rd.

VI. Red Dog I will lead at least 3 autos in front of the police station stopping
— 2 men will take the charge office.
— The next 2 will rush the interior and go take the Communication Office.
— The next 4 will secure the interior and the far exit of the barracks.
— 4 will rush the East entrance of the barracks.
— 2 mercs will go into the Fire Station and keep everyone in station.

Opposition = charge office 3 person, multiple handgun. Armory has had 2 guards on roof but this is irregular and they are not heavily armed. Barracks max 10 persons asleep, maybe some handguns. Fire station no weapons. One police auto also makes patrols around city, no communications.

VII. Red Dog II will rush and secure the prison and hold until Red Dog I will reinforce and free Patrick John and his men approx. 10 to 15.

VIII. *Red Dog will arm Capt. Reid and he, with 3 of his locals and 2 mercs, will arrest the Prime Minister. Dennis Joseph with five local and 3 mercs will secure the radio station across from the Government House, no opposition.*
- *Two locals will be given guns and transport and told to go get reinforcements.*
- *The rest of Red Dog will regroup back of the police station.*
- *Once the Prime Minister is arrested Capt. Reid will go and reinforce Dennis Joseph at the radio station and wait for Red Dog.*

IX. *By daybreak.*
- *The police station, secured.*
- *Patrick John and his men freed.*
- *The Prime Minister arrested.*
- *Communications secured.*
- *Reinforcements coming in.*
- *Walk into Government House and set it up as operation center.*

X. *Secure city,*
- *roadblocks,*
- *patrols,*
- *curfew that night.*
- *Take patrol to airport put some autos on airstrip and leave about 8 locals to keep it closed.*

Perdue went through it all, point by point. If a patrol boat tried to stop them off the coast of Roseau, he said, the mercenaries would be ready with fragmentation grenades made of dynamite wrapped in roofing nails. The Dominicans would first be ordered to surrender.

"If they don't," Perdue said, "we'll blast them out of the water."

WOLFGANG WAS IN THE HOTEL ROOM, but he didn't say much. He brought along his latest recruit, a friend named Larry Jacklin. Tall and gangly, with a thin mustache, Larry lived with his parents on Rural Route 1 in Listowell, Ontario and drove a 1976 Plymouth Fury to the furniture factory where he made five dollars an hour. The balance in his bank account was twenty dollars.

He had met Wolfgang through the Western Guard. Larry was everything that Wolfgang looked for in a recruit: young, naïve, clean-cut, blond and disenfranchised. "He was kind of a true believer, but by the same token he seemed like the type that was exceedingly trustful," says the informant Grant Bristow. Wolfgang was protective of his friend, but Larry was just what he needed for Dominica: a trained soldier. He had spent six months in the Canadian Armed Forces reserves.

When Perdue talked about the communists in Dominica, Larry ate it up. He was captivated by the Texan and his stories of mercenary wars. He had one concern, though. If he went to Dominica, he asked Perdue, would he have to live with blacks? Perdue assured him he would not. Larry said, okay, he would join the Red Dog force.

They still needed more mercs. Larry suggested Bob Prichard, the Vietnam vet they'd met at the American Nazi compound in North Carolina. Jacklin got Bob on the phone.

"Are you interested in doing a mercenary job?" Larry asked.

"What does it pay?" Bob wanted to know.

Bob Prichard was making $3.55 an hour as a security guard in Garner, North Carolina, plus his $54-a-month veterans' disability pension. He was driving a 1966 Ford pick-up worth $100. When Jacklin said they would get thousands of dollars for the mission, Prichard said he wanted in.

"All I knew, I was offered a good chunk of money to do what I do," Prichard said in an interview. "Kill commies for money. That's what it was all about."

Prichard said he agreed to take part "mainly because of my anti-communist feelings," although he didn't even know which island they were going to invade. Perdue did not tell him over the phone. Prichard guessed it was Grenada.

"Now, what about weapons," he asked, "supplies and, you know, medical supplies?"

"It's all taken care of," Perdue assured him.

152

Prichard asked if he could bring along personal weapons.

Perdue asked what kind.

Prichard said he had a Lama .45 automatic pistol, a Colt detective special .38 and a Ruger mini 14 semi-automatic .223.

"Yeah," Perdue said. "They'd be no problem."

ACCORDING TO THE PLAN, Chuck Yanover and McQuirter were supposed to fly to the island in advance of the raid. They would arrange the cars and guide the landing party ashore by signaling with a flashlight. The mercenaries would then hand some of their guns to the local fighters and race to the police headquarters. Yanover was not impressed with Mike Perdue or his team. In the mob, he had been a talent spotter, and he didn't spot any talent in that hotel room. He was even less impressed when he found out that the mercenaries had told everything to a Toronto journalist.

Gordon Sivell was sitting on the scoop of a lifetime. Mercenaries were about to invade a Caribbean island and he had been tipped off in advance. Not only that, these guys had let him record interviews with them as they prepared for the assault. It was the biggest story of his career. A twenty-eight-year-old with high ambitions, Sivell had been a reporter at CJJD radio in Hamilton, Ontario when he first met James McQuirter. The station had a documentary show that featured thirty-minute interview segments with newsmakers, and in 1979 Sivell convinced McQuirter to go on the air to talk about the Ku Klux Klan's attempts to set up a chapter in Toronto. "McQuirter sort of, to a certain degree, intrigued me," Sivell said in an interview.

As the founding father of Canada's KKK, McQuirter needed publicity if he was going to attract a following, and Sivell wanted the story. He had been drawn to investigative reporting since he started in the business at small- and medium-market radio and TV stations in Western Canada. He wanted to make his mark in the world of journalism, and he knew that one way to do that was to seek out stories on the edge. "I sort of gravitated towards these weirdos." Sivell had been feeding stories to CFTR radio in Toronto and, after a friend put in a good word, he was hired as a staff reporter. He anchored the news and worked in the field, covering the legislature for a while. He arrived in Toronto just as the Klan was becoming a big story. He pitched a documentary on the KKK to a nationally syndicated current affairs show called *Sunday, Sunday* and got the go-ahead. He called up McQuirter for an interview and the Klan boss agreed.

McQuirter was not good at keeping secrets, and while Sivell was researching his documentary he mentioned that the Klan had been training mercenaries at a paramilitary camp at a farm near London, Ontario. Sivell broke the story and it garnered national attention. Three months later, just before Christmas, Sivell got a call at the newsroom. It was McQuirter. He wanted to get together for a drink. They met at a lounge on Bloor Street. They had a few drinks and McQuirter said the words that every reporter lives for: "Want a good story?" McQuirter said he didn't have all the details but a bunch of guys were going to take over an island in the Caribbean.

Sivell didn't work at *CBS News* or *The New York Times*. But here he was, sitting with the head of the Canadian Klan, who was telling him about a plot to overthrow a foreign government. It was a world scoop. Sivell was skeptical. He told McQuirter he wanted to know more. Why McQuirter let him in on the coup plot, he cannot say. It made absolutely no sense; the mercenaries were supposed to be an invisible force behind Patrick John. "To this day I personally could not tell you the motivation," he says. To Aarne Polli, it was just another indication of the stupidity of the conspirators: "They were selling their story before it happened. That's how clever they were. These guys confessed before the fact."

McQuirter invited Sivell to the Klan house on Dundas Street, where he met Wolfgang Droege. Despite his soft voice, Droege expressed hardline views. Sivell got the impression that Wolfgang was militantly anti-immigrant, although he preferred to call himself a nationalist. But the reporter never heard him make anti-Semitic remarks or utter racial slurs. Nor did he ever see Droege using drugs. He did drink beer, though.

"Imagine what you could do if you owned your own country," Droege said.

The next time Mike Perdue came to Toronto, Sivell met him at a greasy spoon on Parliament Street. McQuirter and Droege were there, as well as Marion McGuire.

"Do you want to go to Dominica with us?" the men asked him.

"Oh my God, are you fucking crazy?" McGuire interjected. Then she warned the journalist not to get in her way.

Sivell found McGuire rude and aggressive. She didn't like the idea of bringing a reporter along on an invasion. She must be smarter than the others, Sivell thought.

Yanover was equally displeased to learn that Sivell knew everything. Upon finding out there was a reporter in the hotel room, he collected payment for his reconnaissance mission to Dominica and tapped his partner Mikey on the shoulder.

"We're out of here," he said. "Let's go."

He walked out of the hotel convinced that Perdue was possibly the worst mercenary he had ever met.

"I'd be surprised if these guys ever make it to the dock of the boat," he told Mikey.

Yanover didn't care. No matter what happened in the Caribbean, he had already scammed $10,000 and a sun holiday out of Perdue. He was finished with these jokers. The hardest part had been keeping a straight face.

GORD SIVELL WAS NOT IMPRESSED with Perdue either. He thought the Texan was a bully with a big ego. Perdue was the boss and made that clear to all. He boasted about his Purple Heart and how he had rescued fellow Marines in Vietnam. He was at least friendly with Sivell and seemed to warm to him after he heard Sivell had served in the military.

Aside from McGuire, the mercenary team had no hesitation about having a news reporter embedded in the mission. They didn't mind that Sivell had copies of the plans and maps. They wanted him to come along to document the attack.

But Sivell was having a crisis of conscience. When he realized the plot was real, and not just drunken bravado, he agonized over what to do. He had already told his boss at CFTR about the story he was working on. But the more he learned, the more he realized that blood was going to be spilled.

Reporters are supposed to report. They aren't supposed to cooperate with the police unless compelled to do so, and even then some prefer to keep their mouths shut and go to jail. Sivell knew all that, so he was reluctant to tip off the police, but as a citizen he thought he had to do something. "I just felt sort of troubled by it. I felt it would not be right not to alert the authorities."

Sivell went to see a friend named Larry Strange. Strange was from St. John's, Newfoundland. In 1967, the year Canada hosted the world Expo in Montreal, Strange had followed the well-worn trail west to Toronto. He wanted to become a helicopter pilot, so he enlisted in the United States Air Force, thinking he would have more opportunities south of the border than as a member of Canada's smaller armed forces. He drove to Buffalo for recruit testing and walked into a room full of anxious young men on their way to Vietnam. He returned to Toronto and joined the Ontario Provincial Police instead.

After training, he was sent to Niagara Falls, where he was a patrol and community services officer. His job was to visit shopping malls and schools to talk about public safety. He was the face of the police. It was through his work in the community that he came to know Sivell. They became friends and kept in touch even after Sivell had moved on to bigger market radio in Toronto.

Sivell told him about his anguish.

"You're kidding?" was Constable Strange's first reaction. But he trusted Sivell and knew he was an ambitious reporter with a knack for finding stories like this. In that respect, he wasn't surprised that Sivell had found himself in the middle of a bunch of mercenaries.

Foreign coups were not part of Constable Strange's beat, so the detachment commander told him to take it upstairs to the Niagara Falls Intelligence Unit. Strange had a friend there named Marshall Thur, a member of the biker enforcement team that was preoccupied with the local chapter of the Bandidos. Constable Strange never said Sivell was his source, just that he had come across information about a plot to overthrow a foreign government and that there had been meetings in Toronto.

Niagara Falls is a border town, separated from Buffalo by a short stretch of highway and a bridge. Thur's work often revolved around the border, so he had good contacts with his counterparts in the various U.S. agencies that worked the frontier. Thur met an Immigration and Naturalization Service officer attached to what was called the Strike Force. As they were chatting, the American officer mentioned a case he had heard about down South involving a band of mercenaries who were assembling to invade the Caribbean.

"I know," Thur said. "We have a man inside their group."

The INS officer was dumbfounded. When the Americans discovered the OPP had penetrated the conspiracy, they were terrified. They thought Sivell might go to air with his story and blow the ATF undercover operation.

The FBI was unsure about the link between the Toronto plot, which they understood to be focused on Grenada, and the New Orleans plot to invade Dominica. The FBI wrote:

> It is still undetermined how the information developed in
> Canada and the information from New Orleans fits together.
> Whether one is a smokescreen for the other or whether
> there may be a concerted effort by Perdue and his backers to
> attempt to eventually gain control of both islands. In spite
> of the obvious problems and difficulties inherent in such an
> operation and the possibility it may be a harebrained scheme,
> Perdue has, in fact, put up $5,000 earnest money and has
> continued his assurances that he will carry through with the
> operation. No information has been developed to date to
> contrafute this, and all indications are that Perdue is sincere
> and that people he has been in contact with recently are real
> and willing to contribute to his efforts.

Constable Strange called Sivell and asked if he would meet Thur, and he agreed. Thur and Strange drove to Toronto and spent hours with Sivell going over what he had seen and heard. During the interview, Sivell mentioned he had been taping the meetings, and Thur was delighted.

The next day, Strange went to work at the OPP detachment and was told to get his radar gun and go back to traffic work. He can't be sure, but he believes the Americans asked the OPP to stand down. The intelligence unit gave the U.S. authorities what information it had, but it was not to actively pursue the investigation. Sivell felt he had handed them the case on a silver platter but that the intelligence brass had not taken him seriously.

Then another informant came forward. Cecil Kirby was a Satan's Choice biker working for the Commissos, a prominent Toronto crime family. Kirby was their enforcer but after faithfully and violently serving the Commissos, Kirby had grown suspicious that his employer might be plotting his demise, so he went to the cops and was soon feeding information to Corporal Mark Murphy, a Royal Canadian Mounted Police organized crime investigator.

Corporal Murphy was the only cop Kirby trusted. They met at a downtown donut shop, and Kirby said Charles Yanover had offered him a job. Yanover was going to "South America" to participate in a coup, Kirby said, and afterwards, he was going to set up a mob casino. He wanted to know if Kirby wanted a part in the invasion.

It's not clear Yanover did anything more than mention the plot to Kirby, but at the very least the informant had the basic elements right. Corporal Murphy passed the tip to John Toews at the RCMP Security Service, who would have undoubtedly shared it with his counterparts at the FBI. The officer heard another tidbit as well: that Yanover was ordering a tailor-made military uniform from Paris.

THE PLANNING SESSION at the Ramada Inn convinced Gord Sivell that the Dominica coup was all about greed. The plotters clearly had political baggage, but he felt sure the coup was primarily a business venture. "This was not a KKK island. This was all about money, making money," he says. Sivell was also sure he had a career-making scoop on his hands, perhaps a prize winner. He was on the inside of a Third World coup d'état. And he had it all on tape. The mercenaries had not only tipped him off, they had also been allowing him to record exclusive interviews.

"One of the major problems has been finances," Droege said in an interview that Sivell taped during the final planning session at the hotel. "There were times when we were sitting, for instance, for eight weeks in a hotel room, talking every day to possible investors. And sometimes we were turned down, so we just had to go from there."

"You know," he added, "to me, I love the adventure, the excitement of it. I consider myself a little bit of a rebel in society. And, like, I'm not content to have a nine-to-five job. I want to live a real life, you know, I want excitement and adventure in my life. And you know, that's what I'm getting and I'm also, of course, going to benefit financially from it, which will afford me a good life. I hope I'll be fixed for the rest of my life after Dominica."

Perdue talked on tape as well. "I'm thirty-two years old. I want money out of it. The reason I'm even giving interviews is because I want recognition for who I am and what I am. We're going to pull it off ... I've got two men ... here tonight that was there a week. I've got a woman down there now. Know what they say? 'We can do it.' Wolf's been there. I've been there. If they don't arrest me for the next four days, it's all over."

19

Guns purchased for Operation Red Dog

Houston, Texas
April 24, 1981

CHRIS ANDERSON LANDED at Houston airport on April 24. Perdue picked him up and took him to a motel for the night.

"You have a weapon?" Perdue asked.

"No, not with me."

"There's been some people following me. I'm going to leave you with this."

Perdue handed Anderson a .45 and two full clips. Anderson recognized it at once as an M1911 single-action semi-automatic. He had carried the same weapon when he was a sheriff's deputy.

Perdue had a lot of guns. He had been buying equipment for the coup since January—camouflage jackets (small, medium and large sizes), ponchos, ammunition pouches, radios, canteens, sleeping bags and medical supplies. He stored it in a room he rented from a friend in Houston.

The guns were more complicated. His break-and-enter conviction as a teenager in Tennessee meant he was not legally allowed to keep firearms, but he found ways around the law. He asked a friend named Jim Ferguson to sign for an order of assault rifles and shotguns. Perdue gave him $300 but didn't tell him what they were for. "I conned him," Perdue admitted.

Perdue also wanted explosives. He had to break into Stock Farm Prison and, if nothing else, a few loud explosions might intimidate the locals into surrendering. Charles Yanover had failed to come up with any, so he called a few of his recruits and mentioned he needed dynamite. Maybe one of them would come through.

Perdue's initial plan was to load all the guns on a cargo ship that would sail from Texas and rendezvous with the *Mañana* somewhere in the Gulf of Mexico. They would then transfer the arms to the *Mañana* for the journey to Dominica. It was safer that way. If the Coast Guard or police stopped his men as they were leaving New Orleans, all they would find was a dozen guys on a cruise.

But there was a problem: money. Perdue had not been able to win over enough investors, and hiring a second boat was going to be expensive. He was going to have to make do with just the *Mañana*. It was riskier, but there was no way around it now. He had to cut costs where he could. This was a budget coup.

SPECIAL AGENT JOHN OSBURG called Perdue at his home in Houston and reminded him he still owed money for the boat. Perdue said he had just returned from Toronto and that he would be in New Orleans on Saturday. He would bring the $10,000, he said.

He gave Osburg the final headcount for the voyage: ten mercenaries plus the guns and gear. Perdue added that since the meeting in Toronto, he had amassed over one thousand reconnaissance photos of Dominica. He reassured Osburg they were doing the right thing. Even though Patrick John was behind bars, they were just helping resolve a domestic political dispute.

"It's an internal affair," Perdue said. "As long as it's an internal affair, there's no problem that we represent the person that's locked up."

MIKE PERDUE PAID HIS UTILITY BILLS and emptied his bank account. He told a neighbor he had "business in the Caribbean," and then he left, pulling a U-Haul trailer behind his Impala.

His first stop was Chuck Kisling's house, where the gear was stored. Kisling didn't know about the coup. Perdue had told him he was starting a survival camp.

He picked Anderson up at the motel and they drove to an apartment building to meet a licensed gun dealer named Victor Mullen, Jr. Jim Ferguson signed for the eight Bushmaster rifles and five Smith & Wesson shotguns. They were still in their shipping crates. Perdue stacked them in the U-Haul and drove out onto I-10, over the top of Trinity Bay into Bayou country.

Anderson wasn't sure what to make of Perdue but it was hard to turn down that kind of money. It was a lot better than sweeping school floors in Oklahoma City, and he thought invading Dominica was the right thing for America. Anderson had grown up in the shadow of his father, a U.S. Army Ranger who had stormed the beaches of Normandy. He was a hero, and Anderson never felt he could measure up. "This is something he understands," Anderson said, "and if I can be anywhere equal to what he done, then I'll have a light in his eyes."

Sitting in the passenger seat of the Chevy, Anderson filled the silence with small talk as they left East Texas and crossed into Louisiana, through Lake Charles, Lafayette, across the mighty Mississippi River to Baton Rouge, and then north towards Jackson.

They entered Mississippi, the blacktop rolling under them at the top of the Gulf of Mexico. As far as anyone knew, they were just another couple of travelers on the Interstate. There was no way to tell that their car was pulling all the trappings of a coming invasion.

IT WAS A LONG GREYHOUND RIDE from Toronto. The cities rolled by in a blur—Niagara Falls, Buffalo, Erie, Cleveland, Columbus, Cincinnati, Louisville. Larry Jacklin was recovering from acute tonsillitis. He'd spent a week in the hospital before telling his family he was "going to Texas." A marathon bus trip was hardly the ideal way to recover, but he didn't want to miss the coup. The bus stopped in Nashville, Athens, Huntsville and Birmingham, where Wolfgang got off, leaving Larry to continue on to Jackson.

Wolfgang went to Don Black's house. Black wasn't there but he arrived three hours later and packed for the mission, placing his .45 in his travel bag. In the morning, Black's wife drove them to Jackson. Black told Droege not to say anything about Dominica in front of her. All she knew was that they were going to meet someone. They stopped in Tuscaloosa to pick up Mike Norris, crossed the state line into Mississippi and found Danny Joe Hawkins' house without any problem. Larry Jacklin was already there. George Malvaney and Bill Waldrop arrived later.

Waldrop had decided to come despite a last-minute warning from Hawkins, who took Waldrop aside and warned him this might be more dangerous than he thought. They might even get killed. Danny Joe didn't seemed bothered by the risks. He was used to such hazards. But while Waldrop was known at home in Mississippi as a religious man with strong anti-communist views, he was not a soldier. He just wanted to help rid the Western hemisphere of communism, and what he called its "anti-God-like philosophy." Perdue had also convinced him the coup was a covert U.S. government operation, so he decided to go along regardless of Hawkins' warning. But just in case, he brought his .9 mm Astra semi-automatic.

Malvaney had also come well armed. He brought along an AR-180 .223 rifle, Colt .45 model 1911 A1, a .44 magnum Smith and Wesson model 29 pistol and a .30-caliber M-1 carbine he got from Hawkins' mother that he intended to sell to Perdue for $300.

They all went to a movie. Afterwards they rented a Chrysler and returned to the house to load their gear into Danny Hawkins' Ford van. Hawkins' own bag contained a few bottles of prescription drugs and a book, Department of the Army Field Manual FM-5, titled *Explosives and Demolitions*.

MIKE PERDUE AND CHRIS ANDERSON arrived in Jackson at midnight and met everyone at the Howard Johnson's. Two police officers were eating at the restaurant so they went to the Days Inn instead. Perdue said he needed to meet someone to collect some money, so they drove to a dark corner of the parking lot and waited.

A car pulled up. The man behind the wheel looked to be in his sixties and he was gnawing on a big cigar. Perdue spoke with him and then turned and summoned Anderson to come over. The driver handed Perdue an envelope containing $5,000 cash. Perdue told Anderson to open the trunk of the Chevy and take out two silver stags and a vase, which he explained were "collateral." The man with the cigar opened the trunk of his own car. Inside it were three packages, one wrapped in Christmas paper. A Christmas present in April? Perdue instructed Anderson to put the packages in the trunk of the Chevrolet.

Anderson wasn't told what was inside the boxes, but he had a pretty good idea. Before he had left Oklahoma City, Perdue had told him on the phone he was bringing explosives. Anderson guessed that the parcels he had just moved from one trunk to another contained dynamite. He wasn't too happy about it. He was afraid the explosives would become unstable in the heat inside the trunk. He voiced his concern to Perdue, but Mike said this was a type of dynamite that was not sensitive to temperature. Anderson could tell by the way Perdue spoke that he did not have a clue what he was talking about. And why, Anderson wondered, would a CIA-sponsored mission use industrial dynamite. Wouldn't the U.S. government be able to come up with some C-4?

Perdue put the envelope containing the cash in the glove box of his Chevrolet, and the convoy of mercenaries drove off into the night. They stopped once for gas and soon reached the western outskirts of Baton Rouge and got rooms at the Days Inn. A few miles to the east, the waters of the lower Mississippi drifted under the steel trusses of the Horace Wilkinson Bridge on their way out to the Gulf of Mexico.

BEFORE LEAVING FOR LOUISIANA, Bob Prichard dropped by Miller's farm one last time and asked Frazier Glenn Miller if he wanted to come along. Miller considered it.

"It had some possibilities, favourable possibilities," Miller said later in an interview. "It could have been pulled off—kick in the front door and the whole rotten thing would come crashing down."

Miller had left the National Socialist Party four months earlier to start his own organization, the Carolina Knights of the Ku Klux Klan.

Running off to the Caribbean was only going to distract him from his new calling, but it was tempting. "I might have went," he said. "Back in those days, hell ya! The frame of mind I had back in those days, there was a fairly good chance I would have went if I'd have known more about it, but under the circumstances I decided not to go."

Prichard packed his rifle in a travel case and threw some clothes into a bag, along with two handguns, a .45 automatic and a .38 special. He was convinced the CIA was behind the Dominica operation. The agency was fighting communism everywhere else, even in Laos and Vietnam. Why not right here in America's backyard? Prichard threw a Nazi flag in his bag and left for the Raleigh airport.

Wolfgang Droege and Larry Jacklin picked him up at the airport in New Orleans and drove him to the motel in Baton Rouge, where he met the rest of the Red Dog mercenaries. "He was a wild fellow, a character," Waldrop says.

In the darkness of the hotel parking lot, Anderson, Perdue and the others took all the guns out of the U-Haul and loaded them into Hawkins' van.

Perdue was running behind schedule. He wasn't going to make his meeting with the *Mañana* crew in New Orleans. He phoned and said he was having "equipment problems." Perdue asked if he could come by the marina in the morning instead, but Osburg said to come at night.

That way, he said, they wouldn't be seen.

20

A surveillance photo of Wolfgang Droege, John Osburg, Lloyd Grafton and Mike Perdue at the New Orleans marina, April 26, 1981

Baton Rouge, Louisiana
April 26, 1981

MIKE PERDUE RETURNED the U-Haul trailer to the rental shop and took Interstate 10 southeast, following the Mississippi River towards New Orleans. He veered off towards Lake Pontchartrain and the yacht club where his ship and its captain were waiting.

Wolfgang was in the passenger seat. The Canadian wore a dark, short-sleeve shirt. His hair was trimmed but he still had his trademark beard. He looked pudgy and soft-shouldered, hardly in fighting shape, and he wasn't going to get any fitter sitting on a boat for two weeks. Perdue was in better shape; his forearms bulged below the rolled-up sleeves of his combat shirt.

Almost two years had passed since they had met in Toronto. They had spent a lot of time together since then and had become good friends, despite their differences. Perdue could talk a good line about the threat of communism, but Droege breathed politics. Dominica was going to make him a player, more important than Don Andrews and maybe even David Duke. He could pump some of his wealth into the militant white right and help it transform into a political force in North America. He would be a hero of the movement—and a very rich man.

As they approached the Big Easy there was bad news from Dominica. A Review Tribunal had recommended continued detention for Patrick John, Captain Reid, Major Newton and Julian David. The money Perdue had wired to the island to bail them out had not done the job. The only suspected conspirator the tribunal thought should be released was Dennis Joseph, the calypso star. But the government had decided to keep him in custody anyway pending the outcome of the investigation. There was no doubt about it now. The mercenaries were going to have to break them out of jail.

It was seven in the evening when Perdue and Droege arrived at the New Orleans yacht club and found the *Mañana* tied at the wharf. Special agents Osburg and Grafton were waiting with Captain Howell. They all went below into the cabin and sat around the galley table. Perdue opened his briefcase and laid down a stack of $100 bills still bound in bank wrappers. It came to $9,800.

"I'm $200 short," Perdue said.

"Can we trust him for the rest?" Osburg joked.

Howell was at the head of the table. The agents were on one side facing the mercenaries. From his vantage point, Howell had a clear view of the contents of Perdue's briefcase. The ATF agents could not see inside; their line of sight was obstructed by the open lid. Inside the briefcase, Howell saw a loaded handgun.

He was watching it, thinking about whether there was going to be a shootout, when Perdue reached in and picked it up. Howell realized the two agents still couldn't see what was going on, and he thought that if Perdue raised the handgun he would have to grab it and hold on long enough for Osburg and Grafton to reach for their own weapons and take him out.

Perdue put the gun back inside the briefcase, and then picked it up again.

Howell was ready to pounce. He was just about to reach across and make a grab for it when Perdue popped out the ammunition clip and handed him the gun.

"Nice ... pistol," was all Howell could spit out.

Perdue said it was a gift from his business manager.

They passed the gun around and made admiring comments. Osburg recognized it as a Government Model Colt .45. He was still thinking about leads he could chase down. He wanted to find out who else was involved. The gun might open doors. While he was turning it over in his hands, Osburg glanced at the serial number and committed it to memory: 68942B70. He would put a trace on it as soon as Perdue and Droege were gone. He handed it back to Perdue, who returned it to the briefcase. Whether he pulled the gun to impress or to intimidate is unclear, but it was a reckless act.

The agents needed to get Perdue to buy into the elaborate arrest plan they had worked out. Osburg explained that whatever happened in Dominica was up to Perdue—but while they were aboard the *Mañana*, Captain Howell was in charge. All decisions concerning the ship would be made by Howell and Osburg.

The first rule was that nobody would carry weapons on board the ship, and that included knives. Osburg said the mercenaries would have to put all their guns, ammunition and military gear into bags, because the crew didn't want anyone to see them loading weapons onto the boat.

Perdue went for it. "We'll go along with whatever you wish to have done," he said.

Wolfgang wasn't so sure about the whole thing. He looked around the decks of the *Mañana* and thought, there's no way this ship can be ready to sail tomorrow. He was suspicious and raised it with the agents, but they reassured him.

"We can get all this done within a matter of a day. No problem there. We've already got everything, we've got supplies, everything's ready."

Something else bothered Wolfgang. When they were charting their course to Dominica and discussing where they would refuel, Wolfgang pointed to the Yucatan Peninsula as the obvious place to stop. It juts right out into the Caribbean, but Osburg disagreed.

"No, not the Yucatan peninsula," he said.

Wolfgang thought, Osburg doesn't know what he's talking about.

THE ATF AGENTS WANTED TO SHOW Perdue and Droege the spot where they were going to meet the following night so they all got into

Perdue's Chevy. Agent Grafton got behind the wheel. "I know the city," he explained.

Agent Osburg sat in the front passenger seat, and the two mercenaries were in the back. Grafton and Osburg started talking about the next job they would do together, once the coup was over. It was a trick, meant to put their suspects at ease and take their minds off the task at hand, as if it was already done. It seemed to work.

Droege described his plans to open a cocaine-processing lab on Dominica. He promised he'd hire the *Mañana* to smuggle the coke to the United States. This is all a business venture, Droege explained. He said he hoped to make a lot of money, enough to live comfortably for years to come.

Perdue also opened up about money. He boasted he was going to pocket three to five million dollars in five years. The two mercenary leaders intended to make as much as they could from the island, exploit the place and, if they left, it would be with their pockets bulging.

Agent Grafton pulled into Fort Pike State Park and showed Perdue and Droege the parking lot where they would meet. Osburg told Perdue to have his men there at 10 p.m. Osburg said he would bring a van and a truck. The guns would go into the van; the men would get in the truck. Then they'd convoy up the road to the Harbor Inn Marina in St. Tammany Parish where they'd load everything onto the ship. In twenty-four hours they would board the *Mañana* for the long voyage across the Caribbean Sea to Dominica.

They got back into the Chevy and returned to the New Orleans marina. Perdue gave Osburg his maps and charts to help plot the journey. They all went back to the *Mañana* and had a drink. Perdue reminisced about fighting in Vietnam with the 5th Marine Division. Droege excused himself to call the motel in Baton Rouge. He wanted to schedule a pre-mission briefing for later that night.

Before he left the marina, Droege gave Osburg the phone number for the motel and said he would be in room 275 until checkout time on Monday, and then they would all be leaving for New Orleans.

"You see, I told you everything was okay," Perdue said in the car on the highway to Baton Rouge.

Wolfgang got the feeling Perdue was trying to pump him up, to reassure him that everything was going to work out. Or maybe Perdue was trying to convince himself.

AT MIDNIGHT, PERDUE SUMMONED the men into his motel room. He had made it up to look like a war room, with diagrams and reconnaissance photos all over the place. "General Perdue, he had his maps on the wall like he was Eisenhower," Prichard recalls.

Perdue wanted to lay down the rules before they left. He expected strict discipline on the mission. It was another lesson learned from Mad Mike Hoare, who made his men follow ten rules, starting with "Pray to God daily." Perdue had typed up his own rules, which he read aloud.

"At any time the commanding officer feels your behavior, actions or attitude is counter-productive or unprofessional, you are subject to be discharged with total forfeit of bonus and percentage in Nortic," he said.

With that out of the way, Perdue began his operational briefing. He passed around the photos that he and Yanover had taken in Dominica, so everyone could see where they were going and what to expect. He showed them their uniforms and the walkie-talkies. Perdue did not assign any duties that night. He did not want to give away too much right now. They were going to be on a boat for two weeks. There was plenty of time.

"I have some friends," Perdue added, "and if anybody tries to leave, he'll be taken care of."

It was an open-ended comment. It could have meant anything. Anderson took it as a threat. He had judged Perdue to be a seasoned professional when they had first met in Houston. Now he was having doubts. Between the dynamite and the veiled threat, Perdue seemed to be losing it. "He was pretty squirrelly," Anderson says. "He was obsessed with being in power down there. He was obsessed with the league of Aryan nations thing. Anybody who was not Anglo were bad guys." Anderson didn't like Perdue's lieutenant either. Wolfgang's Nazi streak was too much for Anderson. "I thought he was pretty cool, but I didn't like his attitude, a lot of things about him I didn't like. I thought he was pretty secretive." Alarm bells were going off in Anderson's head. "I just figured I'd got myself into something, that I didn't want to be there, but I was there and didn't know how to get out." He slipped out of the briefing room and went downstairs for a coffee.

Wolfgang had already been briefed in Toronto. There was no reason for him to stick around. He left to take a shower, then went to the restaurant with Don Black. "Certainly we were to be paid for this ... we have families that we have to support," Black says. "We can't do something without making a living at it, but our primary reason was that we simply felt we were doing what was in the best interest of our country."

And it was exciting. "Maybe it turned out to be a little more exciting than we thought it would be."

PERDUE HAD PREPARED briefing packages for the men. He wanted to familiarize them with the island and the invasion plan. Each package contained a map of the Caribbean and a map of Dominica. There was also a map of Roseau with notations such as, "Government House has a four-foot wall in front, two destroyed churches, and usually no guards." Perdue had included a copy of his "Rules and Regulations."

The most important document in the package was the assault plan that Perdue had sketched himself, based on what he had learned from Captain Reid. The buildings in the police compound were diagramed with arrows showing the path that each Red Dog team would take.

The plan of attack had evolved considerably since Perdue had set this all in motion, from Grenada to assisting the Dominica Defence Force to the current scenario, in which the mercenaries themselves would have to initiate the coup because of the imprisonment of the DDF commanders.

The police station was the only place Perdue expected any resistance, which is why the main objective of the invasion was to "compromise and neutralize" the compound. Perdue knew the guns were all kept in the police armory, but he also knew, from all the reconnaissance that he and Yanover and the others had been doing for the past two years, that there were only two armed guards on duty at night. The assault plan called for the mercenaries to "neutralize" them.

Perdue placed fourteen copies of the Operation Red Dog packages in his black briefcase, along with his contract. Once they were at sea, he would hand them out and assign each man to an attack team.

The phone rang in Perdue's room. It was Charles Yanover calling from Toronto. He assured Perdue that all was well at his end and wished them luck.

BOB PRICHARD LAY ON HIS MOTEL BED, wondering what the hell he had gotten himself into. It had all sounded good over the phone, but he wasn't so sure after spending time with Perdue.

When he was a kid growing up in Chicago, Prichard had spent his winter nights at an ice rink down the road from his house. He'd lace up his skates at home and slip-slide down the hard-packed snow to the park, where sometimes twenty kids would be playing hockey on the outdoor ice. There were no referees. Everyone just knew the rules. That's what this mercenary job had seemed like at first. Perdue never explained exactly what was going on; everyone just assumed they knew and played along. But now Prichard realized he didn't really have the full picture. He was not impressed with Perdue's planning. He was starting to wonder whether the guy had any military experience at all.

"There's something about that guy that's not right."

21

An aerial photo of the location chosen for the arrests

Baton Rouge, Louisiana
April 27, 1981

THE DAYS INN HAD THREE WINGS that enclosed a courtyard with lounge chairs, patio umbrellas and a big outdoor swimming pool. Mike Perdue was the first to wake. He went downstairs to the pool to take in the morning sun. The air was already steamy and it was only going to get hotter in the weeks to come. If the coup went as planned, he would not be setting foot on American soil again for some time. He might never come back. He was leading his men into danger and uncertainty but he had been doing that for a long time, ever since he was a teenager climbing through the shattered windows of strangers' houses to help himself to their treasures.

Bob Prichard joined him at the pool and they swapped war stories about Vietnam for a while. Prichard was suspicious. He'd done a tough tour of Vietnam. He knew what it was like, and some of the things Perdue said about his combat experience didn't ring true. Perdue said he had fought in the Tet Offensive that began in January of 1968, but at other times he said he hadn't joined the Marines until April 1968. The mercenaries were supposed to leave that night and Prichard still knew very little about what they would be doing. He pressed Perdue for more details about Operation Red Dog, but the Texan was vague.

"We'll have a briefing once we're on the boat," he said.

Even on the day they were to ship out, there was so much secrecy. Larry Jacklin took it in stride, thinking it was a necessary precaution against infiltration by communist spies.

George Malvaney wandered out to the pool and sat with Perdue. He too wanted to know what to expect in the coming weeks. He was worried. He didn't want to step into the middle of a civil war. Perdue assured him they would just be helping out the Dominica Defence Force.

The mercenaries were in no rush. They did not have to be at the rendezvous point until after dark, and Fort Pike was less than two hours from the motel by car. One by one, they emerged from their rooms to drink coffee and eat their last restaurant breakfast for weeks. Someone had the latest *Soldier of Fortune*. There was an article from the frontlines of Afghanistan, where *mujahedin* "freedom fighters" were sticking it to the Soviet Red Army. The magazine was filled with ads for guns, knives, Special Forces Mountain Boots, nunchukas, the Commando Wallet, holsters, berets, books with titles like *Nuclear War Survival* and a T-shirt with a logo that said: "Mercenaries do it for profit." The best ads were in the back pages, the classifieds where private soldiers offered their skills with notices like these:

> *Merc for hire. Anything, anywhere, price is right. 10 years military, 'Nam 66–67, 70–71. Expert small arms, light weapons, demo, ambushes, military intell. Contact Bob.*

> *Merc for hire. All offers considered. Send to M.T.S., P.O. Box 28.*

> *Over/Covert. Local, national, international assignments accepted. Three man team, individuals.*

> *For Hire, Vet, 'Nam 66-67-68, 5'8", 150 lbs., 35 … High risk, ok.*

Wolfgang Droege, Don Black and Mike Norris took the Chevy into town to buy more ammunition. Perdue gave Danny Hawkins and George Malvaney some money and sent them to Radio Shack to buy new walkie-talkies. The ones Perdue had brought from Houston weren't working too well.

When everyone returned with their supplies in mid-afternoon, Perdue gave one of the walkie-talkies to Norris and had him walk around the motel to test out their range. They drank a few beers, went to Droege's room to talk strategy and then crashed for a few hours.

AT 6 P.M., THEY PILED INTO their two vehicles. Wolfgang, George Malvaney and Bill Waldrop were in the Ford van. Danny Hawkins was at the wheel. The rest were in Perdue's car. Perdue was wearing jeans and a green shirt with epaulets on the shoulders. He wore tennis shoes and had brought a straw hat to shade his balding head from the Caribbean sun. For the night of the invasion, he had packed a stylish black beret.

As he drove southeast along I-10, retracing the route he had taken the night before, Perdue briefed his passengers.

"Now," Perdue said, "there's a Russian nuclear submarine base on the north sector of the island. There's no ordinance there. When we secure the government there in Roseau, we're to take some of Patrick John's militia and work to neutralize that base with extreme prejudice."

"That's going to cause an international incident," Anderson interjected.

"That's the orders," said Perdue.

Perdue explained that they were going to rendezvous at Fort Pike and get into vans that would take them to the ship. He didn't foresee any trouble but said that, if any "Barney Fife" should come along, "don't worry about it. I'll take care of him." Anderson got the message; Barney Fife was the bumbling sheriff on *The Andy Griffith Show*.

Anderson thought the plan was reckless. "Who in their right mind is going to get into the back of an enclosed van with a bunch of other mercs and be transported? You can't see what's going on or anything," he said.

Anderson was about ready to bail out. "I had considered taking my bag and hitchhiking out because the setup, it was funky," he said. "He didn't have it together right. When he told everybody how we were going to get on board the boat, I was ready to walk away."

They stopped for coffee at a restaurant in New Orleans, killing time so they'd arrive right at ten o'clock. Anderson thought he spotted an unmarked police car and said so, but Perdue said it was just an ordinary car with a CB radio antennae. When a second identical vehicle came up behind them, Anderson really started to panic. "I knew they was cops of some kind," he said.

He had never been in a situation like this. He tried to think of some way to extract himself from the others and get away, but he remembered what Perdue had said in the briefing at the motel, that anyone who left would be taken care of. Anderson felt particularly vulnerable because he didn't have a gun. He was convinced that if he tried to run, Perdue would shoot him to protect the operation. "I figured, what the hell," Anderson says. "If I'd have had a personal weapon, I would have bailed."

HIGHWAY 90 PASSES the auto shops and boat yards northeast of New Orleans, then hops over the Intracoastal Waterway onto the slim strip of land that separates Lake Pontchartrain from Lake St. Catherine. Egrets wade along the shore among the docked fishing boats whose tow nets are hung up to dry after a day out chasing the shrimp that Louisianans boil, fry, stew, stuff and toss into gumbos and jambalayas.

Just before the narrow bridge to Slidell, a canon at the side of the road marks the entrance to Fort Pike State Park. The old citadel was built shortly after the War of 1812 to defend New Orleans from a naval attack. It served as a staging area during the Seminole Wars and a stopover for troops on their way to the Mexican Wars. The Union forces occupied it during the Civil War. More than a century later it was about to see action again, this time as a jumping off point for the invasion of Dominica.

Special Agents John Osburg and Lloyd Grafton arrived at Fort Pike at 9:30 p.m. They came in separate vehicles, a U.S. Customs van that was to transport the guns and a Jartran moving truck to carry the mercenaries. Both agents had Nagra tape recorders beneath their shirts. A third ATF agent, Robert Rowe, had joined them, posing as one of Captain Howell's crew.

Out on Lake Pontchartrain, the *Manana* lay at anchor, seemingly waiting for the pick up, although in truth Osburg had filled the ship with cold drinks and told federal agents to keep Captain Mike Howell away from the arrest. The last thing he wanted was for the mercenaries to shoot their way onto the ship and slip out into the Gulf.

Osburg had taken one more precaution: he had jammed the passenger door of the van so it wouldn't open. Anyone who wanted in or out of the vehicle had to go through the driver's side door.

The park looked deserted. It wasn't. Behind a picnic shelter, the ATF electronics man, Nick Fratta, was hiding in a surveillance vehicle with a low-light camera, although it wasn't picking up much of anything because it was so dark. Beside him, three FBI special agents and a customs officer were hunkered inside a trailer. Two more FBI agents were hiding behind a bulwark, and the state police were floating just offshore in a patrol boat. Everyone was linked by radio.

MIKE PERDUE DROPPED Bob Prichard at the side of the road outside Fort Pike and handed him a walkie-talkie.

"If there's any cars coming like they're going to turn in here, let me know," he said.

Larry Jacklin heard the comment and thought, "even the local police don't know what we're doing." It only reinforced his belief that this was a covert operation sanctioned by the highest levels of the U.S. government. "If the CIA is going to do anything, or the State Department, they're not going to tell the New Orleans Police Department and private detectives and other small people like that," he reasoned. "Military security is on a need-to-know basis. If somebody doesn't need to know something, he don't tell them."

At 10:10 p.m., Perdue turned his Impala into the parking lot, followed a few minutes later by the Ford van driven by Danny Hawkins. Perdue parked on one side of the Jartran truck, and Hawkins parked on the opposite side.

The men got out and Osburg laid down the rules: once they were aboard the *Mañana*, they were to follow the captain's orders. If the Coast

Guard approached the ship, they were to dump everything overboard. It was another of Osburg's head games, getting the suspects to focus on the future so they would take their minds off their surroundings and the task at hand.

They all went to work unloading the gear from the Chevy and the Ford and putting everything into Osburg's van. The undercover agents were awed by the stockpile of military hardware they saw coming out of the vehicles: ammunition crates, bandoleers, rubber rafts, water jugs, fatigues, first aid kits, PR-6 walkie-talkies, shotguns, rifles. Hawkins reached into his van and took out a black AR-180, which he handed to Osburg, along with someone's luggage.

Some of the guns were in packing boxes but others were loose. There were twenty sticks of dynamite in an ammunition box labeled Federal Cartridges, and a grocery bag containing a tear gas hand grenade. There were safety fuses and blasting caps wrapped in paper napkins. There was a cardboard box in Christmas wrapping paper that held ten electric blasting caps. Busting Patrick John out of prison was not going to be a problem.

The men worked in complete darkness, bumping each other as they passed the guns and explosives from hand to hand. "It was such a circus," Grafton says. At one point, Osburg collided with Don Black, who had a shotgun in one hand and a box in the other. Grafton joked that they needed a stoplight. It took ten minutes to load it all up.

When they were done, the van was stuffed full of guns, ammo, suitcases, gym bags, foam mattresses, canteens, camouflage, flashlights, rubber rafts, paddles and bottles of Jack Daniels. There was a lot of firepower in there: ten 12-gauge shotguns (one J.S. Higgins, one Stevens, three Remingtons and the remainder Smith & Wesson Model 916-As); a Ruger .223 Model Mini 14; a Browning .243 with field-scope; a Plainfield M-1 Paratrooper; a Remington 30.06; a Sterling AR-180; and eight Gwinn Bushmaster rifles.

Osburg told Perdue to put his men in the back of the delivery truck for the ride to the marina.

"I have a man out on the road I've got to pick up," Perdue said.

"Okay, we'll get him on the way."

Hawkins, Black, Norris, Droege, Jacklin, Anderson, Malvaney and Waldrop got into the cargo hold of the truck. The agents closed the door and locked it.

So far so good. Eight of the ten suspects were now confined. Whether they were unarmed was another matter; the ATF agents did not know whether the men were carrying handguns.

They were. Between them, they had nine: a Harrington & Richardson .38; an Astra 9 mm; a Browning 9 mm; a Smith & Wesson .44; three Colt .45s; a Detonics .45; a Llama .45 and a .38 Special, six-shot Detective Model.

Agent Osburg told Perdue to ride with him in the front seat of the van. Perdue tried to get in, but the door wouldn't open, the result of Osburg's handiwork, so Perdue climbed in through the driver's door. Osburg knew he had Perdue now. He couldn't get out of the van without first getting past Osburg.

There was only one man left to get—Prichard.

Osburg backed up the van and pulled out onto the highway. Agents Grafton and Rowe followed in the truck.

Perdue pointed to a spot beside the road and said Bob Prichard was there somewhere. Osburg stopped. Sure enough, Prichard came out of the bushes with a walkie-talkie in his hand and a Colt pistol in his back pocket. Osburg yelled out the window for him to get into the truck and Prichard climbed in next to Grafton.

"Did you see anything?" Grafton asked.

Bob said he hadn't.

The two vehicles headed slowly north over the Rigolets Bridge and turned right into the Harbor Inn Marina. Like Fort Pike, the marina was crawling with law enforcement agents. Osburg was not taking any chances.

Even on the night the mercenaries were scheduled to embark on their mission, Osburg had no idea who they were, aside from Mike Perdue himself. All the agents knew was that this was serious. Ten mercenaries might not seem like much, but they had firepower and Dominica was a small, poorly defended country. They just might pull it off.

There were eight arrest teams, each consisting of two officers, hiding behind two trailers. Three more arrest teams were over by the boat shed. Altogether, there were eight ATF agents, ten from the FBI, eight State Police, seven Customs agents and one member of the Slidell Police Department. A U.S. Coast Guard vessel was docked nearby.

Osburg backed the truck towards the bay, where the *Mañana* was supposed to be waiting to take them to Dominica. He stopped and climbed out.

Mike Perdue followed him out the driver's side door, which is when Osburg broke the news to him. He was under arrest.

Perdue's jaw dropped. He couldn't believe it.

In the other vehicle, Prichard saw Agent Grafton reach under his seat and pull out a handgun. Prichard didn't hesitate. He grabbed the .38 from his waistband and pointed it at someone's head — he doesn't recall whose it was.

"Don't shoot, federal agent."

"What kind of federal agent?" Prichard asked.

"Bureau of Alcohol, Tobacco and Firearms."

"Oh, shit."

Prichard handed his gun to the agent and was immediately tackled by a team of officers. "I never seen so many guns pointed at me in my life," Prichard said. And this from a veteran wounded three times in Vietnam. "I didn't know they had that many federal agents in Louisiana."

A spotlight lit up the two vehicles.

"This is the FBI!" said a voice coming through a bullhorn. "Come out of the van one at a time. No resistance will be tolerated."

Wolfgang was locked in the back of the truck. The doubts he'd wrestled since meeting the agents aboard the *Mañana* the night before suddenly came together into a blindingly obvious conclusion, but he did not get emotional.

"So what are you going to do?" he said. "That's what I said to myself," he reflected later in an interview. "You know as far as I was concerned I hadn't broken any laws. I hadn't done anything really illegal. And I said to myself, so what? So now I'm going to have to spend some time in jail, but so what. What's the big deal about it?"

The arrest teams brought the men out of the truck one by one, laid them on the ground and cuffed their hands behind their backs. Danny Joe Hawkins had been dodging the FBI for almost two decades, throughout the Klan bombing campaign that terrorized Mississippi in the 1960s. Federal agents had targeted him again and again, but they had never been able to put him away. Now they had him.

"You are not going to Dominica!" the bullhorn voice said. "You are going to jail!"

Mike Perdue's two years of fundraising, reconnaissance, recruiting and arms purchases had come to an inglorious end in a parking lot 2,000 miles from Dominica. All the meetings, all the miles, all the planning had brought him nothing but a pair of handcuffs. How could this be happening? Where had he gone wrong? Who had ratted him out?

"We were totally shocked when we were arrested in our own country," Black says. "In fact, when it happened, we thought that the government had its signals crossed. We thought that somebody else, some local agency, had decided we were violating the law and they were going to arrest us. We couldn't believe that we were actually going to be in trouble here. "It was just a total shock to us."

Special Agent Lloyd Grafton laid the guns on wooden tables in the ATF office, along with the boxes of ammunition and walkie-talkies. He draped Prichard's Nazi flag in the background, and propped the seized copies of *Soldier of Fortune*, *Special Weapons* and *National Vanguard* against it, along with Perdue's handcuffs, dark shades and black beret.

A nice display for the cameras.

John Osburg picked up one of Perdue's shotguns and posed in front of the spoils of his undercover work. Captain Mike Howell came by the office to see the arsenal and had his photo taken beside the evidence as well. Someone even had T-shirts printed up that said, *Bayou of Pigs, 4-27-81.*

They could hardly believe these guys had walked into the trap.

"You know," Osburg said to Grafton, "if you were going to get a bunch of mercenaries to try to go attack a country and overthrow the legitimate regime of the country, you sure as hell wouldn't want this bunch of knuckleheads to do it."

Bob Prichard was thinking pretty much the same thing. "It was an exercise in stupidity. The worst part was, I was stupid enough to go along with it."

That night in the parish jail, Perdue reassured the others. "Let me take care of things," he said. "I'll try to get the best deal possible for us."

The arrest was about the closest thing to a slam dunk the ATF could have hoped for. Perdue's briefcase was a treasure trove—his contract, the Operation Red Dog assault plan and an address book that contained the names and addresses of Patrick John, the Dominica Labour Party, Algie Maffei and all the rest of them.

Letters of commendation began to arrive on Osburg's desk from the ATF, U.S. Treasury, State Department and Osburg's SAC, Michael Hall.

Prime Minister Charles has asked the Department of State to express her deep appreciation for the law enforcement activities of U.S. agencies, said a telex from the American Embassy in Barbados.

ATF Director G.R. Dickerson wrote a personal note to Agent Osburg, praising his professionalism and calling his undercover work exemplary.

> *Your professional undercover investigative ability and perseverance exhibited in conducting this successful investigation was exemplary. Such performance and cooperation is a personal credit to you and reflects on the Bureau as a whole.*

Captain Mike Howell got a letter of thanks from the Director of the FBI, William H. Webster.

In the afterglow of the arrests, there was good reason to celebrate. The mercenaries were locked up and investigators in three countries were on the trail of those who had helped them. Federal agencies in the United States, Dominica and Canada thought it was over, that the coup d'état to oust Eugenia Charles was dead.

They were wrong.

Part III

Soldiers of Misfortune

Wherever and whenever mercenaries are detected working the wars, the debate begins anew: are those guys legal?

—Manual of the Mercenary Soldier

22

Mike Perdue outside the New Orleans courthouse, April 28, 1981

New Orleans, Louisiana
April 28, 1981

SHERIFFS ESCORTED THE MERCENARIES to court the morning after the arrests. They arrived in white passenger vans. Mike Perdue stepped out, his wrists and ankles in shackles. His shirtsleeves were rolled up to the elbow and the name of his new home was stenciled on the left knee of his pants: Orleans Parish Prison.

News photographers were waiting to capture the strange scene: ten men in chains and prison uniforms looking disoriented and confused. Wolfgang was laughing but Perdue looked grim, like he still couldn't believe this was happening. As he walked to the courthouse, Perdue held his cuffed hands at his waist. He said nothing, but made a gesture of defiance: the middle finger of his right hand was extended in a salute to the world.

Inside the courtroom, Perdue asked the judge for leniency, pointing out that he was a veteran of the U.S. Marine Corps. The judge was unmoved and set bail at $500,000. A preliminary hearing was scheduled for the following week.

The press had a field day. *The International Herald Tribune* called it a "comic book invasion." The headline in the *Los Angeles Times* described it as "a tragicomedy of errors." *Time* called it "a sitcom version of *The Dogs of War*, after rewrites by V.S. Naipaul and Woody Allen."

In Dominica, *The New Chronicle* said the plot was "an unpardonable crime against the people of Dominica." It said, "Certain powerful and well-heeled persons in the United States ... are being linked with the coup attempt ... Reports filtering in paint a picture of high finance, deals and the burning ambition of certain North American nationals to turn Dominica into a crooks' paradise."

The newspaper called Patrick John a "ruthless criminal despot": "Patrick John, in his greed for power and in his insane ambition to want to govern even after he and his party have been completely rejected by the electorate, was prepared to plot with some of the basest societies on this planet—the Ku Klux Klan and the Nazi Party."

Captain Mike Howell appeared as a guest on a New Orleans television talk show. "If a book was written about this," the host asked, "would it be fiction or non-fiction?"

"It would *sound* fictional, but it would be real," Howell replied. "I don't think you could make up a story as interesting as this is."

The only news outlet that wasn't having fun with the story was CFTR in Toronto. Gord Sivell had been in the newsroom when news of the arrests came in on the wires. He rushed to see his producer. They had lost their scoop. Before long, the Toronto press began reporting that the station had known about the plot for months but had decided to sit on it in the hopes of getting an exclusive. "If we'd gone to the police, we'd have had to work alongside them and then we wouldn't have had the story," the station's news director explained in the *Globe and Mail*.

The issue went all the way to the House of Commons. Liberal Member of Parliament Charles Caccia stood in the House and said CFTR had known about the mercenary plot since October "but did not inform any authorities." "Since there seems to be a trend toward manipulated, sensational reporting these days," Caccia said, "will the minister direct the CRTC [Canadian Radio Telecommunications Commission] to determine whether such so-called 'investigative reporting' is consistent with the commission's regulations? In addition, will the minister ask the Canadian Broadcasters Association to carry out its own inquiry on whether the conduct of CFTR radio station meets the association's professional standards?"

Communications Minister Francis Fox replied that he had asked his officials "to examine the facts of the matter which have been brought to my attention by the honorable member for Davenport. At present I have only initial advice which I am asking my officials to pursue because the matter does not really come within the pervue of the Broadcasting Act. I will, of course, be pleased to draw the whole matter to the attention of the Chairman of the CRTC and also to the president of the Association of Broadcasters."

The politicians did not know Sivell had indeed informed the police about the plot, but he had done it behind his boss's back and the damage was done. He had become part of the story. The station was worried it might lose its broadcast license. Sivell decided to quit. "I suppose [the producer] figured I violated my journalistic principles by telling the OPP," he said.

He had infiltrated a mercenary cell, an unprecedented feat of investigative journalism. Before it all went bad, he thought he might be sitting on a Pulitzer Prize winner. Instead he was left feeling bitter and betrayed, and jobless.

THE CRIMINAL INVESTIGATION went into high gear following the arrests. In Houston, police searched Perdue's house and found a cache of guns buried in the yard. The FBI started profiling the mercenaries, and the ATF headquarters sent a bulletin to all stations that pointed out the obvious national and international implications of the arrests, and urged ...

> ... *further coordination and rapid ATF investigation of new leads being developed.*
>
> *During the next phase of this investigation, a number of high priority collateral investigations will be directed to various parts of the country. In order to expeditiously provide the necessary background information for the proper development of leads, written collateral requests*

will be preceded by telephone contact with effected district offices. These requests for assistance will be given the highest priority possible.

The first thing Osburg needed to know was, "Who are these guys?" Until the takedown, the investigators had deliberately refrained from digging too deeply into Perdue's background. They didn't want to blow the undercover operation and they had not been able to identify them anyway. But now the ruse was over, there was nothing holding them back. The investigators began to "unravel this thing," said the FBI's Edmund Pistey, "find out who they are and what they were doing."

The men locked up at the Orleans Parish Prison ranged in age from twenty-one to forty-one. The youngest, Malvaney and Norris, lived at home with their parents. The eldest was an ex-cop. Five had military training but none seemed to really fit the mercenary profile.

If there was a common denominator, it was the Klan. They weren't all Klansmen, but nine of the ten were somehow associated with white power groups—Droege, Black and Hawkins in particular. It was not a Klan operation, and the motives seemed monetary rather than political, but the recruits had clearly been drawn from the militant fringe of the extreme racist right. During the interviews conducted after his arrest, Perdue said he was "not a member of any white extremist organization and states he only used members of such groups because they were easily recruited," the FBI wrote. There is nothing in the Bureau's files to suggest the coup was a Klan conspiracy. The investigation pointed to financial motives, that "Perdue's expedition may have been part of a larger scheme aimed at acquiring control through the establishment of a friendly government of a Caribbean island which would host operations such as gambling, narcotics and the laundering of monies, as well as the possible creation of financial institutions whose protected records could conceal a wide range of illegal activities." Osburg felt strongly about one thing: these ten guys could not have done this by themselves. No way. Somebody had to be helping them, and he wanted their names.

THE U.S. ATTORNEY'S OFFICE presented its case to a Grand Jury, and on May 7 the foreman, Marion Bloomer, signed a bill indicting all ten men for mounting an illegal expedition against a friendly nation. Six more charges were on the indictment, including exporting firearms without a permit, using explosives to commit a felony and illegally transporting explosives. The indictment said Perdue, Droege and the others "did willfully, unlawfully and knowingly combine, conspire, confederate and agree together" to invade Dominica, "an independent foreign nation with whom the United States is at peace." The mercenaries returned to court for their arraignment on May 13. They were dressed in jeans and T-shirts except Black, who wore a navy suit. All of them entered the same plea: not guilty.

Under U.S. law, there was a thin line between what Mike Perdue did and what hundreds of Cuban exiles did in 1961 when they landed at Bay of Pigs, Cuba to overthrow Fidel Castro. U.S. neutrality laws prohibit "a group organized as a military expedition departing from the United States to take action as a military force against a nation with whom the United States is at peace," U.S. Attorney General Robert Kennedy wrote shortly after Bay of Pigs. "There are also provisions of early origin forbidding foreign states to recruit mercenaries in this country."

It may not have been the clearest of distinctions, but Perdue was on the wrong side of it and he knew it. At the same time, this was about more than the law. Mike Perdue had stumbled into one of the oldest debates in history: when is it right to invade another land? Coming six years after the fall of Saigon, Dominica raised the moral question at the heart of Vietnam, and the wars that were to come in America's future. Catholic thinkers had come up with a set of principles for the use of foreign military intervention. For a war to be just, they argued, there must be a just cause, such as stopping gross human rights violations. Also, war can only be a last resort, and there has to be a reasonable chance of success. Civilians cannot be targeted and war can be waged only by a legitimate authority—individuals and groups cannot take it upon themselves. Mike Perdue's war failed every single test on the checklist.

But for Perdue, this wasn't about morality. It was about numbers. How much money could he make? And after his arrest, it was still about numbers: should he plea bargain for a lesser sentence or risk spending a half-century behind bars? Perdue's lawyer worked out a deal with the prosecutors: he would plead to one count of violating the Neutrality Act and give his total cooperation with the investigation and testify at all pending or future judicial proceedings. In return, six of the seven charges on the indictment would be dropped. He would face a maximum sentence of three years. Perdue took the deal.

That night, he gathered the mercenaries. They had a meeting in one of the rooms at the lock-up. He told them about his decision to plead guilty in exchange for three years, instead of the fifty he could have served if convicted on all counts. "He told us he had an ace in the hole," said Larry Jacklin, "and that he was going to leave us all sitting in the dust. He was going to take the deal and the hell with all the rest of us. He said that we could make up our minds what we wanted to do." Explained Perdue, "After I knew it was over, I tried to convince everyone else to cooperate." It was every man for himself. "The only concern I think they had was what their families may think," Droege said.

Anderson was the most distraught. He regretted ever answering Perdue's recruiting ad. "After we was all in jail, that's when I started to learn this other side of him, this bullshitter side. And hell, if that thing had actually went down, I think he'd a been on his knees begging. At the first firefight, I think he'd a fell apart." The youngster Malvaney put it in perspective. "Well, you know Perdue promised us everything would be taken care of as far as food, shelter and housing and so on," he said. "I just didn't expect this kind of accommodations."

Perdue went to court on May 20 to enter his guilty plea. The whole thing took twenty-five minutes. Once the deal was signed, Special Agent Osburg had the U.S. Marshals escort Perdue to an interview room near his office. Osburg could have gone to the prison to talk to him. It would have been safer but he wasn't concerned about Perdue. "I sat down and talked to him. I felt he was holding stuff back and I told him that. I told his attorney that and I told the U.S. Attorney that he wasn't being truthful to us. He was hesitant about giving us all the information that we wanted. And then he'd give us a little more information but it wasn't sufficient. It was stuff we already knew. He didn't want to implicate anybody, he didn't want to tell us where he got the money or who were the other co-conspirators, how many times he traveled to different places. It's stuff that we had to determine ourselves from passport records from the government of Dominica, their airport log, as far as an individual entering or leaving the country."

Without Perdue's cooperation, the investigators had to do it the hard way. The ATF traced the guns and discovered that some of them had been stolen during a burglary in Mississippi. The investigators traced the money as well. On top of all the stupid mistakes Perdue had made during the planning of the coup, he'd blundered the money. The $9,800 worth of bills he gave Howell aboard the *Mañana* was still bundled in paper bank wrappers. The markings on the wrappers showed the money had been withdrawn from the Commercial Branch of the Deposit Guaranty National Bank in Jackson, Mississippi on April 22. The wrappers even identified the teller who had performed the transaction. Federal agents went to the bank and asked if anyone had withdrawn a large amount of cash in the past few days. It turned out someone had. The teller recalled that L.E. Matthews had cashed a check for $5,000. Armed with the evidence, Osburg asked Perdue once again about his financiers, and this time Perdue acknowledged that L.E. Matthews had given him $5,000 the night before the arrests.

Osburg interviewed Perdue a half-dozen times in May. It was always the same. Perdue wasn't willing to provide a full confession. Osburg got so frustrated he went to the U.S. Attorney's office and suggested they take the plea bargain off the table. He thought they should charge Perdue not only with the Neutrality Act violations, but a lot more offences as well. Maybe when he realized he was looking at spending the rest of his life in a federal prison, he'd be more forthcoming. The prosecutor said no. They had already worked out deals with some of the other mercenaries and all of them got the same offer: one count, three years. Perdue seemed content to do his time rather than to give up his backers.

SPECIAL AGENT CURTIS D. WILLIAMS, an ATF explosives expert, inventoried everything seized on the night of the arrests, then released it all to a technician at the Louisiana State Police explosives unit in Baton

Rouge. Williams also sent a sample of the explosives to a lab in Atlanta for chemical analysis. They tried tracing it, but there was no manufacturing code that would lead them to its source. It was a dead end.

Osburg brought Perdue in again for questioning. "Where'd you get the explosives? Who gave you the dynamite?"

Perdue said it had just turned up in his car. He had no idea where it came from.

"You don't go to a location and all of a sudden there's explosives in your car and you don't know who put the explosives in there," Osburg shot back.

Perdue talked some, but he never gave up enough to allow prosecutors to add charges or conspirators to the indictment. Osburg reconciled himself to the situation. "It's like anything else," he says, "you can't expect too much out of some of these things."

Droege decided to plead guilty as well. He, too, began to cooperate with the ATF and the prosecution prepared him to testify at the trial. Again, Osburg conducted the interrogations. Droege didn't like him. "I felt that I was being intimidated into making false statements towards and against my codefendants," Droege would later complain in a letter to the judge. He said that Osburg, "by innuendo and obliqueness of words implied that I had better go into the court room and tell the truth."

BY JUNE, SEVEN OF THE TEN mercenaries had entered guilty pleas. Explained Droege, "My lawyer said, 'When the captain leaves the ship, you better follow.'"

At the sentencing hearing, Perdue asked the judge to go easy on the others. "These people have never done any harm to the United States," he said. "I hope you will use the same compassion in their sentencing as I would on any prisoner I would have taken."

Judge Lansing Mitchell was unmoved. He opined to the others, "The very fact that you would be willing to follow Perdue into this country, to take over this country and necessarily kill and enslave its inhabitants makes the claims of fighting communism unbelievable."

Perdue, Droege and Waldrop got three years. Everyone else got the same sentence, although Malvaney and Jacklin were sent to a program for young offenders and Prichard, who said he hadn't been right since Vietnam, was sent for psychiatric evaluation. "If the Army ruined your life and messed you up, I want to know about it," the judge said.

Anderson broke down in court, weeping that his wife had left him and his father had suffered a heart attack. "I've learned one thing," he said. "A mercenary's life isn't ever fit for me." The judge paroled him immediately.

Only Black, Hawkins and Norris stuck with their "not guilty" pleas. They were going to take their chances in court.

Don Black held an hour-long press conference on the eve of the trial. After six weeks in custody, he had been released on a $100,000 bond posted by two friends in Birmingham. He told reporters the Klan had played no part in the operation, but he admitted he and the others had been on their way to Dominica when they were arrested.

"It's always been something I've wanted to do," he said. He said they were only helping out the Dominican military. "We were military advisors and our purpose was to stabilize and secure the island against communists," he said. "It was not a crime against the American people and we feel we violated no federal laws."

A jury would have the last word about that.

On the eve of the trial, Judge Mitchell struck several proposed witnesses from the subpoena list, including Republican Congressman Ron Paul. The judge cleared him of any involvement and refused to call him as a witness.

SPECIAL AGENT OSBURG SAT DOWN on June 11 and wrote a long report to his superiors. He summarized his interviews with the defendants and the results of the investigations in the United States, Canada and Dominica. The report was the first detailed account of the plot, and named many of those suspected of having been involved, most of whom had not yet been indicted.

He wrote:

> From those which have been interviewed, evidence has
> been received against the three which are going on trial and

evidence has also been received implicating numerous other individuals in the United States, Canada and Dominica. ATF in New Orleans is cooperating with authorities from Canada and Dominica and future indictments are anticipated in those countries and the United States....

The United States Attorney's Office, Eastern District of Louisiana, New Orleans, Louisiana, is looking favorably upon the indictment of Tommy Thompson (Las Vegas), James White (currently living near Baton Rouge, Louisiana), L.E. Matthews (Jackson, Mississippi), the following on the Republic of Dominica: Patrick John, former Prime Minister; Julian David, head of broadcasting for the Dominica Labour Party; Fred Newton, head of the Dominica Defence Force; Walter Reed, second in command of Dominica Defence Force; Ronnie Roberts, corporal in the Dominica Defence Force; Dennis Joseph, associated with the Labour Party and former minister of broadcasting; Marion McGuire (Canadian citizen), and Roger Dermée. All of those to be indicted on Dominica, except Dermée, are currently imprisoned on the island. Those in Canada to be indicted are: Chuck Yanover (Canadian citizen); James McQuirter, Gord Seville or Sevill ... and possibly Don Andrews and Aarne Polli.

The Assistant U.S. Attorney handling the Bayou of Pigs investigation is reluctant to indict those in a foreign country until that country makes a prosecutive decision. If charges are brought against the Canadian citizens and those in Dominica's jails then they may be unindicted co-conspirators in the United States. Additional information is being gathered towards the possible indictment of David Duke, a New Orleans native and former leader of the KKK.

Agent Osburg typed out ten pages. He flagged the report "Sensitive," signed it and sent it up the chain of command to his superiors. The trial was scheduled to begin in New Orleans in four days.

23

Steve Hammond (in the foreground, before his sex change) at the home of Don Andrews (second from right)

Roseau, Dominica
May 1981

"ALEX IS DEAD. COME HOME AT ONCE."

The woman working at the telegram office in Dominica had no idea what the message meant. All she knew was that it had been sent from Canada and was to be delivered to a guest at the Anchorage Hotel. It was just the latest cryptic telegram that had come in for the same woman, Marion McGuire. Something wasn't right. The prime minister had told Dominicans to be on the alert. She decided to call the police.

Inspector Gene Pastaina of the Special Branch and two other police officers dropped by the hotel to talk to the pretty Canadian with the Irish accent who was receiving these odd-sounding communications.

He was already watching her. A tip that came through diplomatic channels alerted the Dominicans to her possible links to the mercenary plot and Inspector Pastaina began tailing her.

He found that she worked as a nurse in the psychiatric wing at Princess Margaret Hospital in Roseau, earning $600 Eastern Caribbean dollars a month. She had also found her way into the island's circle of political elites. One night, Inspector Pastaina followed her to a party at the home of the former interim prime minister, Oliver Seraphin.

"Shit, she's going to parties now," the inspector said.

Inspector Pastaina was a tall, no-nonsense cop with a bad knee—he wrecked it chasing Dreads through the mountains. He had joined the police force twelve years earlier and rose quickly through the ranks, but he was subjected to steady abuse from fellow officers because of his formal education. In 1981, he found himself in Dominica's "miniature MI-5," the Special Branch.

Two days after the arrests in New Orleans, Inspector Pastaina went to the Anchorage Hotel to search McGuire's room. He found some curious electrical appliances but they turned out to be nothing more than hair curlers. He took McGuire into custody and put her through the wringer. If he didn't slap her, he certainly scared her. But he felt that whatever he did was justified by the circumstances. The country was on the brink of a civil war and foreign invasion.

McGuire broke down and told him everything. She was taken to police headquarters and held in a section of the barracks reserved for female officers, but sometimes at night they would take her out and buy her drinks.

The Dominicans notified the FBI about the Canadian who was "an associate of Perdue" and "possibly in Dominica on behalf of Perdue and his planned expedition against Dominica." Two special agents flew to Dominica and sat in during an interview with McGuire. "The interview was useful and productive," the FBI office in San Juan wrote later. "However, results do not identify other Dominicans that may be involved in, or financial backers of, the attempted expedition against the Republic of Dominica."

STEVE HAMMOND WAS FLOORED when he heard Marion had been arrested. Just a few weeks earlier, he had spent a pleasant evening with her in Toronto, drinking beer and talking. Hammond made his living installing peepholes in apartment doors and painting houses. He was part of the circle that revolved around Don Andrews and Wolfgang Droege and lived in one of Andrews' rooming houses. A former British soldier, who had spent six months in the Royal Army Medical Corps until 1972, he sometimes wore a camouflage combat jacket. "He was a tough guy," Andrews says.

Hammond had been part of the early discussions about invading Grenada but the first he heard of Dominica was when it hit the Toronto newspapers, which is also how he found out that McGuire was in on it and had been caught. He realized she was in deep trouble. And he knew why. Her struggle with alcohol was well known, and it bothered him that Droege had used her like that.

He felt he should do something to help get her out of there. At the time, he was painting a house near the intersection of Yonge Street and Eglinton Avenue in Toronto. He was almost finished and then he would have a $1,000 paycheck. He had no responsibilities. He had a Canadian passport—not his; it belonged to another one of Andrews' tenants, Harold Woods.

"Should I go?"

He realized it was crazy. Dominica had just thwarted a coup d'état, backed by foreign mercenaries. Two of those mercenaries were Canadians and Hammond knew them both. How was he going to fly in there and rescue Marion? But then he thought, "What if she is only under house arrest, maybe at a hotel?" If so, he could help her escape, steal a speed boat and take her to Martinique during the night. When the police found her gone, they would search Dominica, not the neighboring islands. He had grown up around boats; he'd row if he had to. But what if she's in a fortified prison? He'd have to think of something.

"You're alive and young and needed," he told himself. "Don't be a coward."

That night he sat in Don Andrews' kitchen and announced he was flying to Dominica to rescue Marion McGuire.

Andrews thought he was nuts.

Hammond put the last touches of paint on the house the next day and went downtown to buy a plane ticket. Andrews advised him to pose as a tourist, so the two of them drove to the Canadian Tire store to buy a snorkel and mask and some camping gear he might need for his rescue mission.

"He was going to be a one-man commando," Andrews says.

The plane stopped in Antigua and while he waited for his next flight, Hammond strolled to a park. It was hot and the air smelled of sweet blossoms. He heard a bulletin crackling over a transistor radio and asked what was going on. "The Pope has been shot," the man told him.

The plane stopped in Guadeloupe and he thought, "I could get off here," but he chided himself and he was soon in Dominica, where he presented the Canadian passport that identified him as Harold Phillip Woods.

"Hotel," he told the taxi driver.

"Which one?"

"I don't know."

The cabbie dropped him at a small guesthouse and he got a room on the second floor. There was no glass in the windows, just wooden slats, but the sheets were clean. He went out to walk the streets but he felt watched. He realized it was because he was the only white man in sight. He walked past the small bars, afraid to go inside and was on his way back to his hotel when he passed a building with high walls—the police headquarters.

He asked about McGuire at a restaurant in the morning and found out she was detained at the police building he had seen the night before, so he went back for another look. If it had seemed imposing in the darkness, by daylight it resembled a fortress. This was not going to be so easy. He walked the perimeter, peering in the windows and whistling a song McGuire would recognize, hoping she might clue in and respond.

Nothing. "What now?" he asked himself.

He could pretend to be her lawyer and demand to see her, but he knew it would take a police officer about ten minutes to figure out he was a fake. A better plan might be to say he was her friend and that they had the same landlord. It was the truth, even if it wasn't the whole truth. He didn't have to tell them he knew the mercenaries and had come to the island intending to break McGuire out of jail. The problem was, what was Marion going to say when the police told her she had a visitor named Harold Woods? He wasn't Harold Woods. Marion knew him as Steve. There was always the chance that, in the confusion over his identity, he'd be exposed as a liar. There was another problem. Hammond knew Wolfgang Droege personally, and despite being no part of his mercenary plan in Dominica, he might be looked upon with suspicion. He feared he would bear the brunt of Dominican anger. Droege was out of reach in the United States but Hammond was right there.

He ate a lunch of chicken and fries, and thought through his dilemma over coffee and cigarettes. "I decided under no circumstances would I admit to having ever met Wolfgang," Hammond says. He went to the front counter at the police station and introduced himself as Harry Woods of Toronto. He was a friend of Marion McGuire's and he was concerned for her well-being and wanted to see her, he said. Within minutes, a couple of officers appeared and took him upstairs to meet Commissioner Oliver Phillip and Assistant Superintendent Desmond Blanchard, the head of Special Branch.

They threw questions at him relentlessly. Why was he here? How did he know McGuire? How did he know about Dominica? Did he know any of the other mercenaries? Where was he staying? He spent two hours with them. They made it clear there was no way he was ever going to see McGuire. Hammond wasn't angry. "She was known to be party to a bunch of armed-to-the-teeth mercenaries who planned to invade their country." Who could blame them?

It was late in the afternoon when the police officers let him go and he returned to his hotel and changed his clothes before heading out on the town. He watched some kids playing basketball and walked out to the jetty, where three boys threw stones at him and taunted him, shouting "whitey" before running off. At twilight, a hand reached out and grabbed his wrist. It was a woman. She was slim, in her thirties and she was smiling at him. Hammond was not a looker. He was a skinny kid with a bad complexion. When she asked him to take her home, he said "Sure," and they took a bus to Mahaut. She lived in a wooden shack and they picked up some beer at a bar and lay on the bed while the local children banged on the floorboards underneath them. She told him her husband had died four months ago, and he said, "Oh shit. I'll bet these villagers are not pleased." Dawn broke and he took the bus back to his hotel. The proprietor said the police were looking for him. He tipped her, checked out and went to the office of the attorney general. If the police weren't going to let him see McGuire, he would go over their heads.

Government House was two blocks from police headquarters. It was the tallest building in the capital and probably Roseau's most modern structure. Dominica is that rare kind of country where you can just walk into the offices of senior government officials and actually have a shot at speaking with them. Hammond went to the attorney general's office but was told he was not present. As he was leaving the secretary said, "The deputy prime minister is in." He climbed the stairs and followed a corridor until he saw Brian Alleyne standing at his door. They shook hands and sat down, Alleyne behind his desk, Hammond facing him.

Alleyne asked Hammond what he wanted.

"I want to see Marion McGuire," Hammond replied.

The moment Hammond mentioned her name, he noticed a change in the deputy's mood. The pleasantries were over. Alleyne stood up shouting, and Hammond followed suit. Hammond realized what was going on. The Dominicans thought he was a Wolfganger.

"Get off this island today," Alleyne said.

"Release McGuire," Hammond replied, "or you are gone in the next twelve months."

Of all the things Hammond could have said, of all the charming, disarming words he might have spoken, of all the innocent-sounding explanations he might have offered to ease the minds of the Dominican authorities, besieged as they were by both internal revolt and foreign mercenaries, these may have been the absolutely dumbest eleven words he could have possibly uttered.

"He told me basically that this woman was his friend, that if I didn't release her, he would have me killed," Alleyne recalled in an interview. "I called the police, threw him out of my office and that was basically it." Alleyne had been at an international conference in Geneva a few weeks earlier when an American diplomat had pulled him aside and told him that mercenaries had tried to invade the island. "You couldn't be talking about Dominica," Alleyne replied. Only when he saw the newspaper headlines did it sink in. "In so many ways that whole situation was incredible," said Alleyne, who later became Acting Chief Justice of the Eastern Caribbean Supreme Court. "It was almost like a Rambo movie."

Alleyne was still raging over the threat when Hammond slipped out the door, flew down the stairs and headed for the hills. He was on an island, and there was no escape but he thought he could at least hide until things settled down. He stopped at a service station and bought cigarettes and a gallon of gas. He says the fuel was to help start campfires. The dwellings soon disappeared as he walked, following the Roseau Valley as it climbed from the coast. He heard the rev of engines and darted into the jungle. He panicked when he remembered the island's healthy population of snakes, notably the Boa Constrictor. He calmed himself with a cigarette before carrying on. He followed the road, but whenever he heard vehicles coming he ducked into the bush and yanked off his red ball cap. He had been walking for hours when he came to a pool in the river. He stripped naked and plunged into the cool mountain water. Drying on the rocks, he pondered his next move.

"What, really, am I running from? The reason to go to Dominica was to help McGuire, not run in the hills."

Flipping through a travel brochure, he saw that he was only about a mile from a restaurant. It wasn't hard to find. He ordered coffee and sat on the terrace with the owner, an American woman. He confided in her and decided to return to Roseau to brave things out. Before he left, he mentioned he had brought a gallon of gas. He said he would leave it for her, since he no longer had any use for it. A pickup loaded with farm laborers gave him a ride into the city. After he was gone, the restaurant owner called the police and reported the odd visitor with the gas canister. The police thought he was planning a bombing.

Hammond was walking to his hotel when a jeep slammed on its brakes beside him and two police officers jumped out, pointed a gun at him and told him to raise his hands. They cuffed him and put him in the jeep and drove back to police headquarters, passing through the gates into the courtyard. A group of men who had been sitting at tables outside the canteen stood and started screaming when they saw him. All they knew was he was a foreigner, and foreigners had tried to attack their headquarters. The officers led Hammond upstairs to a room on the second floor and took his passport. The questions came in rapid fire. Where had he been the night before? Why had he gone to government headquarters?

The interrogators left him alone and he thought, "This is bad." He also thought their angst was understandable. There was a state of emergency. A coup had been uncovered, involving an invasion by mercenaries aimed at toppling the government of Dominica. And the only suspected conspirators they could get their hands on were Marion McGuire and now Hammond. "I quite understood at that moment, as I do today, how they most dearly wanted to pay retribution to the conspirators," he says. "Now they had me."

Ten minutes passed. The policemen returned and escorted him up another flight of stairs and down a hallway. A door opened to his left and there, accompanied by a female officer, was the woman he had come to rescue. Neither he nor Marion said a word. Hammond was led into a room. A couple of police officers were waiting for him. The windows were open.

"Woods," one of the officers said, "what are you doing on this island?" They were still unaware of his true identity.

He told them he had come to help his friend.

A hard blow landed on the side of his head. "Tell the truth," the officer said.

Again, he was struck on the head. He got out of his seat and moved out of reach of the officer but he was quickly grabbed and felt himself being dragged towards an open window.

They pushed him out the window head first. He felt himself flying but then something caught. Someone was holding his ankles. He dangled upside down over the courtyard, above the men in the canteen, who resumed their taunts. They were on their feet again, shouting. "If they drop me," he thought, "those guys will finish me off like a pack of animals."

But they didn't drop him. They just held him there and then hauled him back into the interview room. Assistant Superintendent Blanchard denied that Hammond was beaten, although he allowed he "was not always around. For some months after disclosure of the conspiracy, tensions ran high in Roseau, and the police were obviously not insulated from it. As for being roughed up, I think the guy's ego may have been bruised, perhaps open insults, jeering, no more. He seemed such a misfit, not in the least bit offensive; he would hardly have been regarded as a really serious physical threat." The police officers took Hammond downstairs through the courtyard, where the men at the canteen erupted yet again, and into the reception area. The inspector opened a door and showed him a cell with a wooden bench.

"Woods, you are lucky," he said. "This is normally where we do interrogations."

They sat him on a plastic chair and when he asked to use the toilet an officer took him outside and across the courtyard. As soon as he got near the canteen, the men who had been sitting there jeering ran over and kicked him to the ground. Now Hammond was really scared. He was waiting in an office, unsure what was coming next, when he saw a razor blade. He grabbed it and slashed his left wrist. He was taken to the hospital and bandaged but the wounds were superficial and he was soon back at police headquarters. A female police officer asked to see his wound. When he pulled back the bandage to show her, she dug her finger into the cut and the pain exploded.

AT 5 P.M., THE POLICE TOOK Hammond by jeep to Stock Farm Prison. He was processed and placed in a cell. Inside, there was a small plastic bucket, a barred window and a muscular Rastafarian named Charlie Brown. Despite his menacing look, Chuck turned out to be timid and kept to himself. He had been arrested for stealing a pair of shoes. The conditions were harsh. The prisoners slept on the concrete floor, with one sheet. Breakfast was green tea and a bread roll. A guard came by to spray down the inmates with a garden hose. That was their shower.

On Monday morning, the police brought Hammond back to the police station and told him he was being deported. They were just waiting for a judge's order. He would be on the 4 p.m. flight that day. But the case on the court docket before his dragged on, and by the time he got before the judge it was 3 p.m. and there was no time to make it across the island to the airport so they told him to be ready to leave at 3 a.m. He spent the night at the police station but nobody returned to get him until 11 a.m., when the inspector took him to the interrogation room for more questioning.

What was his name? Where did he live? The police seemed to have figured out he was not Harold Woods and that he was somehow connected to Droege. The address Hammond had provided did not match anyone named Woods. Commissioner Phillip asked the Canadian police to check into his identity. While that happened,

Hammond was sent back to the prison. A guard fawned over his watch so he swapped it for six packs of cigarettes. It occurred to Hammond that there were only thirty or so other prisoners. Why so few on an island of 80,000? His question was answered after ten days when he was taken to another cell block. Until then he had only been in the temporary remand block.

They all called him Harry. He spent his days reading detective novels he got from the prison library and playing soccer, using a plastic bag stuffed with newspapers as a ball. He did pushups and stretches, and stood watching the lithe young inmates exercising. "Such athletic beauty," he thought, "natural and muscular." In the evenings, the prisoners turned their plastic buckets upside down and pounded them like drums while singing reggae and calypso songs.

EVERY WEDNESDAY, THE POLICE brought Hammond to court, where the magistrate would order him back to prison. It was so hot, he shed his clothes and made a loincloth out of his bed sheet. The mosquitoes were ravenous at night, but the inmates would light twisted coils of toilet paper to keep them away. One day a cook said Patrick John was in the adjacent cell block.

His first visitor was the Canadian high commissioner to Barbados, who was also responsible for Dominica. Hammond told him his real name, hoping it might speed things up. Upon learning that Hammond was actually from England, the high commissioner alerted his British counterpart, who came by later, bringing fruit, cookies and magazines. He promised to return for the trial.

On July 16, Hammond got to court at 2 p.m. The judge told him he had been charged with threatening the life of the deputy prime minister. He pleaded guilty and was sentenced to three months, although he would be out after two, since he was credited with a month for the time he had already served awaiting trial.

THREE WEEKS BEFORE his release date, Hammond asked to see Marion McGuire. The warden said he would think about it. A few days later, Hammond was escorted to the reception area and told he could see her for fifteen minutes.

"No touching," the guard said.

He was taken to a small room with a table and two chairs. He sat and a guard brought in McGuire.

"Hello, you wanker," she said.

She was tanned and her eyes sparkled. She told him she was due in court in a few months. He felt bad knowing he would be out of the country long before she even saw a judge.

On September 15, the police brought Hammond to the police station and put him on the morning flight out.

He was free.

During the stopover in Antigua, the local police chief told him he never wanted to see Hammond on the island again. At 9 p.m., he boarded the flight to London. It was over. Once he was back in Britain, he called Don Andrews and told him what had happened. Hammond realized how foolish he'd been to think he could walk into Dominica and commit a jailbreak. His poor judgment had cost him four months in prison but his experience with the Dominicans left him with no doubt that had Mike Perdue and Wolfgang Droege made it to the island they would have paid an even heavier price. "I believe had they invaded," he says, "none of them would have left Dominica alive."

24

John Osburg with the guns seized from the mercenaries

New Orleans, Louisiana
June 15, 1981

THE TRIAL BEGAN AWKWARDLY.

The attorneys defending Don Black, Danny Hawkins and Mike Norris thought their clients were doomed if the jury found out the mercenary plot was linked to the Ku Klux Klan. The judge agreed with their reasoning and ordered that the Klan was not to be mentioned in the courtroom.

There was just one problem: David Duke. His name was sure to surface in the testimony. Duke was the first person Mike Perdue had approached with his idea of invading Grenada, and it was Duke who had suggested bringing in the Canadians. The mercenaries had hired their ship through a contact they met at a party with Duke. Judge Lansing L. Mitchell decided to confront the issue at the outset by polling the jurors to find out whether they recognized Duke's name and associated him with the KKK.

"Aside from anything you may have heard in connection with this case, do you recognize the name David Duke?" he asked the jury. "Just hold up your hand if you recognize the name David Duke."

Almost all the jurors' hands went up. The defense lawyers were not happy. They approached the bench to talk it over with the judge, and as they did, they thought they saw a conspiracy afoot in the jury pool.

"The black man in the front row of the jury box is making faces to other black jurors to tell them to stay on the panel," David Craig complained.

"He can't make faces. How?" the judge replied. "He's talking to them?"

"He's doing it," Craig insisted.

The man in question, Charles Simmons, Juror Number 4, was asked to step up to the bench, but he denied he had been up to anything. The judge sent the jurors into the hall. He decided to summon them into the court one at a time to ask what they knew about Duke. Sure, they might recognize the name, but did they know he had been the leader of the KKK?

First up was Abraham Abadie. "With what or with whom do you associate Mr. Duke?" the judge asked.

He did not hesitate. "With the Knights of the Ku Klux Klan."

The defense lawyers asked for a mistrial but the judge said no. The prospective jurors were all brought in to face the same question, and with rare exception, they all knew Duke had been a Klan boss. But the judge also asked them whether that would influence their verdict and they all said it would not, except for one woman who said, "I would have to be truthful; I think it would." She was sent home.

That would be the last mention of the Klan for the duration of the trial. This was to be a case where certain things would not be said, where there would be references to "organizations" but not their names, where witnesses would talk about the flags they had packed for the mission, without daring to say what provocative emblems were on those flags. Whenever the prosecution danced too close to a Klan link, the defense would object and ask for a mistrial. The jurors would have to fill in the blanks on their own. It would be like reading a novel that had key pages torn out of it.

THE 212TH CRIMINAL CASE to come before the U.S. District Court, Southern District of Louisiana, got underway the next day.

The first witness was a U.S. State Department officer named Richard D. Howard, who was Deputy Director of the Office of Caribbean Affairs in the Latin American Bureau. He testified that Prime Minister Eugenia Charles was on friendly terms with the United States and that she was not the kind of leader you could describe as a communist.

Mike Perdue was the star witness. His plea deal required him to testify, so he took the stand to help convict the only three men who had ignored his advice to admit guilt.

"What did you want to get out of this?" prosecutor Lindsay Larson asked him.

"Money," he replied.

"Did you do it for an ideological purpose?"

"I'm very anti-communist. It doesn't bother me kicking the communists out at all."

"But the main purpose was what?"

"Was financial."

Perdue named Charles Yanover and Don Andrews as members of the conspiracy. He named James McQuirter, Patrick John, Malcolm Reid, Fred Newton, Wolfgang, Jacklin and Roger Dermée. He also named Gord Sivell, but said he had nothing to do with the plot. "He was interested in the story, that's all."

Perdue spent the day walking the jury through the whole story, from the Grenada coup to Toronto, Las Vegas, the recruiting, fundraising, contracts, meeting Patrick John, the DDF and the Dreads. And the lies.

During the cross-examination, defense lawyer John Unsworth zeroed in on Perdue's weakness. He asked Perdue whether he had told those he approached to participate in the coup that he was a former U.S. Marine.

"Were you, in fact, an ex-Marine?" the lawyer asked.

"No, I'm not."

"Have you ever been in Vietnam?"

"No, I haven't."

Nor had he ever worked as a mercenary in Nicaragua, or Uruguay. He was a fraud.

The man who loved to tell stories about Vietnam and his mercenary campaigns was just a con man living out a soldier-of-fortune fantasy. The truth was not nearly as interesting as the lies he told. Perdue had enlisted in the Marine Corps on April 1, 1968. He was given the rank of Private, and service number 2371183. Two weeks later, he broke into a house on Old Hickory Lane and got arrested. Upon learning Perdue had been charged with petty larceny, the Marines dumped him. His service record shows he was discharged on May 21, 1968. His military career had lasted all of seven weeks.

Instead of going to basic training, he spent a year in Tennessee State Prison. He was released on probation a year later and got a job minding the patients at LaRue D. Carter Psychiatric Hospital. Next, he drove a truck but was laid off and moved to Houston. He spent six months looking for work before landing a job at a local psychiatric hospital, although he had no formal training as a mental health professional.

The Marines-mercenary routine was, he admitted, just "a fantasy of mine, yes, sir, a desire, yes, sir." Perdue said he told his recruits the story to "give them the impression that I had seen combat before to give confidence in my leadership ability."

Perdue was exposed as a fake. But that was not his only secret.

DANNY HAWKINS TESTIFIED that he thought the coup was a CIA operation. He talked about the cryptic hints that Perdue had muttered about the CIA and his "friends" in the State Department. Dominica was going communist and it was in the U.S. interest to make sure it didn't, Hawkins said. The red tide had to be stopped. This was the kind of thing the CIA did all the time, he added. How could he be faulted for helping his government protect America through covert ops?

"Now, sir," prosecutor Pauline Hardin asked. "You're a convicted felon right?"

"Yes."

"And you're a househusband?"

"Yes."

"You don't have any military experience, right?"

"No."

"Why would the CIA or the American government be recruiting you to go down and take over the government of Dominica in the Caribbean?"

"Do you have any idea the kind of people the CIA *do* recruit?" Hawkins replied.

"Do you?" Larson said.

"Yes, I do, lady."

"Have you ever talked to anybody in the CIA?"

"I sure have."

"Who?"

"I don't remember."

Hawkins said that every time the U.S. government tried to clean up the communists in its backyard, it failed. "And if they would have left us alone on this, we would have probably worked it out pretty good."

YOUNG AND CLEAN-CUT, Don Black stood out during the trial. He came to court in three-piece suits, while the others wore jeans. He was neatly groomed, good looking and charismatic compared to his unkempt co-accused. He was also the most educated of them all and began the trial representing himself.

"Ladies and gentleman of the jury, perhaps we were naïve in all of this," he said in his opening statement. "Perhaps we were stupid. Perhaps I was duped. It wouldn't have been the first time it's happened. But what we were doing was motivated by the highest principles, by patriotic motives. We thought we were doing what was in the best interest of the United States."

Before long, Black accepted the help of a public defender named Patrick McGinity. In his testimony, Black said all he had done was accept a job from the Dominica Defence Force, and there was nothing illegal about going abroad to work for another government. Patrick John had been deposed by riot, he said, and Eugenia Charles could hardly be called a legitimate leader since, he claimed, she had been elected by fewer than 500 voters, most of whom were illiterate. He thought the whole thing was completely legal and backed by the U.S. government.

"You don't think it's illegal to go break someone out of jail?" Larson asked.

"It was our understanding that we were going to work for the Dominica Defence Force. Any action they took would be theirs. We were working for them. It was one faction of the government and it certainly was not a violation of the United States law, in my opinion."

"You say that the Dominican government is an oppressive government that's communist-oriented? You still say that?" Larson asked.

"I believe it is, and I believe by this time next year it's going to be a full-fledged communist nation and you'll call that a legitimate government, too."

"You have a lot of strong beliefs, sir, I take it?"

"I certainly do."

Black was argumentative, and the judge had to repeatedly tell him and the prosecutor to cool it down. At one point, the judge told Black to try to keep his answers to a thousand words or less. He was a strong debater, a skill honed during years engaging his foes in the ring of racial politics. But he knew next to nothing about Dominica and it showed. For example, he thought the island was only forty miles from Grenada when in fact the distance between them is more than 200 miles.

"You've never been to Dominica?" the prosecutor asked him.

"No I haven't."

"You've communicated with the government down there?"

"No, I haven't."

"You've read a few *National Geographics* about it."

"I've read a number of publications about it."

"And based on that, you have made your determination that Dominica is ready to go communist ... Do you see communist boogeymen all over the world, Mr. Black?"

"I see one-third of the world controlled by communists, yes, sir. I consider that a very serious threat."

The prosecutors let Black wrap himself in the American flag, then they unleashed the hard questions. If he believed in the America ideal, that people have the right to choose their own government, why was he going to overthrow Dominica's democratically elected leader? If this expedition was above board, why was he leaving at night, without going through U.S. Customs, without a passport. For all his talk about his beliefs, Black was forced to admit he was low on money and he was going to get paid well for his part in deposing Eugenia Charles, at least $36,000 a year after three years.

"So the money played a pretty good part in this, didn't it?" the prosecutor asked.

"It certainly did. I had to be paid."

The parallels between Operation Red Dog and *The Dogs of War* did not escape the prosecution team, and Black had handed them a way of introducing the novel when, on the eve of the trial, he had talked about it with a reporter for his hometown newspaper.

"Do you remember telling the *Birmingham Post Herald*, 'I take a lot of risks?'" Assistant U.S. Attorney Larson asked.

"Yes, sir," Black responded.

"Mr. Black," Larson asked a few minutes later, "in that same article in the *Birmingham Post Herald*, did you not say, in speaking of this enterprise you engaged on, 'It's always been something I've wanted to do. Frederick Forsyth's novel *The Dogs of War*…'"

"Sir, that's an inaccurate quote."

"You said that *The Dogs of War*, about mercenaries and invasion, had not been the group's inspiration, but that book's plot and the plan, and our plan had striking similarities," Larson said. "Did you say that?"

"That's not the quote, no, sir, that's not an accurate quote."

"You didn't say that? What did you say about *The Dogs of War*?"

"I was asked about *The Dogs of War* and they said, 'Was this thing inspired by *The Dogs of War*?' And I said, 'Not to my knowledge.' Certainly there may have been some similarities."

"There may have been some similarity to *The Dogs of War*, the book you're talking about?"

"Yes, sir."

ON THE FINAL DAY OF THE TRIAL, prosecutor Pauline Hardin tried to shatter the defense of patriotism and focus on the money. This was all about greed, she said. These men were going to rape Dominica for profit. They were going to get rich by rounding up a lawfully elected government in the night and putting it on a plane, or worse.

"Who made them God?" she asked.

Mike Norris' lawyer, John Unsworth, begged the jury to go easy on his client, whom he described as a dumb farm boy conned into taking part. The whole thing was like *Fantasy Island*, the popular television show about a mysterious island where guests pay money to live out their dreams, he said. Mike Perdue was Mr. Roarke, the proprietor in the white suit played by Ricardo Montalban. Wolfgang Droege was Tattoo, the midget sidekick played on the show by Hervé Villechaize and whose cries of "De plane! De plane!" became the show's catchphrase.

"The island of Dominica was truly *Fantasy Island*. You've got Roarke and Tattoo. They're directing this whole thing."

Norris, he went on, was like one of the show's guests who fly to the island each week, but whose fantasies never turn out like they thought.

"I'm sure Mike Norris had this fantasy that he was going to go down there and fight communism and come back a hero. Well, what's happened? He's become an embarrassment to himself and his family because of all this, and it's a shame, because of a young man's foolishness, because of a young man's patriotic beliefs that were misused and used really against him."

Twenty-one years old, Norris was just a "naïve foolish kid" raised in Small Town USA, in the South, spawned on Fourth of July picnics, patriotic speeches, pro-American, arch-conservative, the lawyer continued. "He's already going to be labeled a fool for the rest of his life because of it. But the real tragedy would be if you, as members of this jury, would convict this man, this kid, and label him a criminal for the rest of his life."

If this was *The Dogs of War*, he added, Norris was a puppy.

Prosecutor Lindsay Larson got the last say.

The case had gone well for the state. But what did the jurors make of Perdue? The case rested partly on his testimony, and he had been revealed as a liar and a con, who had kept up a two-year ruse about being a veteran, mercenary and CIA operative.

"I'm sure Mr. Perdue would have liked to have been all of that," Larson said. "But you know poor souls who would like to be something and they're not, but they brag about it, and sometimes they get to believe this. Have you ever noticed—maybe you've done it yourself, I suppose, I've done it—sort of embellish an incident a little bit to make yourself seem a little better or a little nicer, or something, and you've said it so many times that you sort of believe it? I don't know if that's Perdue or not; I've never gotten inside his head."

The jury came back to court with their verdict on the morning of Saturday, June 20.

Norris was found not guilty.

Black and Hawkins were guilty.

"From talking to some of the jurors I got the impression that since Norris was the youngest of the defendants, they did not think he had either the sense or judgment to be involved in the operation," Osburg says. "Grafton and I lost no sleep over this verdict, as this may have been his first screw-up and put him on another path in life."

AS SOON AS THE COURT was adjourned, U.S. Marshals served Black, Hawkins and Norris with subpoenas ordering them to testify before a grand jury. The prosecutors were now going after the financiers of the operation. Before they agreed to testify, all three requested—and received—immunity. They could not be prosecuted for anything they told the grand jury.

Less than two months had passed since the bust at Fort Pike. Nine of the ten mercenaries had been convicted. But the investigators felt that Perdue and his men had gotten help. From the very beginning, they were getting advice and assistance and money from more powerful men, and the ATF wanted them. No less than forty names of possible co-conspirators had come up during the investigation, but the probe focused on the three Perdue identified as his money men.

The investigation determined that Perdue had received at least $75,000 from his backers. Perdue claimed that $10,000 of it came from Canada. The remaining $65,000 seemed to have come from the Memphis lawyer J.W. Kirkpatrick, the Klan bomb expert L.E. Matthews and James C. White.

During his interviews, Perdue talked about meeting Kirkpatrick in Memphis. He said he had explained "in detail" the plan to return Patrick John to power "by arranging a coup in Dominica," says an FBI memo. Perdue said Kirkpatrick had contributed $10,000. The FBI found Kirkpatrick and phoned him at his law office in the First Tennessee Bank Building on July 17 to arrange an interview. Kirkpatrick asked what it was about, and when the agent explained, "Kirkpatrick stated he cannot discuss Perdue, and the conversation was terminated," reads a memo written by the FBI office in Memphis. Four days later, the day after the jury found Black and Hawkins guilty, a Crittenden County Sheriff's Deputy found a car parked alongside Highway 149, nine miles north of Earl, Arkansas, near the Tennessee border. In the front seat, a body lay slumped, clutching a .410 shotgun.

It was Kirkpatrick. The Memphis lawyer had put the barrel of the rifle in his mouth and pulled the trigger. He left a note to his family. It made no mention of Dominica but his law partner, Max Lucas, said Kirkpatrick was distraught that his name had been linked to the invasion plot. "When he was contacted [by Perdue] and advised that the U.S. government supported and encouraged private contributions to prevent a communist takeover of Grenada, he donated money," Lucas was quoted as saying in the *Jackson Daily News.* "He forgot this effort until almost two years later when the man who contacted him testified that Mr. Kirkpatrick's money had been used to aid a planned invasion of Dominica." Why would a sixty-one-year-old man take his life if he was innocent? How could a prominent lawyer get duped by the likes of Mike Perdue? The answers to those questions died with Kirkpatrick. Lucas' explanation: "He preferred death to dishonour."

The remaining pair of suspected financiers went to trial in October. The indictment charged White, age thirty, with contributing $45,000 to the coup, and Matthews, age fifty-eight, with providing $13,000. Earl Jones, manager of the Commercial Branch of the Deposit Guaranty Bank in Jackson, and the head teller, Sherri Lambert, testified that Matthews had signed three checks that financed the coup. One of them was made out to Perdue and another to his roommate. Matthews cashed the last check himself, asking for the $5,000 to be paid out in

$100 bills, they said. Perdue testified that White and Matthews had provided the money for the coup, and that in exchange they were to get shares in Nortic Enterprises. "They were the bankrollers of the deal," Pauline Hardin said. "They weren't going to go down there and risk their necks. They were only interested in the money."

While the case revolved mostly around bank records, the prosecution also called Ronald Lynn Cox as a witness. Mike Perdue and Cox had lived together on and off for eleven years. Asked by the defense to describe their relationship, Perdue said they lived "as man and wife."

Perdue was out of the closet.

On the witness stand, Cox went on to claim that it was "sort of general knowledge" that White had also had a sexual relationship with a man. As the trial degenerated into stories about gay sexual liaisons, the judge hauled in the lawyers to say he had heard enough.

"I am surprised you are going into this on such flimsy evidence," the judge admonished the prosecutors. "It's almost like someone saying he swished through the courtroom and therefore he is a faggot."

The defense complained the case was straying into dangerous territory and the judge agreed the trial was at risk. In the trial of Black and Hawkins, the court was concerned the jury might convict on the basis of Klan ties. Now the concern was that White might not get a fair trial because of prejudice against gays. It was never established that White was homosexual, but the defense felt that Cox's testimony might be enough to sway a bigoted juror.

District Judge Jack M. Gordon instructed the jury to disregard anything Cox had said "pertaining to any sexual conduct or proclivity by defendant White." He then explained why "you have heard so much testimony about the sexual relationship that exists between Mr. Perdue, the witness, and Mr. Cox, the witness." Jurors, he explained, had to weigh the credibility of witnesses. In this case, they had to ask themselves whether Perdue and Cox might be lying to protect their relationship. "It looked like a scene from the *Three Stooges*," said Matthews' son, also named L.E. Matthews, who sat through the trial.

Agents Osburg and Grafton testified about the ATF undercover operation, in particular about the money that Perdue had paid for the boat and supplies. John Osburg explained how Perdue had given him $5,000 in $100 bills, four money orders totaling $600 and, just prior to the arrests, another $9,800 in cash. He said that Perdue had talked about his "backers" and "business manager," and that he had mentioned White, and that White's bank accounts "did reflect funds going from Mr. White to Mr. Perdue."

As for Matthews, Osburg explained how ATF officers had traced the wrappers on the bundles of $100 bills that Perdue had paid to hire the *Mañana* to the Deposit Guaranty National Bank in Jackson. Osburg said that in interrogations Perdue had implicated Matthews as a source of money. The prosecution introduced checks from Matthews Electric Company, one of them to Ron Cox.

It wasn't enough. The defense lawyers depicted Perdue as a chronic liar, and it worked. The jury found both men not guilty.

25

Major Fred Newton (center) in police custody

Roseau, Dominica
December 19, 1981

THE COUP BEGAN BEFORE DAWN. Armed with his .38 service revolver, Major Fred Newton led his men to police headquarters. Constable Mathias Alexander never had a chance. He was just a young man, with a three-year-old boy born on November 3, the day Dominica achieved its independence. As a tribute to the former prime minister, he had named his son Patrick John.

The gunmen opened fire before Constable Alexander could defend himself. He took a shotgun blast at close range—so close it burned his skin. The shell blew a two-inch hole in his gut and broke his spine. He fell to the floor and bled to death.

Upstairs in the Criminal Investigations Department office, Corporal Duke Severin and Corporal Casimir Joseph heard the gunfire but thought a careless officer had accidentally discharged his firearm. Then they heard more shooting and knew something was wrong.

Corporal Joseph ran downstairs towards the Charge Office to see what was going on, but he ran into one of the rebels and was felled by a gunshot. Corporal Severin headed upstairs for the telecom office on the third floor, where he found Constable George Challenger. They were at the window, looking down on the shooting, when they heard the door open and saw Fred Newton step in. "He leveled his weapon at Challenger," Severin says. "I heard a click." The gun had misfired. Newton turned and fled back down the stairs.

Bullets were flying everywhere. One of them hit Commissioner Oliver Phillip in the head as he was approaching the police station in his car, having been summoned from his sleep and told of the attack.

The long-awaited coup was finally underway. All was going as planned. A few more hours of fighting and it would be over. Major Newton and the Dominica Defence Force would control the police station, break Patrick John and Captain Reid out of prison, and then the island would be theirs.

SATURDAY IS MARKET DAY IN ROSEAU. The tables next to the river are piled high with bananas, coconuts, fish, goat, chicken and whatever else Dominicans have harvested during the week. The market opens early and it is not unusual to see traffic on the roads hours before daybreak, so even though the island remained tense following the coup attempts in March and April, the police would not have been suspicious of a few vans full of men moving across the city.

The Dominica Defence Force no longer existed, at least on paper. Prime Minister Charles had disbanded the militia. She had given it a chance to prove it could serve Dominicans responsibly, that it was more than just the private army of Patrick John, but it had failed the test and she had put it down, for the sake of the nation. The DDF commander, Major Newton, was placed under arrest but there wasn't enough evidence tying him to the mercenary plot and the public prosecutor let him go on October 16. Even if everyone knew he was involved, what danger did he pose? The DDF had been dismantled and its weapons were locked in the police armory. But the Defence Force was a brotherhood. It could not be done away with so easily. Two weeks after Newton was released, two former DDF soldiers came to see him. Howell Piper and Ronnie Roberts had both been held temporarily under emergency powers, but were set free like Newton.

"What we were doing about Marley?" Piper asked.

"The same procedure it took to get us out," Newton replied.

Piper said Ashton Benjamin had been working on a plan.

The plan was just the latest adaptation of Operation Red Dog: storm the police headquarters, raid the armory, free PJ and Marley Reid from prison and round up the cabinet. The only difference was they were going to have to do it without the American and Canadian mercenaries and their Bushmaster rifles, but the DDF soldiers still had a few guns they had stashed away before the police had come to collect them. Newton was still recuperating from his jail time. He had his freedom and he was enjoying it, but he also knew that his colonel, Patrick John, and his best friend and deputy, Malcolm Marley Reid, were still locked up. Major Newton took charge of the coup, but Piper and Benjamin played prominent roles. At least five other ex-DDF members were involved: Walton Phillips, Hilroy Garraway, Jones Sampson, Romaine Roberts and Garner Willis.

On the night of the assault, they all met at the Botanical Gardens, forty acres of lawns and manicured trees, shrubs and a cricket field, at least what remained after the hurricanes. It was secluded and the police station was just down the valley, a few minutes away by car. Garraway arrived in his van at 3 a.m. and Newton told him the plan. Garraway said he had to pick up his mother in Cockrane and take her to market.

"Which hell, mother," Newton responded. "Tomorrow the whole place will be under curfew."

Garraway drove Newton and Piper to the police station. When he heard gunfire in the charge office, Garraway returned to the Botanical Gardens to tell the rest of the rebels to come join the attack. The scene at police headquarters was surreal. The DDF soldiers went for the armory, but they could not break the lock. That gave the police time to organize a counter-attack. After getting over the initial surprise, the police began to fight back and reinforcements arrived from all over. When a few of the officers caught sight of Major Newton's boyish face, it only confirmed what everyone in the city had already surmised: the DDF was mounting its long-anticipated coup d'état to oust Eugenia Charles.

The gun battles were still raging when Newton and Piper commandeered a police jeep and made their way to the prison to free Patrick John and Marley. But the Special Branch had anticipated an attempted prison break, and had posted officers in the bushes. When Newton's jeep neared the prison gate, the officers stepped out and opened fire. Piper died on the spot. Newton fled, stashed his two guns under an acacia tree and went home. By daybreak, the police had the upper hand, although they had lost one officer and another six were wounded, including the commissioner, who was flown to Martinique for surgery and somehow survived his head wound.

Outnumbered and outgunned, the DDF retreated and scattered. The police went after them. Ashton Benjamin bolted but the police caught up with him and shot him dead on the street.

Eugenia Charles declared a state of emergency and went on the radio to appeal for calm.

"We wish to exhort you not to gather in crowds and to take no action which might hinder police in their endeavors to bring this grave situation to an end," she said.

Major Newton was arrested at 9 a.m. He and six others were charged with the murder of Constable Alexander and causing grievous bodily harm to Commissioner Phillip, Corporal Stephen Anselm and constables Stephen Pascal, Glenis Popo and Campbell Esprit. Newton was charged with two additional counts, causing grievous bodily harm to Corporal Joseph and attempting to discharge a loaded firearm at Constable Challenger.

The FBI field office in San Juan asked the U.S. Embassy in Barbados to find out if American mercenaries or arms were involved, but the New Orleans field office reported back that Perdue's men were all locked up. "It would appear that this coup attempt is local (Dominican) in nature and does not involve United States citizens," said the FBI teletype.

All those arrested on the morning of the coup were convicted except Ronnie Roberts. The only evidence placing him at the scene came from a police officer who thought he had heard his voice. The Court of Appeal of the Eastern Caribbean States upheld the convictions. All six were sentenced to death.

Dominica had dodged yet another coup attempt. "Skeptics may snigger at the mention of divine intervention, but that is their folly," read the editorial in the next edition of *The New Chronicle*. "There can be no other possible explanations for the many times that this country has been delivered from the evil intent of certain persons."

THE BROWN WOODEN DOORS of the High Court of Justice face the sun-speckled Caribbean Sea. It is a solid two-level building, made of heavy stone. The hurricane winds that pound Dominica can collapse houses and wipe out whole plantations, but the tradesmen who built this rectangular fortress made sure that no storm could ever interfere with the administration of justice.

The most sensational trial in Dominica's history began on May 12, 1982. Patrick John, Julian David, Dennis Joseph and Malcolm Reid were up on two charges: conspiracy to overthrow the government by force and conspiracy to assault police officers. All four pleaded not guilty. His Lordship Horace Mitchell warned the nine jurors at the outset that they should not allow their politics to influence their verdict. Prosecutor Lloyd Barnett opened by appealing to the jurors' sense of national pride. Only months after Dominicans had chosen their first government since independence, a plot had been hatched, in cooperation with foreign mercenaries, to overthrow it by force, he said.

"Now Mr. Foreman and Members of the Jury," he said, "if you conceive of the idea of taking action involving the overthrow of a lawfully constituted government of a country, you do not seek to enlist the support of scout masters, you seek to enlist the support of disgruntled persons, soldiers, or you seek to enlist the support of foreign adventurers, and you seek to enlist the support of those who by their criminal conduct appear to you to be likely to lend assistance in a scheme of that type."

Barnett was preparing the jury for his star witness.

ALGIE MAFFEI WAS the one conspirator who had managed to escape arrest. He was studying in Guyana when the arrests began and he had not returned to Dominica since. Assistant Superintendent Desmond Blanchard of the Dominica Police knew Algie was involved. It just isn't that easy to keep a conspiracy secret. Word eventually gets out. Blanchard also knew that Algie was in Guyana and got in touch with him. "He wanted my story," Algie said in an interview, "to hear the story directly from me." It was a sensitive matter for the Guyanese. Dominica was accusing them of harboring a felon. There were rumors Algie was living at a military camp. Algie refused to talk to Blanchard.

He didn't know what to do. He was a wanted man. He had a murder investigation hanging over his head and his name had turned up in Mike Perdue's address book. His college course in Guyana was finishing. He was going to have to leave. He flew to Barbados and lived on a ship in Bridgetown harbor for ten days before catching a flight home. Desmond Blanchard was waiting. They went straight to police headquarters to talk. Algie said he would cooperate with the police investigation under one condition—he wanted his wife and three children protected. Eugenia Charles talked to the Canadian High Commissioner in Barbados and arranged to send Maffei's family to Canada for a while. "I was living in fear for my children and my wife," he said. "Anyone could attack them because I was a witness for the Crown." The Dominica police paid their airfares to Montreal and sent a monthly check to Mrs. Maffei. The instructions came right from the prime minister. The money came from the government's consolidated revenue.

Two months later, the Director of Public Prosecutions signed a brief letter: *By virtue of the powers vested in me under Section 72(2) of the Commonwealth of Dominica Constitution Orders 1978, I hereby discontinue the Criminal proceedings instituted by the Police against the above-named defendants.* The murder charges that had been stalking Maffei and Leroy Etienne for the past two years were dropped.

Algie took the witness stand on the second day of the trial. He told the jury about the meetings with Captain Reid, the contract that Patrick John had given him to take to Antigua, the negotiations with Mike Perdue and the discussions about the Black Revolutionary Council. He answered questions for hours, interrupted only by the judge, who periodically stopped the proceedings to say that he would not tolerate sloppy dress in his courtroom.

"Persons who come into court should be properly attired," he said. "We don't really want people coming into court with shirt tails over their pants. That person who came in just now, let him go outside and put his shirt in his pants."

The defense lawyers attacked Algie's credibility. They portrayed him as a criminal, a Dread, and not the type of person the jury should believe. They went over his rap sheet in excruciating detail, and noted that his murder charge had been dropped shortly after he had agreed to testify.

223

"I am putting it to you that you are a man of violent character; you are a violent person," said lawyer Berthan Macaulay.

"It's true," Maffei responded.

Algie was asked, "What is a Dread?"

"A Dread is one that carries hair, dread locks and have certain habits which is different from society's."

"Are you a Dread?"

"I used to be part of the cult."

The judge interrupted as a police officer was taking the stand. "Would you put your shirt in your pants?" he said. "It shows how slack, with all due respect, policemen are."

JOHN OSBURG AND LLOYD GRAFTON were asked to testify against Patrick John. It was a struggle convincing their boss to let them go; he seemed to think they were going to spend two weeks tanning on the beach. Osburg suspected his boss wanted the assignment himself. The supervisor eventually relented.

"Don't bring your guns down there," he told them.

The supervisor drove them to the airport. "Did you bring your guns?" he asked.

"Damn right I brought my gun," Osburg said.

The Dominican police posted a guard outside their hotel. Noticing he was armed with nothing but a miniature pistol, Osburg handed the sentry his Magnum.

"Just don't play with it," Osburg said.

The ATF agents took all their evidence with them, all the rifles and shotguns. The trial in New Orleans was over, and the courts had rejected an appeal filed by Don Black, so it was just taking up space in the evidence room. Osburg thought he might as well bring it to Dominica.

The ATF office manager wanted it all back, but when the Dominican police asked what they were going to do with the guns after the trial, Osburg said, "Keep them." That was justice. The guns that Mike Perdue had bought to attack the island would now help defend it.

An FBI agent had accompanied them to the island. In a memo, he wrote that the Dominicans were friendly and had thanked the United

States for thwarting the coup. "The country, devastated by hurricane[s] and actively courted by Cuba in the form of free university scholarships for their high school graduates, is desperately poor but struggling hard to avoid the fate of Grenada to the south (now a virtual Cuban satellite). They are very politically aware but were much more pro American than had been expected by members of the delegation."

Osburg's testimony was crucial for the prosecution because it backed up what Algie Maffei had said and linked the DDF with foreign mercenaries. He went through the undercover operation and what it had discovered about Perdue's plan to invade the island. He talked about the maps and diagrams that Perdue had showed him.

"He stated that their main objective on the island was to attack the jail and police facility, to free Patrick John, the ex-prime minister and his men," Osburg testified.

"Yes, anything further?" asked the prosecutor.

"That he had a contract with Patrick John to supply arms, ammunition, men and military equipment in their attempt to over-throw the government of Dominica."

In addition to the guns, Osburg had brought along the documents found in Perdue's briefcase, including the contracts, the letter of intent signed by Patrick John and a handwritten note that appeared to be a legend to a diagram of the police station. The deputy clerk of the U.S. District Court in New Orleans, Theophille Duroncellet, testified that the papers had been part of the evidence at Perdue's trial.

Special Agent Grafton gave a detailed list of the weapons that Perdue purchased for the assault. He told the jury Perdue was going to land north of the capital and that he was to be rewarded with a position in the Dominican government. "He advised us that he had people on the island that were going to assist him."

Dominica is a small island, the kind of place where everyone knows everyone else. Inspector Gene Pastaina, the Special Branch officer who had arrested Marion McGuire, had worked with Malcolm Reid for years. The police and the DDF had not always been enemies. They had worked together, and that is how Pastaina knew Reid. The inspector thought he knew Reid so well that he swore he could recognize his handwriting, so he was called as a witness. He said he believed Reid had penned the letter that the police had intercepted in March, the one that urged Fred Newton to call Mike Perdue about the "strike" at the police station. He also said the note found in Perdue's briefcase that described the buildings in the police compound was written in Reid's handwriting.

On day eight of the trial, the jurors returned to the courtroom at 9:40 a.m. The judge explained that, at the request of the defense lawyers, he had determined that the evidence was unreliable. He instructed the jurors to find all four men not guilty on all counts.

"How say you," the deputy registrar asked the jurors, "is the prisoner Patrick John guilty, or not guilty, on the first count?"

"Guilty," the jury foreman replied.

The deputy registrar repeated the question and again the answer was, "Guilty."

"You have to return a verdict of not guilty," the judge interjected.

"Not guilty," the jury foreman said.

Patrick John, Julian David, Dennis Joseph and Malcolm Reid were discharged.

"I was amazed," Algie said.

After all he had gone through to testify, all the stress and the taunts, the judge had thrown out the case. Nobody believed him. "The mistake I made was going to Antigua without a camera," he said.

The director of public prosecutions filed a notice of appeal that same day, and the case went before the Court of Appeal of Eastern Caribbean States, which ruled on December 7, 1982. The judges agreed that there was no evidence linking Joseph to the conspiracy. But they said that, in the cases of John, Reid and David, the judge had made a mistake and that the case should have been left to the jury. The trial was going to have to take place all over again.

WHILE HE WAS OUT ON BAIL, Patrick John ran in the 1985 elections as the Dominica Labour Party candidate for St. Joseph. He won. On the eve of the re-trial, he told a gathering of Labour Party supporters he was certain he would be found guilty. "I know I will go to jail not because there will be evidence against me but [because] the Freedom Party members of the jury will be sleeping through the trial and then find me guilty," he said.

Algie testified all over again at the second trial.

This time, all three of the accused made statements. Julian David said he had nothing to do with the coup and that his dealings with Mike Perdue concerned the sale of onions and potatoes.

Malcolm Reid explained his trip to Antigua by claiming he was on a business trip when he ran into Algie at the airport. He said Algie introduced him to Perdue, whom he described as a scoundrel and a scamp.

"When Maffei introduced me to Perdue and the discussions which followed, I realized that these two men were up to nothing good," he said. "In fact, they attempted to use me to meet their own ends. They tried to give me a job and to effect this, they made certain real fanciful promises, childish, wild promises. From the discussion, I formed the opinion that these two had made certain promises to bigger people and that if those promises were not kept, if they did not perform, they would be in serious trouble. I got sick. In fact, I really got afraid and I will venture to say [it was] from the fear of the position I found myself in."

Patrick John gave a masterful address that made it seem he had been framed by his political opponents. He was prime ministerial in his choice of words, reminding the jurors he had led the delegation to London that had won Dominica its independence and its own system of justice. He believed in that system, so why would he subvert it with armed force?

Then he invoked the crucifixion: "It was only two thousand years ago when evidence of untruths and half truths, evidence contrived for obvious reasons and designed and created by persons with special interests, was given against a man who was charged with conspiracy to overthrow a government and install himself as king, and the court then condemned [him] and found an innocent man guilty. They raised and praised and claimed a murderer, Barrabas, and set him free, giving him all he desired, and up to today, descendents are living with their consciences. I am not guilty and I am totally and completely innocent of any charge."

The judge warned the jury that Algie's testimony had to be treated with caution. He was, after all, an accomplice, and his murder case had been dropped shortly after he had agreed to help convict Patrick John.

"He is here maybe to save his own neck," the judge said, "so proceed with caution, members of the jury. The law says it is a dangerous thing to accept his evidence without corroboration but you can do so if you feel, having seen and heard him, that he is speaking the truth."

He described Algie as a violent revolutionary, but added, "if you want someone to assist you in a revolution, what type of person would you look for?"

The jury convicted all three of them.

John's lawyer asked the court for mercy for his client, describing him as a man who had "fallen from great heights." He talked about his "indescribable suffering," his "humiliation of regret, sorrow, embarrassment and shame."

Reid's lawyer said his client was a poor man, the sole breadwinner for his two children. "Reid regrets," he said.

John and Reid were sentenced to twelve years' imprisonment. Julian David got five. An appeal court upheld the verdict and the sentences, although the judges noted that, "David appears to have been very fortunate."

26

Released from prision in 1983, Mike Perdue was soon arrested again and gave his occupation as: mercenary.

Toronto, Canada
September 1982

DON ANDREWS WAS a little worried when he got a call from the police. He had nothing to do with the Dominica coup, but he thought his contact with Mike Perdue, his visit to the island and his involvement in the early stages, when Grenada was the target, might get him in trouble. The Ontario Provincial Police gave him a choice: take a lie detector test or they would charge him as an accessory in the Dominica affair. "After consulting with my lawyer, I took the test," Andrews says. He went to OPP headquarters on Lakeshore Boulevard in downtown Toronto. It was the first time Andrews had been wired up to a polygraph machine, but he felt alright about it because in his mind he was innocent.

The questions were easy at first.

"How old are you?"

"Thirty-nine," he answered.

"What's your name?"

From time to time, out of nowhere, the officer would throw a tough question at him, to measure his body's reaction.

"Did you finance the takeover of Dominica?"

"No!"

Afterwards, Andrews waited in the cafeteria to see how he'd done. Three hours went by before the police constable emerged with the results.

"You passed," the constable told him. "Just."

THE DOMINICA COUP INVESTIGATION became a top priority for Canadian police following the arrests in New Orleans. The government was worried about the way the Canadian Mafia and Klan had apparently worked together on the plot. The prospect of an alliance that combined the cold brutality of the mob with the zeal of the right-wing extremist movement was disturbing, to say the least.

"The fact that organized crime might feel the Klan is a fertile ground for recruiting people they feel may assist them in their criminal activity is a matter of concern," Attorney General Roy McMurtry told reporters.

McMurtry had good reason to go after the Klan. The last time police had targeted the far right, in 1977, he had received a letter from David Duke warning of "grave consequences" unless he backed off. McMurtry kept the letter. He framed it and hung it on his office wall. "I was kind of proud of it," he says. "To me it was a large compliment to be threatened by the Ku Klux Klan."

Soon after the plot was thwarted by the ATF, the government of Canada suddenly came to the realization that it had no laws that dealt specifically with mercenary crimes. Douglas Fisher, a member of Parliament in the Liberal government of Prime Minister Pierre Elliott Trudeau, stood in the House of Commons to point out that "Canada lacks any legislative instrument comparable to the United States Neutrality Act designed to outlaw such plots and actions."

He tabled a motion in Parliament saying:

> That this House urges the government to bring forward legislation to prevent mercenary armies and other private citizens from using Canada as a safe haven from which they can launch armed activities against legitimate foreign governments.

MP Stanley Hudecki seconded the motion but it never went anywhere. The only charge police could lay against the likes of McQuirter and Yanover—if it came to that—was conspiracy.

James McQuirter behaved as if he was untouchable. He was so sure he would not be charged that he talked openly to the press about his involvement. He confirmed that he and Perdue had met several times in Toronto to discuss the plot. "Mike, Wolf and I are quite sure this whole thing wouldn't have caused any deaths," reporter Peter Moon of the *Globe and Mail* quoted him as saying. "If so, it would have been negroes doing it to negroes." He said a lawyer had advised him he had not broken any laws. "It's hard, in Canada, to prove a conspiracy."

It turned out to be lousy advice.

CHARLES YANOVER WAS already onto his next criminal scheme by the time the OPP came looking for him. After Perdue and Droege were arrested in New Orleans, Yanover was approached by a friend named James Choi about another job. The North Koreans wanted to kill the president of South Korea, Chun Doo Hwan. All they needed was an assassin. Yanover flew to Vienna to tell them he would do it. He also said it was going to be very expensive. He signed a contract and left for Hong Kong with his partner, Mikey. At a meeting in Macau, they collected two briefcases stuffed with cash.

The time and place for the assassination were already decided. President Chun would be golfing with President Ferdinand Marcos at the Puerto Azul resort in the Philippines between July 6 and 8. A well-aimed gunshot from out of the blue, and that would be that. Yanover made his way to Puerto Azul to scout things out. He knew what was going on. He was being used. The North Koreans could have killed President Chun themselves but they wanted a scapegoat. When the president's body went limp and the finger-pointing started, Yanover would take the blame. The North Koreans could sit back and deny involvement, pointing instead to the mob. That's what they were buying for their $1.5 million.

But Yanover had a plan. He began secretly tape-recording and filming his conversations with the North Korean agents. Then, through a lawyer, he approached the Royal Canadian Mounted Police with an offer. In exchange for revealing the assassination plot, he wanted $1.5 million dollars and immunity. And he wanted police to drop all charges against his mob friends including his boss Paul Volpe. But before he could make a deal Yanover was arrested over the Dominica coup. He and McQuirter were charged with conspiracy "to use force or violence for the purpose of overthrowing the government of the Commonwealth of Dominica, West Indies." The charge sheet accused them of conspiring with Perdue, Droege, Jacklin and McGuire. Neither Don Andrews nor Aarne Polli were charged.

MARION MCGUIRE WAS still imprisoned on Dominica. The judge had sentenced her to three years for her part in the invasion plot. Hours later, guards found her bleeding. She had slashed her wrist with the metal stand of a mosquito coil. They took her to Princess Margaret Hospital for treatment and she survived. She passed the days scrubbing the prison floors. She lived on a diet of tea and bread, with the occasional pig snout, chicken neck or codfish. She was the only woman in the prison. The Canadian Ambassador to Barbados, Allan Roger, lobbied on her behalf, trying to get her back to Canada, and in March 1982, she was told her appeal for mercy had been granted. She was free to go. Three days later, she was back in Toronto. She had lost twenty-five pounds and her skin was cinnamon brown. All she wanted was coffee and scrambled eggs. She said she had done a lot of thinking during her ten months in the Caribbean, and she had changed her way of thinking. She was a new person.

"I'm not bitter," she told the *Toronto Sun*. "I'm just tired."

BY THE TIME Special Agent John Osburg was subpoenaed to appear as a prosecution witness in Canada, he had already testified at three trials in two countries, as well as too many preliminary hearings and bail hearings to count, all stemming from the arrests of Mike Perdue and Patrick John. The subpoena arrived in New Orleans on August 11,

1982. This time he was told to appear in Room 21 of the Old City Hall courthouse in Toronto at 9 a.m. on September 7.

McQuirter decided to plead guilty. His public statements were going to be used as evidence against him, including a tape-recorded interview in which he had said, "If you have control of a country, you can make a lot of money. Our purpose was to make a lot of money for white nationalist circles." The case went to court for sentencing on September 24. The Crown prosecutor, Paul Culver, told the judge that McQuirter was supposed to guide the mercenaries ashore with lights and then secure a communications center. He added that police believed the coup could have succeeded if it had not been detected early on. Defense lawyer Frank Fay called the coup "a harebrained, crackpot scheme" that was "unsophisticated, undermanned, underfinanced, ill-led, misdirected and adolescent. In short, it was virtually a comic opera. Idiotic." Judge Patrick LeSage imposed a two-year sentence, the maximum. "Your participation was criminal, the type of conduct that is abhorrent and cannot be tolerated anywhere in the world," the judge said.

Yanover pleaded guilty as well. The judge sentenced him to six months for his role in the Dominica coup. The next day, he was sentenced to two years for his involvement in the Korean assassination plot. Police never did recover the $600,000 the North Koreans had given him as a down payment for killing the president. All they found was $21,000, which was in his partner's safety deposit box.

Constable Larry Strange, who had been the first Canadian police officer to find out about the coup when Gord Sivell confided in him, received a commendation from the acting commissioner of the Ontario Provincial Police, J.L. Erskine. Unfortunately, the letter thanked him for saving the wrong country. Constable Strange was commended for the "high professionalism" he displayed in the "investigation of the attempt to overthrow the government of the Dominican Republic."

IN THE END, FIFTEEN MEN and one woman were convicted for their involvement in the coup, plus another seven when Fred Newton and his men are included. The harshest sentences went to those caught in Dominica; nobody caught outside the island got more than three years. Even though they were lucky to get off so lightly, the mercenaries continued to lobby for lesser sentences.

From his prison cell in Tallahassee, Mike Perdue wrote letters to the judge begging to be released.

> *I could justify our punishment better if I felt that we were doing wrong to America*, he wrote. *If the United States government really feels that it is protecting an ally in Dominica and that the present government is accepted by the populace, it is being fooled. The government has made sure that its best friends on Dominica are now standing trial, and the best leaders for Dominica to keep it out of communist hands are Patrick John and the military leaders.* He asked the judge to go easy on the others as well. *Their fault was wanting a better life. They aren't criminals.* He called the ordeal a nightmare. *At the risk of repeating myself we never meant any harm to the government or the people of the United States. We wanted to help stop the spread of communism and make money for ourselves.*

Larry Jacklin's mother and father drove to the Federal Correctional Center in Milan, Michigan. "An awful experience," is how his mother Twyla describes the visit. Larry sent four letters to the judge pleading for leniency, one of them describing his parents' despair.

> *They cried seeing that I was behind barbed wire with drug pushers, homosexuals, murderers, and rapists*, he wrote. *They want me home and that's where I want to be. I never realized how lucky I was before and I would like to ask you, your honor, to re-sentence me, and I can assure you I'll never brush with the law again once this is over. I've had three offers of jobs (good) that will utilize my skills in the construction industry and give me a chance to offer something to the world, instead of being an overfed parasite of the Federal Bureau of Prisons burdening the taxpayer.*

Jacklin said he didn't think he should have to serve the same time as Perdue and Droege when "[he] was the one who was conned." He said he was "only a pawn and not a organizer or director ... I played only a minor role in the crimes and feel that I have learned a lesson." He wanted to help others avoid the bad choices he had made, to help them see right from wrong, he told the judge. If he could "save just one person," he said, it would be worth it. He wanted to go to college and work at his father's construction business. "We all make mistakes when we are young," he said. Although, not all of them involve the invasion of a foreign country.

Wolfgang Droege was held at Sandstone Prison, "up in the middle of nowhere in Minnesota." He passed the time working out a system for racetrack betting and doing "what everybody else does. You read, watch TV, you know, like maybe do a little bit of exercise here and there," he said. "Ya, you know, keep in touch, write some letters."

He sent letters to the judge apologizing and explaining his conduct.

> On several occasions I had my doubts and reservations concerning Mr. Perdue's planned mission, as well as his character. But due to the fact that I lack mature reasoning and understanding I was easily influenced into taking part in the planned mission, other than that I would have declined his offer to be a participant. He said he had been misled and used like a puppet by Perdue. He thought invading Dominica would be a good favor to the U.S. government. I did not receive any financial gain from my active participation in this mission. My expenses were paid by my codefendant Mr. Michael Perdue, I did however receive promises of money and perhaps a position in Mr. Perdue's administration once the mission was accomplished.

Droege's friends wrote the judge as well. His girlfriend Anna-Maria Edmonson wrote from Vancouver to say that she and Wolfgang were planning to get married as soon as he was out of prison. She said Droege's interests included reading the Christian magazine *The Plain Truth* and listening to classical music, and that:

He is a responsible, law-abiding member of society, with
no connections to the criminal element ... he does not
smoke; he does not drink alcohol; he does not use drugs; he
is not violent; and he is very even-tempered. He is greatly
respected by his friends and acquaintances.

Al Overfield sent a letter offering Droege a job at his bailiff service in Scarborough, Ontario. And a company called CMP Films in Toronto said it wanted to hire Droege as a key grip for its documentary film crew.

In his letters to the judge, Droege wrote in the voice of a teetotaling churchgoer whose naiveté had been exploited by bad people. All he wanted, he said, was to return to his simple, quiet life.

I would like to return to Canada, and to my home and live
a more positive and productive life. I do not drink any kind
of alcoholic beverages, nor do I use any kind of tobaccos.
I am a member of the German/Canadian Club and I
have helped with a young boys soccer team in my home
community. I am also a former member of the conservative
party of Canada.

He was wrenched with remorse. If the judge would let him out of prison, he said, he would "rectify and correct my behavior pattern in society." It was a fine performance. It was also a magnificent lie.

As Droege's parole date approached, the U.S. government began deportation proceedings. At a hearing in Chicago he fought the immigration department's attempt to kick him out and ban him from re-entering the United States for five years. "I felt I hadn't done anything to warrant deportation," he said later. "I mean, a violation of the Neutrality Act? I said to myself, you know, it was a vague law which was rarely ever used and ... I hadn't done anything really against the U.S. government ... so I thought to myself, why should I be barred from the States?"

PERDUE WAS RELEASED to a Houston halfway house. It had been four years since he had picked up a newsmagazine and come up with the brilliant idea of invading a Caribbean island for profit. It was Manifest Destiny gone stupid. Although Perdue was still on probation in March 1981, the FBI got word he was planning another mercenary expedition. The FBI office in Houston was granted permission to use body recorders to gather evidence against him, and cash was wired to the officers on March 30 for use in an undercover operation. A memo sent out that day advised that Perdue "is continuing with a plot to overthrow the incumbent government of the Caribbean island of Dominica." The investigation lasted months, but the FBI could find no evidence Perdue was capable of orchestrating a second coup and the file was closed.

Droege lived with his girlfriend in Vancouver, a Klan member studying at the University of British Columbia. He made $100 a day playing the horses, using the betting system he'd worked out in prison, until he lost his shirt and had to drive a taxi.

Four months after Droege got out of prison, a police informant got word he was at it again. Droege was overheard expressing an "interest in the takeover of an island," according to an FBI document declassified for this book. "Having just been released from serving a lengthy prison term for attempting the same thing, the informant is not certain if the statement was made in jest or in earnest," the memo said. "There was no further explanation given at that time as to the source or the degree or credibility the information should receive."

It was not clear which Caribbean island Droege had his sights on this time, but if it was Grenada, the United States was about to save him the trouble. In October, the Washington press corps started speculating that the United States was about to invade Grenada to oust the Cuban-backed communists. President Reagan was going to finish the job Perdue and Droege had started.

Don Andrews felt a sense of vindication once the news reached him at the Mansion in Toronto. He was all for invading Grenada. That was how this had all started back in 1979, until Perdue and Droege got greedy and decided to loot Dominica instead.

"It's about time," Andrews said.

27

Ronald Reagan and Eugenia Charles meeting in the White House

St. George's, Grenada
October 25, 1983

IT WAS STILL DARK WHEN the helicopters swept in from the Caribbean Sea and dropped nearly 400 U.S. Marines at the Pearls airstrip on Grenada's east coast. Thirty-six minutes later, C-130 turboprop planes swooped low over the island's south. The Cubans were waiting. They opened up with anti-aircraft guns and small arms. Through the ground fire, hundreds of U.S. Rangers paratroopers jumped from an altitude of 500 feet, landing at Point Salines. Operation Urgent Fury had begun.

President Reagan had grown increasingly concerned about Grenada since taking office. The Cubans were on the island, building a 9,000-foot runway at Point Salines that could accommodate Soviet MiG 23 fighter bombers. With an airbase like that, the Soviets could run flights to Libya, the East Bloc and Central America, and support the hundreds of Cuban troops in Angola. Reagan ordered warships to the Eastern Caribbean in early October for exercises, and to help protect the tiny, poorly defended nations of the Lesser Antilles.

Then it all blew up. Maurice Bishop's four-year revolution came to a sudden end at midnight on October 12. The left wing of his party no longer considered him radical enough. Deputy Prime

Minister Bernard Coard and the commander-in-chief of the armed forces, Hudson Austin, turned against the prime minister, questioning his commitment to the "revo" after he expressed an interest in improving relations with the United States. The leftists removed Bishop from office and placed him under house arrest. Bishop's supporters freed him after a week, but he was recaptured by Hudson's men and executed by firing squad. Austin closed the airport and imposed a round-the-clock curfew, warning violators they would be shot.

When word of the crisis reached Washington, the U.S. Joint Chiefs of Staff met to begin planning the evacuation of the roughly 1,000 Americans on the island. Most were students at the St. George's University School of Medicine, founded seven years earlier by Charles Modica, who catered to would-be doctors who, like himself, had been rejected from mainstream medical schools. The generals were eager to avoid the mistakes of Operation Eagle Claw, the disastrous April 24, 1980 attempt to rescue fifty-three U.S. hostages held in Tehran. Two of eight Marine Corps helicopters got lost in a sand storm and a third broke down. The mission had already been aborted when one of the Sea Stallion choppers crashed into a C-130 transport plane. Moreover, the legacy of Vietnam weighed heavily on the military commanders. With two Cuban ships moored off Grenada's shore, the U.S. generals assumed the worst. Ever since the New Jewel Movement revolution of 1979, the U.S. had only limited tactical intelligence about the island's military strength. Outdated estimates put the size of the Grenadian forces at 1,200 regulars, twice that many militia, and about 240 Cuban combat troops. Those estimates turned out to be low. The Soviets had shipped at least six BTR-60 armored personnel carriers and four 23-mm anti-aircraft guns to Grenada. The Cuban presence worried the American generals, and so the mission grew. In addition to rescuing the stranded American citizens, the U.S. troops would also have to disarm the Grenadian and Cuban forces.

The Organization of Eastern Caribbean States met in Bridgetown, Barbados on October 21 to discuss the crisis. The chaos in St. George's had unnerved the OECS leaders; they feared the fire of revolution could—with Soviet, Cuban and Libyan help—spread to their own islands. They voted to ask "friendly countries" to help them confront "the unprecedented threat to the peace and security of the region created by the vacuum of authority in Grenada." The request was relayed to Washington by the spokesperson for the OECS, Prime Minister Eugenia Charles of Dominica. President Reagan was roused from his sleep at 4 a.m. and briefed on the developments while still in his pajamas.

The next day, the governor general of Grenada, Sir Paul Scoon, who was under house arrest at his official residence near St. George's, asked the OECS to help liberate his country from the Marxists. Reagan decided he could not say no to Dominica and the other five nations that had requested U.S. help. "We'd have no credibility or standing in the Americas if we did," he wrote in his memoirs.

On October 24, four teams of Navy Seals boarded Boston Whalers and made their way through rough seas to Point Salines and Pearls. The reconnaissance teams ruled out a shore landing; the terrain wasn't appropriate for amphibious vehicles. A helicopter and airborne assault would be needed. The Joint Chiefs decided the invasion force would consist of Marines, Rangers and Special Forces as well as a Caribbean Peacekeeping Force made up of the Jamaica Defence Force, Barbados Defence Force and troops and police from Antigua, St. Lucia, St. Vincent and Dominica. President Reagan gave the "go" and the countdown began. At 5 a.m., the Americans were going in with overwhelming force.

THE U.S. GENERALS HAD HOPED for a surprise attack, but word soon spread that American warships were on their way. Fidel Castro sent an experienced officer named Pedro Tortola Comas to Grenada to direct the Cuban defenses.

"An invasion of our country is expected tonight," Radio Free Grenada announced over the airwaves. "The revolutionary council has made it clear that the people of Grenada are prepared to fight to the last man to defend our homeland."

The assault got off to a bad start. The Marines landed at Pearls on schedule and quickly captured the airport, but the Rangers were late getting to Point Salines. The navigation system in the lead C-130 failed and by the time the troops made their jump more than half an hour later, they had lost any hope of surprising their adversaries. The Cubans at Point Salines fought hard for the first few hours; many were veterans of the wars in Angola and Ethiopia.

President Reagan announced the invasion in the White House Briefing Room at 9:07 a.m. "We have taken this decisive action for three reasons: first, of overriding importance, to protect innocent lives, including up to one thousand Americans whose personal safety is, of course, my paramount concern; second, to forestall further chaos; and third, to assist in the restoration of conditions of law and order and of governmental institutions to the island of Grenada, where a brutal group of leftist thugs violently seized power, killing the prime minister, three cabinet ministers, two labor leaders and other civilians, including children. Let there be no misunderstanding. This collective action has been forced on us by events that have no precedent in the eastern Caribbean and no place in any civilized society."

The invasion was Reagan's chance to push back against Soviet expansion in the Americas. To Reagan, Grenada had become a Soviet colony, a military base and a future hub of communist revolutionary violence. Officially this was a rescue mission and a humanitarian intervention, but it was also the beginning of the end of the Cold War. And standing at the president's side during the news conference was a stately woman who represented the leaders of the Eastern Caribbean, the prime minister of Dominica, Eugenia Charles. "A truly great lady," Reagan called her. The woman that Mike Perdue and his far-right mercenaries had tried to depose because of her supposed communist leanings had turned out to be one of the best friends the United States ever had.

FACING TOUGHER CUBAN RESISTANCE than expected, the Americans continued to flood the island with troops. Eight thousand U.S. and Caribbean combat soldiers landed by air and sea. As one town after another fell to the invasion force, the Cuban and Grenadian soldiers began to surrender. After four days of fighting, the mission was pretty much over. The medical students had been rescued, along with the governor general. Bernard Coard and his junta were captured. The U.S.

forces entered the Cuban embassy and found weapons hidden in false walls, along with documents spelling out the Soviet plan to turn the island into a communist outpost.

Combat operations ended on November 2. The U.S. had lost nineteen troops, the Cubans twenty-five and the Grenadians forty-five. Two dozen civilians had also lost their lives, many of them mental patients at a hospital that was mistakenly bombed. The "revo" was over. Reagan wrote in his memoirs that the Grenada operation was the best day of his presidency. "Success seems to shine on us," he recorded in his diary that day. Lebanon was a different story. At 6:20 a.m. on October 23, suicide bombers had attacked the U.S. Marines barracks in Beirut, killing 241 servicemen.

In his radio address that week, Reagan linked Grenada and Lebanon. In both cases, the president said, the Soviets had encouraged violence through surrogates. "The world has changed," the president said. "Today our national security can be threatened in far-away places. It's up to all of us to be aware of the strategic importance of such places and to be able to identify them."

ON NOVEMBER 7, the FBI field office in San Juan sent a telex to headquarters advising them about Wolfgang Droege and how he was "once again involved in planning to participate in a coup attempt in the Caribbean, preferably on an island with a militant left-wing group." Agents were told to "Locate Droege, and determine the authenticity of the report to enable appropriate preparation in Dominica, and possibly some of the other territories in the region." FBI agents in New Orleans, Ottawa and San Juan chased leads, trying to "determine the seriousness of his supposed intentions to overthrow a Caribbean island," according to a confidential memo declassified for this book. Droege's plot was said to be in the planning stages, but it never went anywhere and within a month the FBI dropped its investigation.

STOCK FARM PRISON SITS ON a plateau at the north edge of Roseau, above the electrical plant. Across the valley, the homes in Fond Colé cling improbably to army green slopes. Rockaway Beach, where the Operation Red Dog mercenaries were to land, is below at the edge of the brilliant sea that washes through the Caribbean islands, a curving line of emeralds that have eternally tempted ambitious thieves.

Patrick John was held in the Security Block at Stock Farm Prison. He read books and, once a day, was let out to walk. "In the security area there was a large area where you could exercise, and that was enclosed also," he says. "So they would open my cell and give me two hours out in the sun, and then return to my cell."

Marley Reid eased the boredom of prison life by taking an electrician's course. The Dominica Defence Force was through; he was going to need a new trade when he got out. He spent a lot of time alone in the dark. His cell had no windows but he taught himself to "see" what was going on outside by listening to the sounds. He knew when the police were chasing the Dreads in the mountains because he could hear the rifle shots echoing down the valley. He would listen to the murmur of conversing inmates and the guards in the corridors killing time with shop talk. Sometimes the guards were loud, like they knew he was eavesdropping and wanted him to hear what they were saying.

On August 8, 1986, Reid woke early and sensed something was up. It was before dawn and there was a commotion outside. Security sounded heavier than normal. Then he heard the guards talking loudly about Major Fred Newton and how he was in the prison reception room. The next news he heard was that Newton was in the prison chapel. He knew then that Major Newton, his commanding officer and closest friend, raised by his own mother as if they were brothers, was on death row.

The courts had dismissed Newton's appeal. The government had commuted the sentences of the other five convicted coup conspirators to life imprisonment. Not so for Newton. He was going to hang.

It was all happening quickly. It tore Reid up inside to be locked in his cell, knowing what was going on, hearing it but only able to imagine the scene as the Major was marched to the gallows. He imagined the expression on Fred's face and the thoughts running through his head.

Reid heard the quiet anticipation of the gathered crowd of police officers and guards, then noises he knew could only be the sounds of a life ending at the end of a rope. It was Dominica's first execution since independence.

"This," Reid later said, "is probably the first activity that has taken place in Dominica on time."

Epilogue

Where Are They Now?

AS THEY WERE released from prison, the mercenaries went back to their everyday lives. Some returned to their families and jobs and never looked back.

Bill Waldrop still lives in the same house in Mississippi that he left when he set off for Dominica. "Well, if we could do it all again I guess we'd all probably wind up making worse mistakes than we did the first time, wouldn't we?" he says.

"On rare occasion" he talks to Malvaney. "George is a real good fellow. He's cleaned up his act real good, went to college, got a degree. George is real intelligent, comes from real good folks. He's made a good life." Malvaney still lives around Jackson and works for an environmental services company. When Hurricane Katrina hit New Orleans, he drove down the next day to help out. He says the coup attempt "is not something that I'm ashamed of by any means, but it's definitely something that I've put way behind me."

Chris Anderson learned welding in prison and opened a shop in Wichita when he got out. He has since changed his name to Chris Bearsiron and moved to a small town in southern Colorado. He lives in an RV. "Shit happens," he says. "It's all in the past."

Mike Norris went to work at his family's convenience store in Alabama and died at the age of forty-five. "His heart just gave out," a relative says. "He gained a lot of weight and that had a lot to do with it, I think."

Larry Jacklin worked at his family's construction business in Listowell, Ontario and tried to forget the whole thing. "He never talked about it at all," his mother Twyla says. "He just felt as if he had no friends, but with time and especially motorcycling, he had a lot of friends, and good friends." On August 31, 2002, Jacklin and his friend Dennis Wright were riding their motorcycles on Oxford County Road 17 at twilight when a poplar fell across the road. There was no wind, no rain. "It was just time for that tree to fall," says Constable Dennis Harwood of the Ontario Provincial Police. The bikes hit the tree at full speed.

The police and Township of Zorra Volunteer Fire Department got to the scene around 9 p.m. The OPP issued a press release with the headline, "Motorcycles Hit Fallen Tree, One Driver Dead." It said the "names of the two drivers are not being released at this time until relatives can be located and notified." The police woke Twyla at 3 a.m. to tell her that her forty-four-year-old son had died instantly at the scene. The OPP issued a second press release naming Jacklin, but it did not mention his mercenary past, nor did the local press make the connection.

Bob Prichard left the right wing, married and had a son who also served in the Army. Prichard was treated for Post Traumatic Stress Disorder and now lives on his military disability pension in rural North Carolina, where he is active in the Veterans of Foreign Wars organization. "I behave myself, I stay out of trouble," he says.

Not Mike Perdue. He returned to Texas and almost immediately launched a new scam. "They couldn't figure out how he did it," his brother Bill says. Mike boasted he was making more money than Bill earned at the Ford plant. He worked as a handyman at Stonecreek Apartments and used his access to the suites to steal checkbooks. Mike drove from town to town in a 1977 Datsun, repeating the same fraud until he was caught out in a simple traffic accident. "He had all kinds of checks and stuff in his car and this Mexican ran a red light, knocked him out. The police came and they found all this shit scattered over the car," Bill says.

When the police searched him they found bogus checks and papers detailing his plans to move to an island off Haiti. On his arrest forms, he listed his occupation as: mercenary. The judge sent Perdue to prison for six years, but he was soon out again and the ATF continued to get tips about his mercenary schemes. On September 11, 1987, a woman called the ATF office in Houston and said she had overheard Perdue "talking about the shipment of $15,000 worth of weapons, including automatic weapons, plastic explosives and RPGs, being sent from the Houston area to the Miami, Florida area," read an FBI bulletin declassified for this book. "The weapons were shipped via rail to the Miami area. Perdue [was] overheard discussing elections to be held in Dominica and that 'they' had to be in Dominica before September 15th. The female was unable to provide more explicit information than that above and stated she would recontact BATF if she were to receive further information. She would not provide any information about herself and did not want any contact with federal authorities due to fear for her life." The FBI could not find Perdue. His last known address was in Lewisville, Texas, but he hadn't been seen there for two months.

The FBI sent out yet another teletype on March 10, 1989, saying that agents in New Orleans had interviewed a source who told them someone was recruiting to fly arms to Central America. Perdue's name does not appear on the heavily censored report but it was located in his personal FBI file, suggesting he may have been involved.

Purdue turned up next in Utah, where he weakened and was admitted to hospital. He was diagnosed as HIV positive and his organs were shutting down.

His mother and brothers Bill and Jim flew to Salt Lake City, but Mike was already in a coma when they got there. He was being kept alive by the hospital machines. The family decided it was best to let him die, and he took his final breath at the foot of the Wasatch Range, whose sawtooth peaks reach more than twice as high as the dark green *montany* of Dominica. He was buried at the Sherron Cemetery in Sumner County, Tennessee, alongside his father and a Confederate war hero.

Nobody who read the newspaper obituary would have guessed he was the same Mike Perdue whose mercenary adventurism had once caused so much grief:

> West Point native Michael Eugene Perdue, 42, of Dallas,
> Texas, formerly of West Point, died at 8:05 p.m. Nov. 11

in Salt Lake University Medical Center, Salt Lake City,
Utah. He was visiting in Salt Lake City when he became
ill. Born August 19, 1948, in Crawfordsville, he attended
grade school at West Point, then moved to Portland, Tenn.,
where he was affiliated with the Church of Christ. Mr.
Perdue was a self-employed over-the-road truck driver.

The obit was more than a little dishonest, but it would be the last scam for Mike Perdue. Make that the second to last—years later, the new owner of his house in Houston dug up a handgun in the garden.

WOLFGANG DROEGE COULD NOT stay out of trouble. When the Vancouver Police Department found out he was driving a taxi, they would not approve his license. The only way he could get a permanent taxi license was to go before the mayor and city council and make his case, and he was too proud to do that. "A city council meeting consisted of people who I knew would be my natural enemies, and so I felt I wasn't going to go before people where I would have had to humiliate myself," he explained in an interview. "I certainly wasn't going to beg anybody for a job."

He decided to return to the United States. He was barred from entering the country but he managed to slip in undetected and made his way to Minnesota, where he had friends. From there, he went south: "I knew some people in Alabama who I felt I could rely on and who could help me set up a network in narcotics, and so that's what I was working on." With the help of his prison friends, he started selling cocaine and marijuana to dealers. He justified being a drug dealer by telling people he was only doing it to help the racist far-right movement.

"I was intending to raise large amounts so I could support the cause I believe in," he said. "Ya, you know, for instance if I … knew people needed money for political goals or if I felt they had a worthwhile project, well, I would give them a few hundred, or maybe even a couple of thousand dollars …Ya, regularly. I was making like six, seven thousand dollars a week. Maybe not quite that much, but that would have been probably a good week. But quite often, there was times I made about six, seven thousand dollars a week."

Within a year of his release from prison, Droege was mixing with the most extreme fringe of the North American neo-Nazi movement, a group called The Order. They respected him. His attempt to attack Dominica had showed a level of militancy that got the attention of hardcore white supremacist leaders. "That elevated him," Andrews says. "What does that tell you about the movement?" What impressed them most was their belief that Droege had not betrayed the cause following his arrest. Although Droege had testified for the prosecution as part of his plea agreement, they were convinced he knew far more about the plot's connections to the far right and had kept quiet. Instead of ratting out his friends, they felt he had just served his sentence. And when he got out of prison, he soon discovered that those two years were a cheap price to pay for the credibility they earned him in the racist movement.

They gave him sensitive assignments, such as spying on American Jewish leaders who were confronting the far right. On November 29, 1984, he flew to Huntsville, Alabama on one such assignment. He didn't realize he was being watched.

Droege was still airborne when the Supervisory Criminal Investigator of the Immigration and Naturalization Service in Atlanta contacted the FBI and, according to a declassified FBI memo, "advised that WOLFGANG WALTER DROEGE, an illegal alien, was to arrive at the HUNTSVILLE MADISON COUNTY JET PLEX later that day and would be carrying a quantity of drugs." FBI agents were waiting for him. They watched as he got off the Republic Airlines flight carrying a soft Samsonite suitcase. They watched as he walked through the airport lobby and waited by the street for a ride. At 3:40 p.m. a car pulled up next to Droege, and when he approached it, he was arrested. A search of his bag turned up a black Teflon dagger, 4.5 ounces of cocaine and $3,754.18 in cash.

Although the arrest was reported in the press as a simple drug and weapons case, declassified records show that the Domestic Terrorism Unit of the Terrorism Section at FBI Headquarters was involved. The FBI had linked Droege to the Aryan Nations and had sources indicating that he "was on a mission at the time of his arrest by FBI." Droege pleaded guilty and was sentenced to thirteen years at Lompoc Prison.

BY THE TIME HE WAS PAROLED on April 21, 1989, Droege was forty years old. He was penniless when he arrived back in Toronto; all he had was his reputation as the bad boy of the far right. Fed up with Don Andrews, he wanted to form his own movement. Droege's idea was to unite the Canadian KKK and Aryan Nations under a single organization that would become the primary instrument for the country's white supremacist movement. He was going to call it the Society for the Preservation of the White Race, but later he came up with the White Heritage Front.

The Heritage Front was launched at a gathering in the fall of 1989. Droege envisioned two wings. The political wing would engage in propaganda: leafleting and lobbying. The covert wing would do the dirty work. It would attack so-called race traitors (whites who disagreed with the Front's ideals); raise money by robbing armored cars and black drug dealers, for example; and attempt to create a white enclave. Droege hoped to sell information on Canadian Jewish groups to Libya.

Among those present at the founding meeting was Grant Bristow, who became the security chief and office manager of the Heritage Front. Bristow had started attending far-right meetings at Don Andrews' house in 1988 and, by the time Droege had been released from prison, he was a regular fixture in movement. He was also an informant for the Canadian Security Intelligence Service. A private investigator, Bristow was hired in 1986 by the South African embassy in Ottawa to help with security. But when he was asked to spy on anti-apartheid demonstrators, he met with CSIS and the foreign diplomat who tried to hire him was subsequently expelled. The agency began using Bristow to keep an eye on the extreme right. Bristow reported the creation of the Heritage Front to CSIS, which opened a formal investigation. Droege never suspected a thing. He fell for Bristow's ruse the same way he had fallen for Mike Perdue. For a career militant, Droege was awfully gullible.

Bristow believes Droege owed his reputation to Dominica. "Droege dined out on Dominica for a long, long time. That's what gave him his original bona fides in the United States." Although the Dominica plot was about money, it was later spun as an operation whose aim was to create a white bastion, or make money to finance the white supremacist movement, which was only partly true. But what most impressed the leaders of the white right was their belief that when he could have talked to save his skin, Droege had maintained his silence. "I think," says Bristow, "he looked at it as a good tradeoff—did a little bit of time, got himself a bit of a rep and a lot of doors opened for him in the white supremacists movement."

Droege learned from Dominica. "I think that he looked at it two ways," Bristow says. "One was that it was one of the best lessons that he'd ever had in life … because it taught him a lot about people, and it taught him about who he could trust. He felt that … he was more of a naïve individual prior to that happening and he became less trusting and more discerning after that. Now the jury's still out on the comment given how much he trusted me.

"But you know, the fact was that Droege was a lot more surveillance conscious and a lot more security conscious in 1989 than he clearly was in '81 and clearly was in '84. He believed that he was likely going to be the target of an investigation. He sort of had a sense for how it was going to happen. He believed that likely there was going to be a fair amount of electronics played against him, like wiretaps." Droege was right. CSIS threw everything at him. But Droege had not counted on CSIS having an informant inside the Heritage Front from the very start.

In 1990, Bristow gave CSIS his first bit of actionable intelligence. He found out that Steve Hammond was back in Canada. Following his bungled attempt to rescue Marian McGuire from Dominica, Hammond had quietly returned to Toronto. Bristow's information was passed from CSIS to Canadian immigration authorities, who issued a warrant for Hammond's arrest. The Toronto police picked him up and he was deported to England. Hammond considers the Dominica escapade "very stupid and very immoral … No thought for innocent people, to be shot or blown up. No consideration for the social structure of the populace, welfare of the people, or thought of retaliation from allied neighboring countries." Hammond later underwent a change in sexual identity and now lives in Blackpool, Lancashire as a woman named Andrea.

Steve Hammond was the first of six foreign nationals, identified by CSIS as "leading white supremacists," who would be deported over the following two years because of information supplied by Bristow. With Bristow at his side, reporting his every move to Canadian intelligence, Droege began to unify the assorted hate groups under the Heritage Front. The Heritage Front held rallies, tried to establish links with the conservative Reform Party and set up a telephone hate line that spewed racist messages until it was shut down by legal action from the Jewish and aboriginal communities.

On Droege's instructions, members would phone up anti-racist activists to harass and threaten them. Bernie Farber of the Canadian Jewish Congress was one of their targets. "You fucking Jew," said a message left on his answering machine. "I'm gonna fucking kill you." One Front skinhead beat a Tamil refugee so severely that he was partially paralyzed. The Heritage Front became increasingly violent. Bristow reported to CSIS that Droege was gathering information on "enemies" such as Jewish leaders. A hit list of twenty-two names was compiled. Droege told Bristow that a Heritage Front member was planning to walk into the Canadian Jewish Congress office and "take some people out." Bristow was sure the primary target was Farber. But by 1994, the Front was beginning to collapse under the strain of legal troubles and high-level infiltration. Tired and stressed, Bristow was pulled out of his undercover assignment in March 1994.

Bristow says Droege had no contact with Mike Perdue following the Dominica affair. "I believe that Droege took the position that Perdue essentially rolled on everybody. He talked about him, but not in flattering terms. I think Droege continued to … believe they could have beaten or at least minimized what happened in the Dominica trial had Perdue not rolled so quickly." He adds that Droege sometimes talked longingly about Dominica. "He believed that it would have been easy street had it worked out."

Dominica may have been Droege's ticket into the top ranks of the far right, but it was also his downfall. His involvement in the violent overthrow of a country allowed Canadian intelligence to brand him a national security threat and make him a target of a state surveillance and disruption campaign. The undercover intelligence investigation not only brought down Droege, it discredited his entire network. In that sense, Dominica was the beginning of the end of Canada's right-wing extremist movement.

THE DOMINICA CASE put Charles Yanover out of action, but only for a while. After serving sentences for the Dominica coup, the Korean assassination plot, and the bombing of the Arviv Disco, he started selling guns again. He sold handguns and submachine guns equipped with silencers, their serial numbers removed. He didn't know it, but his customers included undercover police officers. On April 10, 2003, following a fourteen-month investigation by the Provincial Weapons Enforcement Team, he was charged with conspiracy to traffic in firearms and a hundred other weapons offences. He was sentenced to nine years. The National Parole Board reviewed his case on June 13, 2007. It said there was a "high risk" the sixty-one-year-old would re-offend. "If released," the board wrote, "the psychologist recommends that you not participate in any covert government organizations or have any links with legitimate military related activities as they could serve as magnets for criminal activity." His parole was denied.

Don Andrews still lives in the Mansion in Toronto and posts commentary on his Internet site. He keeps a photo of Wolfgang Droege above the shaving mirror in his kitchen. Don Black moved to West Palm Beach, Florida and runs an Internet site for the "white nationalist community" called Stormfront. Gordon Sivell worked for Environment Canada for several years and then returned to journalism as the producer of the popular television show *Don't Forget Your Passport*. He lives in Thailand.

IN LOUISIANA, MIKE HOWELL and the *Mañana* rode out Hurricane Katrina on Lake Pontchartrain. He still lives at the New Orleans yacht club aboard his ship with a cat and four stray dogs. He is a popular fixture on the lakefront, where he is active in the U.S. Coast Guard Auxiliary. Lloyd Grafton retired from the ATF in 1990 and worked as an assistant professor of criminal justice at the University of Louisiana at Monroe. John Osburg also left the ATF but still works as a contract firearms consultant. In 1985, the ATF closed its Dallas regional office. During the process, as years of paperwork was being moved, the ATF discovered that the cash from the Bayou of Pigs investigation was missing. The $14,800 worth of hundred dollar bills that Perdue had given Special Agent Osburg during the undercover operation—and that Osburg had carefully locked in the ATF evidence vault—was gone. An internal investigation failed to get to the bottom of it, and the money was never found.

The ATF, FBI and U.S. Customs continued to uncover coup attempts out of New Orleans. In 1984, police arrested thirteen men at a motel in Slidell as they were meeting to plan an invasion of Haiti. Two years later, another thirteen people were arrested as they were leaving for Surinam to overthrow the government. Federal agents seized two dozen guns and other military supplies. "Apparently this is a strategic location and is viewed as a jumping off point for Central and South America, which have been the targets of coup attempts," U.S. Attorney John Volz was quoted as saying by the *Dallas Morning News*. In California, following a joint ATF-FBI investigation called Operation Tarnished Eagle, ten people were arrested on June 4, 2007 for allegedly plotting to overthrow the government of Laos. They included a West Point graduate and a former General in the Royal Lao Army. Like Perdue, they were charged with Neutrality Act violations. "We cannot tolerate our country being used as a staging ground for foreign coup attempts," Assistant Attorney General Kenneth L. Wainstein said.

PATRICK JOHN WAS RELEASED on May 29, 1990, after serving four years of his prison sentence. He ran for public office again but lost. He lives in his house overlooking the sea in Canefield, where he is working on his memoirs. He continues to maintain his innocence. "I can tell you straight off the bat, I was never involved in any coup with Perdue," he said when the author of this book arrived at his front door unannounced. "I was very close to the Defence Force, and because of my closeness, both through Malcolm Reid and Newton, well, they felt that I must know something about it." The DDF was acting on its own, he says. Moreover, he believes the Defence Force planned to execute him and make it look like the killing had been ordered by Eugenia Charles. That way, he explained, the military could get rid of John and also have a pretext to execute Prime Minister Charles. "They were going to make me a martyr," he said.

He brushed off his conviction as a setup. "As I told you," he says, "the majority of the members of the jury were members of the Charles administration." His explanation for the Letter of Intent he signed with Perdue: he thought he was agreeing to purchase a printing press for the Labour Party offices. "When he met me, he called himself an import-export businessman." There was no mention of mercenaries, he claimed. "If these things would have ever come out, Perdue would have been cut off from the get go. He never appeared to me as a scam artist because he was quite, you know, good selling what he was selling, and he came in as a man who was import-export and tried to show me that he could get this printing machine for me for nothing. And you know in exchange, when we would get into office, he would get some favors. And I said, 'OK, *quid pro quo.*' I took him at face value, and I think that was my error instead of probably trying to find out more of his background."

The former prime minister is now a lay Eucharistic minister in the Anglican Church. On May 11, 2007, the Confederation of North, Central American and Caribbean Association Football inducted Patrick John into its Hall of Fame. The press release noted his "profound impact on football in the Commonwealth of Dominica, CONCACAF and the Caribbean Football Union." It made no mention of his conviction for attempting a military coup.

Malcolm Reid completed an electrician's course in prison and, since his release, has been active in the Dominica truckers' association. He lives in Mahaut. He was deeply affected by the camera phone images of Saddam Hussein's hanging. He had only heard the sounds of Fred Newton's hanging, but after seeing the Iraqi dictator's execution, he had pictures to put to the soundtrack. "Nothing disturbed me and troubled me worse than when I looked and saw what happened to Saddam." The government refuses to tell him where his friend is buried. He found the prisoner who buried him but he wouldn't tell. Reid said the man was wearing Newton's sneakers. Julian David works at a small convenience store called the Mini-Mart south of Roseau, selling cold bottles of Kubuli beer. He would not speak to me about the coup attempt. Dennis Joseph runs an advertising company in Roseau. "I think the whole thing was set up by Eugenia Charles," Joseph says. No convincing evidence has ever surfaced to support that claim.

The government gave Algie Maffei a security job at the port. In 2000, his close friend Rosie Douglas, whose political rise was funded partly by the Libyans but who had become far more moderate with age, became Dominica's prime minister, only to die eight months into his term. "Rosie was always like a brother," Algie says. "What hurt me most of all when he died was that, for the short time he was prime minister, we never had a rapport because he was always busy and I was always busy." Algie still takes heat for testifying against Patrick John but he says he just did what he thought was right and never received any money or favors in return. "I didn't do it for prime minister or police," he told me. "I did it for the nation. And if I had to do it again, I would do it again." He has a house in Fond Colé but spends most of his time in the country, living close to the land.

Eugenia Charles was knighted by Queen Elizabeth and remained prime minister of Dominica until 1995, when she retired from politics. She died on September 6, 2005. She was eighty-six.

Dominica remains among the least developed islands in the Caribbean, but it has begun turning that to advantage, marketing itself as the Nature Island, where tourists can experience the authentic West Indies. Dominica was named one of the world's top ten eco-tourism destinations in 2006. Hollywood has also discovered the island's allure. *Pirates of the Caribbean: Dead Man's Chest* was filmed largely in Hampstead, Portsmouth, Vielle Case and Soufriere. More than 400 Dominicans were employed during the shoot, and Disney returned for the third *Pirates* movie. The CBS reality show *Pirate Master* was also filmed in Dominica.

Hurricane Dean struck the island in August 2007, toppling the banana trees once again. The Venezuelans quickly arrived with offers of assistance.

WOLFGANG DROEGE WENT BACK to dealing drugs. One of his regular customers was a broken young man named Keith Deroux.

Deroux had never in his whole life been lucky. He was one of those lost souls who can't seem to get from A to B without somehow going astray. Even after somehow putting a bullet in the back of

Droege's skull, he could not bring himself to run away. Instead, he ran back into Droege's apartment and hid in the closet.

There was no shortage of people who would have liked Droege dead. The list was infinite. He had made himself an easy person to revile.

On April 13, at 2:50 p.m., a woman called 911 to report that she had heard gunshots in her building. She had also seen a man sprawled in the second-floor hallway. He was not moving.

Keith Deroux could have fled. If he had, there would have been endless theories. The murder might have never been solved. But he made it easy for the Toronto Police homicide squad. Instead of bolting, he called his brother and then dialed 911. When the police got there he refused to come out of the closet and claimed he had a hostage. He snorted more cocaine and downed two of Wolfgang's beers. That was the story of his life.

After his father had left home, Deroux had experimented with alcohol and drugs. He was expelled from school; his formal education ended in the eighth grade. His mother got him a job at a newspaper but he was caught using amphetamines and asked to leave.

At nineteen, he went north and worked at Cominco Mines, alongside his father, but on a trip back to Toronto he went on a bender and was too drunk to return to work. He tried quitting drugs and managed to stay sober for five years while he worked at Sears and later drove a cab for Toronto Taxi, then Beck Taxi. It didn't last. He fell back into it and in 1998 he was convicted of impaired driving, which cost him his driver's license and his job as a cabbie.

Cocaine led to heroin. He tried to go clean. He even checked himself into rehab and started methadone treatment. Another three years of sobriety followed, and he held down a job with a vending machine company, but then the cycle started all over again. Booze, then cocaine. He was asked to leave his job.

The cocaine made him paranoid and delusional. After breaking up with his girlfriend, Carrie, he convinced himself that someone had been entering his apartment when he was out, and that people were watching him from the street. He was sure that listening devices and cameras had been installed in his apartment, and that someone was sending him coded messages through his computer.

He blamed his girlfriend's new partner, but then he started to think it had to be his drug dealer. He knew Wolfgang was a big shot, with connections; he was the only one who could have done it. Deroux had laughed at Droege's white supremacist views once; maybe the former mercenary was doing it for revenge or maybe just for perverse amusement.

Deroux skipped town and moved to Vancouver, but the paranoia wouldn't go away. He felt he was being watched by bikers. He decided the only way to stop the harassment was to go back to Toronto and confront Droege.

He bought a .22 and mailed it to himself at his aunt's address. On April 7, 2005, he flew back to Toronto and started planning his confrontation with Droege. The gun arrived in the mail the next day.

He visited Droege on April 8, 9, 10 and 11 but didn't take the gun with him. He just bought cocaine, trying to come up with a plan. In the forty-eight hours before the shooting, he went overboard, downing coke, Tylenol and alcohol.

He hadn't meant to kill Droege, he said. But it all went wrong and before he knew it he had cranked out four bullets and now Droege was shot and Keith was in the closet. He put a single bullet in the chamber of his revolver and thought about ending it right there. He couldn't do it. He put the gun down, opened the door of the apartment and surrendered to the Emergency Task Force.

"Is Droege dead?" he asked. "I didn't mean to," he added. "I just wanted to know what was going on."

THE OFFICER ASSIGNED TO THE CASE, Detective-Sergeant Peter Callaghan, knew all about Wolfgang Droege. The homicide detective had been stationed at 14 Division when Droege's thugs had clashed with anti-poverty demonstrators. Detective Callaghan had even been to Dominica once while on a Caribbean cruise.

He knew how easily the case could go astray. Conspiracy theories were inevitable. He checked over the crime scene and interviewed the neighbors. They told him Droege was dealing drugs. He also talked to friends of Droege and Deroux. He quickly realized the link between them was drugs. It had all the makings of a drug deal gone bad. The case was quickly wrapped up and Deroux pleaded guilty.

At the press conference the next day, the reporters all wanted to know if the killing had anything to do with Droege's militant past, but Sergeant Callaghan tried to put that to rest.

"I think Mr. Droege is of interest to a lot of members of the community here. There was no ongoing investigation of Mr. Droege at this time. In fact, I think it had been quite some time since Mr. Droege had come to the attention of the Toronto Police Service."

"Sorry about the question," a female reporter asked, "but do you have sort of any explanation as to why he was in his underwear at three in the afternoon?"

"No, I don't," he said. "I can't explain that."

Author's Note

This was an odd story, to say the least—mercenaries, the Mob, the Klan, militant Rastafarians, a Third World strongman. I had to talk to all of them. Finding them after twenty-five years was a challenge. One had changed his name; another his sex. One was in prison. But I eventually tracked down all the key players, at least those still surviving. To find out more about those who had died, I spoke with their friends and families. Those I did not visit in person, I spoke to by phone, e-mail or letter. I also interviewed the lead investigators and others who were involved on the law enforcement side. Although most of the people I approached had never spoken to a reporter about Operation Red Dog, almost all were cooperative—and some wanted to know who would play them in the Hollywood movie. A few did not want it known they had helped me. Only a few people would not talk to me, notably Don Black, Danny Hawkins and Julian David.

I read thousands of pages of documents from the Bayou of Pigs investigation and the subsequent court cases in the United States, Canada and Dominica. I also requested and obtained the FBI's files on Mike Perdue and Wolfgang Droege, which were released in declassified version under the Freedom of Information Act. Gordon Sivell found an old cassette tape of an interview he conducted with Wolfgang Droege about Dominica in the early

1990s. He kindly shared it with me. It was one of the few times Droege ever spoke on the record about the plot. Sivell was one of several people who had intended to write books about Operation Red Dog but for various reasons never did. Everything in this book is true, to the best of my knowledge. I have not changed any names or dramatized any scenes. Every little detail is presented just as it was described by those who were there. I corroborated the veracity of their recollections by checking everything from hotel receipts and plane tickets to immigration landing records and old photographs. I visited the locations where the key events took place to see them for myself. The dialogue is exactly the way it was recalled by those who were present. In some cases, the dialogue comes directly from recorded conversations such as wiretaps. Most of the reporting and writing was done in Toronto, New Orleans and Dominica.

One question nagged me throughout my research: was the CIA behind this? Is it possible that Mike Perdue really was doing the agency's dirty work in the Caribbean, as he insinuated so many times? My conclusion is, I don't think so. Would the CIA recruit a bunch of far-right Nazis and Klansmen for a job like this and not tell U.S. law enforcement agencies what it was doing? It's possible. But the reason I believe the theory has no merit is that it was not in the U.S. interest to replace Eugenia Charles with Patrick John. Of the two, Charles was clearly the more pro-American leader. The day she was elected, she openly declared her hostility to communism and later supported the U.S. invasion of Grenada.

Another theory I heard repeatedly was that Operation Red Dog was a government trap to ensnare the most dangerous figures in North America's resurgent far right. I don't think that one has much value either. Perdue's recruiting was far too haphazard, and the ATF did not even know they were dealing with Nazis and Klansmen until after the arrests.

Finally, in Dominica there is a theory that Eugenia Charles or her supporters staged the coup to get rid of Patrick John. I don't buy that either. John was already out of the political picture by then, and there was no indication he had enough popular support to make a comeback as prime minister—through democratic means, anyway. Such a conspiracy is also completely out of character for Ms. Charles. In my view, Operation

Red Dog was Mike Perdue's ultimate get-rich scam. He scammed Patrick John, Malcolm Reid and the DDF into believing he was a veteran mercenary who could get the job done. He scammed his recruits into believing they were fighting communism. If it had all worked out, Perdue would have been a millionaire with his own island. I think *The New Chronicle* had it right when it wrote that Perdue and Droege wanted to build a "crooks' paradise."

The first investigative reporting I ever did was about the militant right wing. As a junior newspaper reporter, I found out that a candidate running in a local election was a closet Nazi. I wrote an article and he quit. It was a valuable lesson about the power of journalism. This book marks my return to writing about the far-right-wing movement and I am grateful to those who helped me, particularly John Osburg, Lloyd and Frances Grafton and Mike Howell. Thanks also to Gordon Sivell for sharing his research. Bill Perdue kindly invited me into his home to talk about his brother, and he sent me family photos. Don Andrews loaned me his photo collection and scrapbooks. Aarne Polli shared his collection of photos and documents from Dominica. I owe a particular debt to those journalists who covered these events at the time, and whose reporting was crucial to telling this story, especially the staff of *The New Chronicle* as well as Peter Moon and Ed Anderson.

I would like to thank Robert Harris, Don Loney, Meghan Brousseau, Liz McCurdy and everyone else at John Wiley & Sons for supporting this book. Andrew Borkowski did a masterful editing job.

Thank you to Bernie Farber, Desmond Blanchard, Gene Pastaina, Scott Baldwin, Grant Bristow, Kenneth Dean, the Honorable Roy McMurtry, Jack Nelson, Bill Minor, Jerry Mitchell, Jim Ingram, Alex Rose, Parry Bellot, Reginald Winston, the *New Orleans Times-Picayune*, the National Archives of Dominica, the U.S. National Archives in Fort Worth, Texas, Markham Public Libraries, Toronto Reference Library, Houston Public Library, Salt Lake City Public Library System, Ronald Reagan Presidential Library and Foundation, FBI Records Management Division, Roseau Public Library, Detective Sergeant Peter Callaghan and the Toronto Police Service, and others who prefer not to be named.

Thanks to my editors and colleagues at the *National Post*, Adrian Humphreys, Gord Fisher, Doug Kelly, Steve Meurice, Anne Marie Owens and Mick Higgins.

Thanks to Anne, Bob and Kay.

Most of all, thanks to Laura and the girls.

Notes

Part I

The account of Michael Perdue's involvement is based on his court testimony at the trial of Don Black, Danny Hawkins and Mike Norris.

Wolfgang Droege described his role in the coup during his testimony, as well as in a previously undisclosed taped interview with journalist Gordon Sivell.

Andrews suggested my book title should be *KKK on King Kong Island*. Polli's suggestion was *The Fantasy Island Chronicles*.

Malcolm Reid admits he brought Perdue to his house but denies anyone else was there. Patrick John denies meeting Perdue in the mountains.

The quote regarding the *Hamilton Report* is from "The A-to-Z of Dominica's Heritage," avirtualdominca.com/heritage.cfm.

Excerpts of the report of the commission into the May 29, 1979 incident were published in *The New Chronicle*, April 18, 1981.

The description of Droege as a "diligent recruiter" comes from "Metro Klansman One of 10 Nabbed in Invasion Plot," *Toronto Star*, April 29, 1981.

The "last free men" is a line from the jacket of *The Dogs of War*.

The song "You Could Have Been a Lady" was later covered by the Canadian band April Wine.

Part II

All ten of the accused mercenaries told their stories during the trial. The two ATF agents also testified. The transcripts of their testimony are the backbone of this account. Additional details come from interviews. Danny Hawkins declined to be interviewed. Don Black responded to a few of my queries but never said anything of substance and would not agree to an interview. He did, however, review a list of facts about his involvement in the coup plot that I sent him. He responded that "there were no egregious errors" in my account. He added that he would not talk because, "it would be a betrayal of trust, whether for the living or dead." This account of their involvement in the coup is based on their own court testimony in New Orleans.

Malvaney told me he does not recall the parade permit incident. "I don't remember that I got any parade permit or anything like that. I'm not going to say I did or didn't. I don't recall." But it was documented in two newspaper articles: Kuhl, Greg and Binz, Larry, "3 Men: Background of a Plot," *Jackson Daily News*, April 29, 1981; and Pendergrast, Loretta and Flagg, Michael, "Accused Conspirators No Newcomers to Crime," the *Clarion-Ledger*, Jackson, Mississippi, April 30, 1981.

I requested Chris Anderson's military service record, but the archives was unable to find it. Anderson insists he did in fact serve.

Malcolm Reid wanted it known that he never tried to buy drums of acid in Guadeloupe, as some have claimed.

Algie Maffei claims his letter to Mike Perdue was simply an attempt to get money.

Part III

Andrea (formerly Steve) Hammond wrote a fifty-page account of her trip to Dominica in longhand. I also spoke with her many times and verified parts of her account with other sources.

Maffei told me that it was Rosie Douglas and his brother Mike Douglas, both politicians, who told the police he was in Guyana, but a police source told me that was not the case.

Two credible sources told me that the FBI contacted CSIS in 1984 to say that they were holding Droege and that he had volunteered to become an informant for Canadian intelligence. The offer was apparently declined because Droege was a service target, was considered untrustworthy and CSIS felt it did not need him. But in fairness I only learned of this after Droege's death and was therefore not able to put the question to him.

Bob Woodward wrote in his book *Veil: The Secret Wars of the CIA*, that the CIA had sent $100,000 to Dominica following its support for the invasion of Grenada, but Eugenia Charles said that was not true.

Peter Moon's reporting on the conspiracy was so far ahead of the pack that *Maclean's* magazine wrote a laudatory article about him.

Sources

Prologue

Transcript of sentencing, *Her Majesty the Queen and Keith Deroux*, Ontario Superior Court of Justice, Toronto, June 16, 2006. Interview with Detective Sergeant Peter Callaghan.

Part I

Key Interviews

Bill Perdue, David Duke, Don Andrews, Aarne Polli, Andrea (Steve) Hammond, Patrick John, Malcolm Reid, Algie Maffei, Parry Bellot, Grant Bristow, Kenneth Dean, Jim Ingram, Roy McMurtry, Mike Howell, Ted Thorp and Carlton Van Gorder.

Documents

"Report of Investigation, Michael E. Perdue," Department of the Treasury, Bureau of Alcohol, Tobacco and Firearms, June 11, 1981.

Transcript, *United States* v. *Michael S. Norris, Joe D. Hawkins and Stephen D. Black*, United States District Court, Eastern District of Louisiana, Criminal Action No. 81-212.

Transcript, *The State* v. *Patrick John, Julian David, Dennis Joseph, Malcolm Reid*, Criminal Suit No. 27 of 1981, High Court of Justice, Dominica.

Perdue's military service record was released under the Freedom of Information Act by the National Personnel Records Center, National Archives and Records Administration, Washington, D.C.

Details on the rise of the Western Guard come from three scrapbooks of documents and clippings compiled by Don Andrews.

Security Intelligence Review Committee, "The Heritage Front Affair," Report to the Solicitor General of Canada, Dec. 9, 1994.

Lauder, Matthew A., "The Far Rightwing Movement in Southwest Ontario: An Exploration of Issues, Themes, and Variations," Guelph and District Multicultural Centre, 2002.

Dominica Laws, Acts, Statutory Rules and Orders and By-Laws for the Year 1974, Government Printery, Roseau.

"Eastern Caribbean: Rising Cuban Influence," CIA, July 20, 1979, declassified under FOIA, available online at *http://www.foia.cia.gov.*

Chapter 10 is based largely on the court testimony of Algie Maffei. It should be noted that the others implicated by Maffei disputed his version of events. But Maffei's account was ultimately accepted by the jury, which convicted the men. Maffei's account is also consistent with Mike Perdue's testimony in New Orleans. I also interviewed Maffei at his home in Dominica.

The landing cards that Mike Perdue filled out when he arrived in Dominica, as well as the various drafts of his contract, letters and other documents were obtained from the office of the Director of Public Prosecutions.

For information on Miller's farm as a paramilitary training base see, Southern Poverty Law Center, Legal Action, *Person v. Carolina Knights of the Ku Klux Klan,* http://www.splcenter.org/legal/docket/files.jsp?cdrID=22&sortID=4

For information on the Greensboro Massacre see report of the Greensboro Truth and Reconciliation Commission, *http://www.greensborotrc.org/.*

Mike Howell's military commendations are posted on his website, *manana.com.*

Articles

AP, "It's Business As Usual in Grenada One Day After Regime is Ousted," March 14, 1979.

Barrett, William P., "Bayou of Pigs: A rag-tag band of mercenaries barely missed the boat," *Dallas Times Herald,* May 10, 1981.

Darroch, Wendy, "Western Guard Chief Cleared of Assault, Criticized for Bigotry," *Toronto Star,* Jan. 30, 1975.

Jones, Tammy, "Deposed Ruler Determined to Return," *Los Angeles Times,* April 10, 1979.

Kaufman, Michael, "Grenada's 'Destined' Leader," *New York Times,* Feb. 7, 1974.

Kaufman, Michael, "Grenada Chief Reports Evidence of Plot," *New York Times,* Feb. 9, 1974.

MacGray, Ken, "Toronto Was a Heartbeat Away from Fascist Mayor," *Toronto Star*, December, 1974.

New Chronicle, "Dominica Passports for Iranians," May 3, 1980.

"Reds, Western Guard Clash," *Toronto Sun*, July 30, 1973.

Stoneman, Brian, "Anti-Semitic Slogans Are Blamed on Western Guard Splinter Group," *Canadian Jewish News*, Sept. 28, 1973.

Thomas, Jo, "Dominica Is Racked by Political Upheaval and Depression," *New York Times*, August 8, 1979.

Thomas, Jo, "Radical Grenada Symbolizes Political Shift in Caribbean," *New York Times*, August 20, 1979.

Time, "Let Them Eat Bananas," Feb. 18, 1974.

Time, "Poor Little Paradise," Nov. 13, 1978.

Time, "The Fall of a Warlock," April 2, 1979.

Treaster, Joseph, "Rebels in Grenada Said to Stage Coup," *New York Times*, March 14, 1979.

"2 Musicians Shot Critically, Wounded Outside Yonge Club," *Toronto Star*, Jan. 28, 1975.

Ward, Fred, "Dominica," *National Geographic*, September 1980.

Books

Balor, Paul, *Manual of the Mercenary Soldier: A Guide to Mercenary War, Money and Adventure*, Dell Publishing, New York, 1988.

Bishop, Maurice, *Forward Ever: Three years of the Grenadian Revolution, Speeches of Maurice Bishop*, Pathfinder Press, Sydney, 1982.

Bishop, Maurice, *Maurice Bishop Speaks: The Grenada Revolution and its Overthrow 1979–83*, Pathfinder, 1983.

Douglas, Rosie, *Chains or Change: Focus on Dominica*, Committee in Defence of Black Prisoners, January 1974.

Fanon, Frantz, *Black Skin, White Masks*, Grove Press, 1968, U.S.A.

Fontaine, D'jamala, *Dominica's English-Creole Dictionary*, 2003.

Higbie, Janet, *Eugenia: The Caribbean's Iron Lady*, The MacMillan Press, London, 1993. The definitive account of the life of Eugenia Charles.

Honychurch, Lennox, *The Dominica Story: A History of the Island*, MacMillan Education, 1984.

Lanning, Michael Lee, *Mercenaries: Soldiers of Fortune, from Ancient Greece to Today's Private Military Companies*, Ballantine Books, New York, 2005.

Martin, Tony (ed.), *In Nobody's Backyard: The Grenada Revolution in Its Own Words, Vol. 1: the Revolution at Home*, The Majority Press, Dover, Mass., 1983.

Minor, Bill, *Eyes on Mississippi: A Fifty Year Chronicle of Change*, J. Prichard Morris Books, Jackson, 2001.

Ojito, Mirta, *Finding Manana: A Memoir of a Cuban Exodus*, Penguin Paperbacks, 2006.

Wade, Wyn Craig, *The Fiery Cross: The Ku Klux Klan in America*, Oxford University Press, New York.

Part II

Key Interviews

Bob Prichard, Chris Anderson, Bill Perdue, John Osburg, Lloyd Grafton, Mike Howell, Frazier Glenn Miller, Steve Hammond, Kenneth Dean, Jim Ingram, Mark Murphy, Larry Strange, Marshall Thur, Gordon Sivell, Algie Maffei, Patrick John, Malcolm Reid, Desmond Blanchard, Gene Pastaina. George Malvaney and William Waldrop also helped me understand their involvement in the events. One other key source directly involved in the coup did not want to be identified.

Documents

"Subject Michael Eugene Perdue," FBI files 2-2850 and 2-2489, released under the Freedom of Information Act on June 12, 2008. Of the 511 pages located by the FBI, 325 were released.

Transcript, *United States v. Michael S. Norris, Joe D. Hawkins and Stephen D. Black*, United States District Court, Eastern District of Louisiana, Criminal Action No. 81-212.

"Statement of John L. Osburg, Special Agent," Bureau of Alcohol, Tobacco and Firearms, New Orleans, May 5, 1981.

The military service records of Malvaney, Black and Prichard were released under the Freedom of Information Act by the National Personnel Records Center, National Archives and Records Administration, Washington, D.C.

Her Majesty the Queen against James Alexander McQuirter and Charles Yanover, In the Court of General Sessions of the Peace for the Judicial District of York, File no. 1544-22, Sept. 22, 1982.

Sources

Her Majesty the Queen against Charles Yanover, In the Court of General Sessions of the Peace for the Judicial District of York, File No. 1544-82, June 8, 1983.

National Parole Board Decision, Charles Yanover, Government of Canada, June 13, 2007.

Letter of Commendation to Larry Strange, Ontario Provincial Police, Nov. 27, 1981.

Articles

Canby, Vincent, "Movie Review: Dogs of War," *New York Times*, Feb. 13, 1981.

Charles, Eugenia, Partial text of radio address, *New Chronicle*, February 21, 1981, Roseau.

Charles, Eugenia, address to the nation, *New Chronicle*, March 14, 1981, Roseau.

Grove, Noel, "The Caribbean: Sun, Sea and Seething," *National Geographic*, February 1981.

Moon, Peter, "Raiding Party Was Set to Blast Dominican Boat," *Globe and Mail*, May 15, 1981.

New Chronicle, "Treason," January 17, 1981, Roseau.

New Chronicle, "High Treason," March 7, 1981, Roseau.

New York Times, "Ray's Brother Acquitted in Shooting of Nazi Youth," Nov. 25, 1970.

New York Times, "Reagan Criticism Fails to Alienate Klansman," Sept. 3, 1980.

New York Times "Small Klan Group Marches," Nov. 30, 1980.

New York Times, "Tennessee Reporter Tells of Joining Klan Groups," Dec. 14, 1980.

Paternoster, Laurie and Winiarski, Mark, "10 Accused of Plotting Dominica Coup," *Houston Post*, April 29, 1981.

Books

Dubro, James, *Mob Rule: Inside the Canadian Mafia*, MacMillan, Toronto, 1985.

Forsyth, Frederick, *The Dogs of War*, Bantam Books, 1975, New York.

Hoare, Mike, *Congo Mercenary*, Robert Hale Ltd., London, 1967.

Murphy, Mark, *Police Undercover: The true story of the biker, the mafia & and mountie*, Hushion House, Toronto, 1999.

Nelson, Jack, *Terror in the Night: The Klan's Campaign Against the Jews*, University Press of Mississippi, Jackson, 1993.

Part III

Key Interviews

John Osburg, Lloyd Grafton, Bob Prichard, Chris Anderson, Twyla Jacklin, Gordon Sivell, Algie Maffei, Patrick John, Malcolm Reid, Andrea (Steve) Hammond, Gene Pastaina, Desmond Blanchard, Roy McMurtry, L.E. Matthews III and Don Andrews.

Documents

"Report of Investigation, Michael E. Perdue," Department of the Treasury, Bureau of Alcohol, Tobacco and Firearms, June 11, 1981.

"The Media," Commons Debates, House of Commons, Ottawa, May 15, 1981.

"Canadian Neutrality: Outlawing of Private Armies—Motion Under S.O. 43," Commons Debates, House of Commons, Ottawa, May 15, 1981.

Transcript, *The United States v. L.E. Matthews and James C. White*, United States District Court, Eastern District of Louisiana, Criminal Action 81-301.

Record of Proceedings, In the Eastern Caribbean Supreme Court, Court of Appeal, Dominica, Criminal, *Appeal Nos. 13, 14 and 15 of 1985, Julian David, Malcolm Reid and Patrick John, Appellants, and The State, Respondent*.

Trial Record, In the Eastern Caribbean Supreme Court, Court of Appeal, Dominica, Criminal, *Appeal Nos. 13, 14 and 15 of 1985, Julian David, Malcolm Reid and Patrick John, Appellants, and The State, Respondent*. Filed January 20, 1986.

Transcript, In the Judicial Committee of the Privy Council, *On Appeal From the West Indies Associated States Supreme Court, Between Patrick John, Malcolm Reid, Julian David and Director of Public Prosecutions, Dominica*.

John and Others v. Director of Public Prosecutions for Dominica, in *West Indian Reports*, Vol. 31, Butterworths, London, 1985.

The State of Dominica v. Newton and Others, in *West Indian Reports*, Vol. 35, Butterworths, London, 1986.

John and Others v. Director of Public Prosecutions for Dominica, in *West Indian Reports*, Vol. 32, Butterworths, London, 1986.

David, Reid and John v. Commonwealth of Dominica (No 2), in *West Indian Reports*, Vol. 38, Butterworths, London, 1986.

"Michael Perdue," From ATF HQS (Criminal Enforcement) to All Stations, April 29, 1981.

"A commendation for law enforcement efforts concerning a plot against the Government of Dominica," From Secretary of State, Washington, D.C.

Letter of Commendation to John Osburg, From G.R. Dickerson, Director, ATF, Department of the Treasury, May 27, 1981.

Letter of Commendation to John Osburg, From Michael Hall, Special Agent in Charge, New Orleans Field Office, ATF, Department of the Treasury, June 2, 1981.

Letter of Commendation to John Osburg, From Director G.R. Dickerson, ATF, Department of the Treasury, July 22, 1981.

Letter of Commendation to John Osburg, From John M. Walker Jr., Assistant Secretary, Enforcement and Operations, Department of the Treasury, August 13, 1981.

The letters that Mike Perdue, Wolfgang Droege, and Larry Jacklin wrote to the judge were obtained from the U.S. National Archives in Forth Worth, Texas.

"Subject Wolfgang Droege," FBI, Files 163-HQ-61345, 2-HQ-2680 and 12-HQ-10490, released under the Freedom of Information Act on December 27, 2007. Of the 133 pages located by the FBI, 94 were released.

Cole, Robert H., *Operation Urgent Fury: The Planning and Execution of Joint Operations in Grenada, 12 October–2 November 1983*, Joint History Office, Office of the Chairman of the Joint Chiefs of Staff, Washington, D.C., 1997.

"Remarks of the President and Prime Minister Eugenia Charles of Dominica Announcing the Deployment of United States Forces in Grenada," October 25, 1983, Ronald Reagan Presidential Library.

Articles

Anderson, Ed, "3 Given Immunity in Dominica Plot Probe," *New Orleans Times-Picayune*, Aug. 6, 1981.

Anderson, Ed, "Indictment Charges 2 Financed Coup Plan," *New Orleans Times-Picayune*, Aug. 7, 1981.

Anderson, Ed, "2 Plead Innocent In Coup Plot," *New Orleans Times-Picayune*, Aug. 10, 1981.

Anderson, Ed, "Man Charged In Dominica Plot Is Released on $50,000 Bond," *New Orleans Times-Picayune*, Aug. 11, 1981.

Anderson, Ed, "Trial Set for 2 Suspected of Financing Plot," *New Orleans Times-Picayune*, Aug. 20, 1981.

Anderson, Ed, "Dominica Suspect Free After Bond Is Reduced," *New Orleans Times-Picayune*, Sept. 18, 1981.

Anderson, Ed, "Coup-plot Trial of Two Starting," *New Orleans Times-Picayune*, Oct. 5, 1981.

Anderson, Ed, "Ringleader of Coup Plot to Testify in Trial of 2 Men," *New Orleans Times-Picayune*, Oct. 6, 1981.

Anderson, Ed, "Handwriting Testimony Due in 'Bayou of Pigs' Coup Trial," *New Orleans Times-Picayune*, Oct. 8, 1981.

Anderson, Ed, "Coup-plot Judge Denies Mistrial," *New Orleans Times-Picayune*, Oct. 9, 1981.

Anderson, Ed, "2 Freed of Coup Charges," *New Orleans Times-Picayune*, Oct. 10, 1981.

AP, "Toronto Nurse Faces Dominican Court," *Toronto Star*, August 15, 1981.

AP, "10 Held in New Orleans in Plot to Overthrow Caribbean Regime," *Houston Chronicle*, April 28, 1981.

AP, "7 Sentenced in Dominica Plot," *Houston Chronicle*, July 2, 1981.

Hall, Joe, "Husband Still Loves Dominica 'Spy,'" *Toronto Star*, May 1, 1981.

Graham, Bob, "Bitter Plotter Says She Was a Sucker," *Toronto Star*, May 17, 1981.

Hall, Joe, "Nurse From Metro Held in Island Invasion Plot," *Toronto Star*, April 30, 1981.

Hodges, Sam, "Broke No Laws, Black Says About Aborted Invasion," *Birmingham Post-Herald*, June 10, 1981.

Logie, Stuart, "Prisoner Returns 'A New Person,'" *Toronto Sun*, March 25, 1982.

Moon, Peter, "Klan Linked to Plot to Seize Dominica; 2 Canadians Held," *Globe and Mail*, April 29, 1981.

Moon, Peter, "The Ku Klux Klan, A Mobster's Money and a Foiled Coup," and "Toronto Mobster Gave Funds to Klan," *Globe and Mail*, May 13, 1981.

Moon, Peter, "Police Investigate Role of Mobster in KKK Plot," *Globe and Mail*, May 16, 1981.

Mulgrew, Ian, "Nightly Talk Led to Dominican Jail," *Globe and Mail*, May 5, 1981.

New Chronicle, Editorial, May 2, 1981, Roseau.

New Chronicle, January 9, 1982, Roseau.

Oakes, Gary, "Dominica Plot Jails Former KKK Chief," *Toronto Star*, Sept. 25, 1982.

Oakes, Gary, "Koreans Bilked in Assassination 'Sting,' Court Told," *Toronto Star*, Feb. 17, 1984.

Oakes, Gary, "Man Gets 2 Years for $500,000 Con", *Toronto Star*, Feb. 18, 1984.

Pendergrast, Loretta, "Conspirator denies Florence man financed Bayou of Pigs," *Clarion-Ledger*, Jackson, June 23, 1981.

Paternoster, Laurie, "Perdue Gets 3-year Sentence for Role in Attempted Coup," *Houston Post*, July 2, 1981.

Reuters, "Jailed Nurse Tries Suicide," *Toronto Star*, September 19, 1981

Thomas, Jo, "'Comic-Book' Invasion Attempt Unsettles Dominica," *International Herald Tribune*, June 8, 1981.

Time, "Bayou of Pigs: A coup that fizzled," May 11, 1981, http://www.time.com/time/magazine/article/0,9171,949118,00.html

Toronto Star, "Dominica Plotter Back Home," March 23, 1982.

UPI, "Coup Attempt Fails in Dominica," *New York Times*, December 20, 1981.

Books

Reagan, Ronald, *An American Life*, Simon and Schuster, New York, 1990.

Sher, Julian, *White Hoods: Canada's Ku Klux Klan*, New Star Books, Vancouver, 1983.

Epilogue

Press Release, "Plot to Overthrown the Government of Laos Thwarted," Department of Justice, June 4, 2007.

Associated Press, "Jumping Off Point for Coups: Five Plots Foiled in New Orleans," *Dallas Morning News*, Dec. 27, 1986.

Transcript of sentencing, Her Majesty the Queen and Keith Deroux, Ontario Superior Court of Justice, Toronto, June 16, 2006.

"News Conference—Detective Sergeant Peter Callahan Updates the Media on Homicide #15, Walter (Wolfgang) Droege," Toronto, April 14, 2005. http://www.torontopolice.on.ca/media/audio/2005.php

Photo Credits

Index

Index